The Services Challenge: Integrating for Competitive Advantage

Edited by:

John A. Czepiel
New York University

Carole A. Congram
Consultant

James Shanahan
MasterCard International

 Proceedings Series

American Marketing Association

250 S. Wacker Drive • Chicago, Illinois 60606 • (312) 648-0536

American Marketing Association

1987

Printed in the United States of America

Cover Design by Francesca Van Gorp

Library of Congress Cataloging-in-Publication Data

The Services challenge.

(Proceedings series / American Marketing Association)
Papers presented at the 5th Annual services marketing
conference held in Boston, Mass., Sept. 7-10, 1986.
1. Service industries—Marketing—Congresses.
I. Congram, Carole A. II. Czepiel, John A. III. Shanahan,
Jim. IV. American Marketing Association. V. Series:
Proceedings series (American Marketing Association)

HD9980.5.S4255   1987   658.8   87-12543
ISBN O-87757-188-O

The Services Challenge: Integrating for Competitive Advantage

TABLE OF CONTENTS

MANAGING MARKETING SYSTEMS

EXPLORING THE SERVICE ENVIRONMENT

MANAGING LONG-TERM RELATIONSHIPS

MASTERCLASS

PREFACE

This, the Fifth Annual Services Marketing Conference to be sponsored by the American Marketing Association, is devoted to the concept of <u>integration</u> as the unifying concept in successful service firms. Four types of integration are included. First, integration means coordinating all of the functions within the firm to focus on the customer. Second, integration means achieving unity of purpose and unity of action in functionally organized and geographically widespread service businesses. Third, it means coordinating integration of the elements of the marketing mix. Fourth, integration means the melding of the theoretical and the practical. Yet it can be achieved and the results are obvious for those firms which have committed themselves to the effort.

This proceedings contains the thoughts of those firms and individuals who have and are working at the forefront of their field. We invite you to read their ideas, improve on them, put them into practice, and then to share them with all of us at the next Services Marketing Conference.

John A. Czepiel   Carole A. Congram   James Shanahan
New York University   Consultant   MasterCard International

Olli T. Ahtola	University of Denver
Alan Andreasen	UCLA
John Bateson	London Business School
Kenneth J. Bernhardt	Georgia State University
Leonard Berry	Texas A & M University
Mary J. Bitner	University of Washington
Bernard Booms	Washington State Univ.
David Bowen	University of S. Calif.
Stephen Brown	Arizona State University
Kay Clarke	Templeton, Inc.
Clare Comm	Babson College
Carole A. Congram	Consultant
John A. Czepiel	New York University
David Davidson	AT&T
Jim Donnelly	Univ. of Kentucky
Gerald Faulhaber	Wharton
Sandra Fiebelkorn	New York University
William Francis	GTE
William George	Villanova University
Peter Gillett	Univ. of Central Florida
Thomas Gillett	GTE
Mary C. Gilly	UCLA/Irvine
John B. Gragnola	Allstate
Christian Gronroos	Swedish School of Economics
Michael Houston	Univ. of Wisconsin
Charles W. Lamb	Texas Christian University
Eric Langeard	I.A.E.
Jarmo Lehtinen	Service Marketing Institute
A. Dawn Lesh	The New York Stock Exchange
John H. Lindgren, Jr.	University of Virginia
William Locander	SMC
Christopher Lovelock	Christopher Lovelock & Assoc.
Ian MacFarlane	MacFarlane & Company
Tom Maronick	Federal Trade Commission
John Martin	Boston University
Sarah Maxwell	ARA Services
William Mindak	Tulane University
Parsu Parasuraman	Texas A & M University
Gordon W. Paul	University of Central Fla.
James Peckham, Jr.	A. C. Nielsen
Debra Ringold	The American University
Thomas Rooney	Purolator Courier
Diane Schmalensee	Marketing Science Institute
Benjamin Schneider	University of Maryland
James Shanahan	MasterCard International
G. Lynn Shostack	The Coveport Group, Inc.
Michael Solomon	New York University
Carol Surprenant	New York University
Fred B. Thiemann	Bank of America
Lloyd F. Thompson	Camp, Dresser & McKee
Greg Upah	Merrill Lynch
Charles Weinberg	Univ. of British Columbia
William Wells	Needham, Harper Worldwide
Valarie A. Zeithaml	Duke University

Achieving Internal Integration in Service Organizations:
Five Propositions

Carole A. Congram, Consultant
John A. Czepiel, New York University
James B. Shanahan, MasterCard International

Why are some service organizations more successful than others in attracting and retaining customers? Experienced service marketers are coming to realize that success in the marketplace is a result of success in integrating the organization's complexities to achieve unity or wholeness. While this is true for all types of business, it is especially true for service firms. For within service firms the responsibility for service delivery, for achieving customer satisfaction is spread throughout the firm. As a result, everyone in the firm--regardless of function or department --shares responsibility for the customer.

For this reason, a significant portion of the Fifth Annual Services Marketing Conference focused on organizational issues and sought to identify the sources of success in internal integration. This paper presents five propositions which represent a synthesis of points which recurred in conference sessions. Most of the supporting examples are drawn from the opening plenary session, "Integrating Functions to Achieve Organizational Goals." The speakers in this session were James L. Heskett, (1907 Foundation Professor of Business Logistics--Harvard Business School), Edward A. O'Neal (Executive Vice President-Operations Division Chemical Bank), Thomas W. Rooney (Executive Vice President-Marketing and Sales Purolator Courier Corp.), and Susan L. Wall (Regional Director-Human Resources Hyatt Hotels Corporation).

WHAT IS INTERNAL INTEGRATION?

Heskett offered a definition of psychological integration: "the organization of various traits, feelings, attitudes, etc., into one harmonious personality." He continued: "We in services are beginning to learn the significance of some reasonably intuitive relationships between such facroes as employee satisfaction, employee motivation, service quality, customer satisfaction, and, indeed, increased volume of business or profitability." The service organization's "personality," then, is determined by organizing a complex set of interrelated factors. Many of these factors relate to the service organization itself and are under management's direct control. There is evidence that success in the market place is predicated upon successful integration within the organization.

FIVE PROPOSITIONS ON INTERNAL INTEGRATION

The propositions underlying success in internal integration are deceptively simple in concept. The challenge lies in implementing them within the organization so that their positive benefits are fully realized. The objective is to overcome functional parochialism and to direct the organization to fulfill its central purpose, creating and keeping customers.

Understand the customer's perspective

Basic to success in marketing services is understanding the needs of the organization's customer--from the customer's point of view. In service organizations for which marketing is new, management all too frequently "knows" what customers want. In fact, service organizations conduct market research less frequently than do goods-producing companies. Customer feedback can be used to help top management understand how the marketing concept applies to its organization. At Purolator Courier, for example, top management

personally observed a long series of focus groups in each of which customers insisted that before-noon delivery at a 95% consistency level was required. It was this personal experience with the market that led them to commit the organization to that target. Research, conducted properly, can indicate what must be done to succeed in the marketplace.

Equally important is to establish a system to obtain customer perceptions of expectations delivered, service quality, changes in needs, and competitive performance. At Hyatt, according to Wall, "Our customers' perceptions are what count." To gather customers' perceptions systematically, Hyatt uses such approaches as the traditional guest comment cards as well as ratings by independent consultants of Hyatt's facilities and employees' responsiveness. Reports are sent to corporate, regional, and individual property managers.

Help employees become customer-conscious

In service organizations, the employee is integral to the service offered; in high contact services, the contact employee "is" as well as "produces" the service. Customers evaluate a service organization, in large part, on the basis of their experiences, or interactions, with employees. The goal of internal marketing is to help each employee understand that his primary responsibility is to retain a customer. As Wall explained: "A knowledgeable, satisfied employee is our best marketing agent...We treat our employees the way we want them to treat our guests."

How do you help employees increase their consciousness of customers' needs? Selecting the best employees is the first step. The Cambridge Hyatt hires only one out of every 15 people interviewed. Ongoing educational and training programs are another prerequisite.

Regular communication with employees is essential. Leading service organizations use all media--print and electronic newsletters and video magazines--to help employees understand different aspects of service. Personal communication within the organization must be high in quality and frequency.

Top management must deliver the message that the focus is on the customer and demonstrate its support of the employee who serves the customer. At Purolator Courier, members of top management went into the field three or four times a year to meet with employees and to explain each employee group's role in customer retention. Some service organizations use customer feedback to help employees improve their service delivery performance and to determine bonuses and promotions.

Upward communication is also important. At Hyatt, the general manager of a hotel holds monthly meetings in which hourly employees identify operational problems. Hyatt also uses surveys to assess employees' perceptions of service quality and working conditions. The results are sent to corporate and regional management, as well as to the appropriate hotel's manager. Action plans are developed by the hotel's management group and results are discussed in employee meetings.

Some service marketers believe that it is not possible to keep the focus on the customer because the work force of the 1980's is so self-centered. However, research findings suggest that people who choose to work in services want to provide good service. For example, Red Cross workers make a conscious trade-off between psychic and economic income. Similarly, Weight Watchers' seminar leaders, many of whom are themselves former seminar attendees, are infused with a missionary zeal. They do want their clients to succeed in the program.

A service organization's culture affects the success of internal integration. At Chemical Bank, management emphasizes partnership, teamwork between and among departments and functions, and ties career advancement to working with other areas. O'Neal observed, "A culture is very, very hard to change, and it takes years, perhaps decades to build. . .We have found that creating a different kind of culture starts with recruiting and involves almost every aspect of the organization, but it seems to take years before you begin to see it take effect."

Build cooperation between functions

When a service organization's focus is on the customer, each function defines its responsibilities in terms of its impact on the customer, as opposed to its function, e.g., finance, human resources. This shift focus helps to minimize "turf" problems and other barriers between functions. Marketers tend to become the integration facilitators in this process. The integration of operations and marketing is particularly important. Rooney, describing Purolator Courier's recent financial situation, cited this as crucial in a situation in which "senior management had to speak with one tongue."

O'Neal noted that the integration of operations and marketing was one of his top priorities at Chemical Bank. One approach used at Chemical is to change the organizational structure. For example, retail and wholesale operations were reorganized "to more closely align them to the marketing groups they serve." Compensation systems also can be used to effect functional integration. Chemical Bank asks middle and senior operations management to set goals related to marketing priorities, and compensation reflects the degree to which these goals are achieved. Hyatt has a detailed point system of incentive compensation designed to promote functional integration. The top level of management at a hotel can earn up to 30% of annual income in a cash bonus. Points are awarded, and a manager cannot achieve the maximum number of points unless there is cooperation with other functional managers.

Assess the impact of technology on service

Technology affects service organizations in significant ways. The increasing use of technology can change the nature of the customer's relationship with the organization and its service. Technology can make the relationship less personal. Marriott's video checkout system saves time, but it also eliminates a personal encounter. In banking, the technology of the ATM similarly eliminates a personal encounter but it also puts customers into direct contact with operations. It cannot be predicted whether this will mean a decrease in a satisfying human interaction, a reduction in an unneeded frustrating encounter, or an increase in the effectiveness and delivery of the core service desired. It will depend on the situation and the importance and desirability of the personal, human encounter.

In some situations technology can strengthen a relationship. Customers of Decatur Federal Savings & Loan, for example, can obtain their checking account balance by telephone 24 hours a day. The "touch tone" phone enables the bank to insure confidentiality and verify that the caller holds an account. Customers receive added service without additional bank staff.

Technology can help a service organization lock a customer into a relationship. Inventory and reordering systems can be developed between members of a distribution channel so that high-quality and cost-effective service is insured. Technology affects internal integration, too and can break down departmental barriers. At Chemical Bank, for example, information technology has imposed discipline; as people access data from other departments, communication has become more precise and more open.

Develop systems to support the integration process of marketing

Systems extend to all parts of the organization and include not only automated but manual systems too. Every activity in an organization affects its service delivery system in some way. The systems developed must be evaluated and modified continually to support the organization's support of its customers' changing needs. One significant example is an organization's financial reporting system, which frequently focuses on operations, rather than markets or customers and can seemingly work against marketing. To meet this challenge, Chemical Bank created shadow profit centers for each product. As O'Neal described it: "Rather than pense guidelines, performance and bonuses were tied to product profits, thus making coordination with marketing managers more important."

Another area which can be significantly affected by systems thinking is human resources. Having a corps of customer-conscious employees begins with the development of a selection and hiring system, which dovetails into employee training and education, which complemented by career planning. American Express and Hyatt are two service companies that attribute market leadership to their human resource systems.

NEEDED: THEORY AND RESEARCH

Organizations differ dramatically in their inner workings and culture. Services marketers would benefit greatly from informed thinking on the nature of service organizations and in identifying tested approaches to achieving goals. Ideally, this work would come from the integrated efforts of marketing educators, organizational development specialists, and marketing practitioners. Unlike their counterparts in product marketing, services marketers cannot divorce their "product" from the organization which produces it. The two are one to the customer and must be integrated.

INTERNAL MARKETING

Fran F. Compton, American Red Cross Blood Services, Columbus, OH
William R. George, Villanova University
Christian Gronroos, Swedish School of Economics
Matti Karvinen, John Nurminen Oy

ABSTRACT

This paper first describes the 1986 Internal Marketing Program competition. Then the Internal Marketing MasterClass "mini-case" concerning "The Moment of Truth" internal marketing program at the John Nurminen Corp., Finland, is presented. John Nurminen Oy is an international freight forwarding firm.

INTRODUCTION

The concept and phrase "internal marketing" are relatively new to the marketing discipline. Internal marketing ideas appeared for the first time in the mid-70s. A growing and diverse literature base is emerging. The content is becoming more substantive each year. The Internal Marketing Program competition entries and the John Nurminen Oy "mini-case" provide a current picture of the concept. The competitive entries on Monday afternoon described components of internal marketing programs in financial, health care, consumer, business-to-business, and professional services.

1986 INTERNAL MARKETING PROGRAM COMPETITION

This competition was the first effort ever undertaken to solicit examples of internal marketing programs. A four page entry form and 1-1/2 pages of instructions were provided to interested parties.

Entries

The response was limited in number. Several possible reasons are suggested: 1. internal marketing is a new area of inquiry with most organizations that are trying out the idea still at the earliest stages; 2. the proprietary nature of the information; 3. the difficulty of reaching by publicity and other information avenues those organizations that are making progress; and, 4. the entry form may have been somewhat intimidating, especially the questions on budget and evidence of results.

Most of the entries were narrowly focused on a particular tactical problem. In addition, there appears to be no apparent location within organizations yet for internal marketing programs. It should be noted that the three Scandinavian entries were all more comprehensive and structured.

Entry Form

Two sections of the entry form caused problems for those submitting internal marketing programs for review. First, the form required that the "evidence of results" be related back to the internal marketing program objectives. While it may not be easy to establish objectives for what is often a qualitative endeavor, measuring the results of an internal marketing program can be very difficult. In many cases the best evidence available was primarily impressionistic, intuitive and/or subjective. The "evidence of results" section generated the most calls from would-be entrants who were concerned about their lack of quantitative measures.

The other problem section was the question about the budget for the internal marketing program. Most budgets were fairly small, often out of miscellaneous sources or from accounts which appear to be unrelated to internal marketing efforts. For many of the programs it was difficult to determine the total resources spent on an internal marketing program since a number of departments within the organization were involved -- e.g., Human Resources, Communications, Operations, etc. Again, the Scandinavian entries all had far larger budgets for developing and implementing the internal marketing program.

"Scenario for the 1995 entries"

There is a vision that internal marketing will be recognized as an effective approach for integrating the various functions within the service firm. It will be considered an integral component of management strategy. The internal marketing program will be comprehensive and involve multiple functions within the organization.

The internal marketing program will have "achievement measurements" included in the developmental stage. These will be multiple measures for accessing the impact of the program at stated time intervals. Such measurements could include pre-and-post tests about perceptions, behaviors and the like of the affected employees and their customers, and of changes in levels of complaints and compliments for both control units and experimental units.

Budgets will be specifically established for developing and implementing internal marketing programs. Both service and manufacturing firms will recognize the importance of an internal marketing program as a part of the strategic management process.

INTERNAL MARKETING AS A PREREQUISITE FOR SUCCESSFUL EXTERNAL MARKETING: THE JOHN NURMINEN CASE

Background: Industry and Company

Functions of an international forwarder include: 1. transportation (e.g., own handling equipment or through trucking, railways, air and shipping companies); 2. customs brokerage; 3. pick-up and distribution; 4. warehousing (e.g., bonded warehouses, long term warehousing, packing, loading and unloading); 5. ocean liner, ships clearance and I.A.T.A. Agencies, aircraft brokerage, and aircraft ground handling. The functions cover the home country and, through subsidaries and/or agents, the whole world. (Note: in the U.S. the activities of forwarders have been limited by law both geographically and functionally.) All the activities of a forwarding company are services.

Forwarding in Finland involves 80 companies with 115 branch offices. Forwarders take care of about 70% of all import and export transactions. The industry has a total of 5,500 employees. Yearly turnover/profits for the industry is about $167 million (U.S.) derived as follows: 1. import and export, customs brokerage, and transportation = 74.5%; 2. liner agencies = 7%; 3. stevedoring = .5%; and, 4. warehousing, travel agencies, fuel sales, etc. = 18%. Because of fierce competition and structural changes, the profitability of the industry is diminishing.

John Nurminen Co. was established in 1886 and is privately owned. Invoicing/sales amounts to $527 million (U.S.) with turnover/profit of $37 million (U.S.). Consignments per year are 191,000 with a staff of 638 people. The Company has 23 branches and 111 agents abroad. The market share of John Nurminen Co. is about 16%.

Background: internal marketing

The Nordic School of Services Marketing defines marketing: "Marketing is the task of establishing, developing and commercializing customer relations, so that the goals of the target customer, the firm and the society are achieved." Consequently, the contact persons should perform their tasks so that the trust of the customers in the contact persons -- and thus in the firm itself -- is maintained and strengthened. The same goes for the physical resources of the company and the systems (e.g., service delivery, claims handling, telephone reception, information, etc.) which the customers are expected to live with.

Perceived quality is the essence of services marketing analysis and management. It impacts on expectations (i.e., giving promises via the traditional marketing function -- the marketing mix) and on experience (i.e., keeping promises via the interactive marketing function -- interactions of technical quality (what) and functional quality (how). Perceived quality also impacts on profitability and image. (See Figure 1.) The Central Communications Circle involves expectations and experiences via perceived quality as well as word-of-mouth and interactive marketing. First, managers must develop programs of internal marketing and then develop technical quality, systems and physical resources as inputs for interactive marketing. Only after this is done, should traditional marketing variables (e.g., mass communications, personal selling, direct marketing, etc.) be directed to impact on expectations. (See Fig. 2).

The objectives of internal marketing are: 1. to help the employees understand and accept the importance of the interactions with the customers and their responsibility for the total quality and for the interactive marketing performance of the firm; 2. to help the employees understand and accept the mission, strategies, goods, services, systems and external campaigns of the firm; 3. to continuously motivate the employees and inform them about new concepts, goods, services and external campaigns as well as economic results; and, 4. to attract and keep good employees.

Situation analysis

Internal research provided the following: 1. In 1977 the staff was defined as the most important resource. 2. An internal vocational training program was started -- Nurminen was the first forwarding company in Finland to undertake such a scheme. 3. It was determined that the first objective should be to reach top management.

4. A simplified MBO was implemented. 5. In 1980 the company climate was researched with several positive findings (a. the personnel in general were happy; b. the working atmosphere was good; 3. the company training was perceived very positively) and several negative findings (a. the company was seen as old-fashioned; b. the typical attitude was "We are not responsible for marketing.")

An image study was undertaken in 1979 of freight forwarder users with the following positive findings: John Nurminen Co. was financially sound, experienced, large, versatile, and good in import forwarding, customs clearance, ocean transport, and warehousing. The negative findings included: John Nurminen Co. was viewed as being stagnant, uneconomic (i.e., no real value-added), old-fashioned, bad in customer service and giving information (i.e., this was "The Moment of Truth" situation where the customer and employee come in contact with each other and the customers were saying these contacts were unsatisfactory), expensive, rigid credit terms to customers, and bad in linear functions. The respondents felt the company image was vague and without highlights.

Case analysis by audience

The discussion covered many areas: 1. The meaning of the research results as perceived by the owner (who recognized the need for significant change in order to assure a profitable future), top management (who were not very receptive to change) and the employees (who were unaware of the research). 2. Using the commonalities of the internal and external findings to gain consenses. The question of how to get employees to buy-in to the findings and suggest what they believed should be done. The need to have the employees feel a part of the change and recognize themselves as the agents for change. The issue of the time dimensions in this approach in contrast to an autocratic approach. 3. The objectives of the organization. (This discussion had to be halted in 20 minutes with many areas not yet analyzed.)

What happened -- the internal marketing program and results

Five objectives of the internal marketing program for John Nurminen Oy were set forth and achieved: 1. Attitudes -- marketing is seen to play a role in everyone's work: providing a service (i.e., production of a service) is the most important part of marketing. 2. Information -- as regards distribution of information, both internal and external for present and potential customers, John Nurminen has become the best in the forwarding sector. 3. Company image -- the company is regarded as the best freight forwarder in Finland: a high quality image for the company. 4. Market share -- increase in the market share controlled according to one year and medium-term plans. 5. Profitability -- minimum ROI of 13% before interest and taxes on the present values of assets plus yearly real depreciation of the values of the assets.

The steps of the internal marketing program included creation of structure, internal activities and external activities. Creation of the structure included 4 parts: organization, guiding principles, definition of marketing functions, and definition of service quality. Implementation of theories of the marketing of services raises the question of organization. John Nurminen Oy combined mass-marketing and the internal information functions in the Marketing Development Department. Company training stayed in the Company Planning

8

Department and Personnel Administration in the Finance and Administration Department. Sales was decentralized to profit centers. Because of the right sort of personalities this seems to work. But the lines of responsibility are at the moment to some extent confused and need some rethought.

This structure also included 3 guiding principles: business idea, basic beliefs and policies. As now stated, the business idea of John Nurminen Oy is to produce for the market services aimed at bringing Finnish and foreign markets closer together by minimizing barriers to the exchange of goods in foreign trade. The basic beliefs and policies follow from this business idea.

The third part of creating the structure was the definition of marketing functions. Marketing was now viewed from several different perspectives. John Nurminen is in the service industry and targets its markets mainly at other businesses. Marketing is understood to be a conglomeration of functions in which everyone in the employ of the company participates. Production of services is a marketing function. There is a heavy interaction of marketing and personnel policies.

One of the facts that has come to light during the development of internal marketing at John Nurminen Oy is that the marketing and personnel administration cannot be separated in a service company. They are like two sides of a coin. Consequently, the two policies must be prepared simultaneously and the marketing policy must contain ideas about personnel administration and vice versa.

The definition of service quality is depicted in Figures 1 and 2. Service quality is translated into operational terms as "The Moment of Truth". This means that every one of our customer contacts is a "Moment of Truth". It is the responsibility of the whole organization to provide our contact persons for "The Moment of Truth" with knowledge, skills and support. With the aid of these they are capable of showing their superiority in professional skills and their awareness in the providing of a comprehensive service.

Implementation of the internal marketing program included training, internal information, and management methods and examples. The training was multifaceted and started off with extensive management training with four sessions of one week duration each for top management and three sessions of three days duration each for middle management. Vocational training included basic courses, professional skills courses, language courses, and special subject days. The marketing courses were mostly selling courses, but were not labeled that. Instead they were called courses in "Active Customer Service." The first level course was for two days and included the whole staff, from managing director to truck drivers. Lecturing took three hours, with 15 hours of group work. Truck drivers provided the best ideas during the group sessions. These sessions focused on immediate solutions and/or a listing of problems and action plans with deadlines. The second level course was three days long for 150 contact personnel. Special training courses were also undertaken for EDP personnel and for secretaries. Such training was recognized as an investment in our staff. In total 1,000 training days were accomplished during 1985.

The internal information component of the internal marketing program focused on circulars and the house magazine. Of importance here was the management's role,

the congruence with personnel policy and the integration with external marketing. Various management methods and examples were used based on the premise that "a manager always has subordinates he deserves."

Mass marketing was considered a part of the internal marketing program because of the need to integrate both the external and internal perspectives. The main vehicle to do this was "Nurminen News" which comes out one to two times per month. It is factual in nature with no advertising. It circulates to 4,000 Finnish import and export companies and also to other potential customers. In addition, extensive information campaigns in the press were undertaken: 1981 "Nurminen takes care"; 1982 "100 reasons..." series; 1983 "With knowledge and skill"; 1984 "With knowledge and skill"; 1985 "Our satisfaction through customer satisfaction"; and 1986 "Serving customers for 100 years". Overprint mailing to the addresses of "Nurminen News" media covers the whole country. The third component of the mass marketing was exhibitions and sponsoring: 1. "Finland in Antique Maps", 2. "Transport - '85" exhibition, 3. Nurminen yacht race (yearly), 4. "Salt and Bread of the Sea", a marine painting exhibition. The fourth component here was public relations to the press and the gaining of editorial publicity. Fifth, special subject seminrs were held for CEOs of customer and potential customer companies. Finally, external marketing included career talks in colleges of higher education.

Client research done in 1984 and 1985 attempted to measure the impact of the internal marketing program. The results of this research and other input can be grouped into seven categories. #1: Concerning the first problem about attitudes: according to the research, the service awareness of company personnel and their ability to provide a service is good; deadlines are met and the company operates smoothly; customer problems are examined in detail and resolved; and, the personnel can be relied upon. #2: Regarding information, the data indicated that of the companies in the same sector, John Nurminen Oy was by far the most efficient and the most able at providing detailed information. #3: The company image was found to be that of the best freight forwarding company in Finland. Also, it was the best in all the different service sectors within the freight forwarding business. #4: Market share measurement reveals that John Nurminen's market share has steadily increased every year. In 1985 the number of import consignments handled by Nurminen increased by 8% and export consignments by 12%. During the same period the percentage increase for the whole country was 6% for imports and 2.7% for exports. #5: Profitability of ROI 13% (before interest and taxes) was achieved during all the years under the program. In many cases this figure was exceeded, with 1985 being an exception here. #6: Concerning recruitment, among students, John Nurminen Oy was considered the best employer in its field. #7: In the award category, John Nurminen was awarded the prize for the training organization of 1984. The award was made by the Training Managers Association of Finland.

Other empirical research confirms the above results. For example, image findings included: a company awareness of 100%, very reliable company, modern, very expanding, good international agent network, a full service house, punctual and precise and reasonable price level with respect to the service. There were two negative findings: the company is in second place in warehousing capacity and in being less bureaucratic.

In summary, the experiences of the internal marketing program include: 1. be strong in your faith <u>and</u> secure the support of the top management for the program; 2. do your homework well and define the subject comprehensively; the subject concers a. creation/changing the company culture, and b. combining and coordinating personal administration, training, management methods and the use of internal and external measures; 3. make your own applications; 4. set your objectives with planning on a yearly basis and include measuring the results; 5. remember, it will take years.

Four pragmatic aspects of the internal marketing program are: #1. Managers: the success or failure of the internal marketing program depends on the change in attitudes and behaviors of the managers. The aspects of service awareness must become part of the daily routine of managers. The behaviors and concerns of managers is quickly reflected in the attitudes and behaviors of employees. It must be remembered that a manager always has subordinates he deserves. #2. Circulars and internal information: the internal marketing must be reflected in the company circulars. The style in which they are written has an indirect influence on employee attitudes - an effect which can snowball in time. But here the role of middle management is emphasized. Giving information, tutoring, advising, controlling is the best way of passing on daily information. The service and customer awareness is an important part of the job orientation of a new employee. #3. Company internal training: the vocational training creates the basic knowledge and skills. After that foundation, it is possible to start to change attitudes. In John Nurminen Oy the whole staff was targeted. The objective was mainly to affect the attitudes. This happened in two-day seminars, where the main teaching method was team work. The groups always consisted of workers and employees of different occupations from different branches and departments. Problems and suggestions for solutions were recorded. Then a time schedule was drawn up of actions to be taken plus a list of people responsible for those actions. #4. Coordination of programs: The coordination of the internal and external marketing programs is essential because of their strong interaction. The second coordination question concerns the time span. A five year plan can never succeed. From the very beginning it is too expensive to be accepted. It is much better to create the structures, define the target and operate with one year plans.

Why it was done -- tenets of the internal marketing concept

Key aspects of internal marketing are #1. motivation (to motivate and persuade the employees to perform in a desired manner); #2. marketing-like approach (active, goal-oriented and co-ordinated activities); and, #3. connection with the external market. Internal target groups should include: #1. top management; #2. middle management and supervisors; #3. contact personnel; and #4: supporting personnel - these people are critical to the success of the internal marketing program, even though they may have little direct contact with customers and other publics.

Internal marketing is a process. The most important component of the internal action process is: THE CONTINUOUS MANAGEMENT SUPPORT provided by every single manager and supervisor as part of the normal daily job. Thus training and/or internal communications are not the most important activity of internal marketing. Goals of internal marketing are: #1. to continue the internal training process where formal courses and seminars stop; #2. to demonstrate how subordinates can combine new ideas and routines concerning, for example, customer service and marketing with their everyday job; #3. to

give information and feedback; and, #4. to create an open internal climate where the marketing and customer service aspects of the jobs are considered important.

As a process, the internal marketing tasks of managers and supervisors can be supported by five components: #1. Training programs and service and marketing seminars where the focus is on a. explaining facts about marketing as a continuous process; b. discussions about mutual problems and opportunities among the personnel; c. offering communication skills; and, d. creating favorable attitudes toward marketing and service orientation among all employees. #2. Mass communication support with a. internal booklets and information materials; and, b. slides, overheads, video cassettes, written material, etc. #3. Administration of the personnel where recruitment, career development, job circulation, salaries and wages, and the like are used as a part of the internal process. These administrative activities must be coordinated with the other components of the internal marketing process. #4. Systems support which allows for changing the organization, as for example, changing the billing system so that employees are more able to give good service. #5. External marketing support with realistic promises by sales persons, advertising campaigns and the like.

In summary, internal marketing starts from a notion that the employees are a first, internal market of a firm. This can first of all be viewed as a philosophy for management of the personnel. And, secondly, it should lead to an internal action program with marketing-like actions, goal oriented and coordinated activities. Thirdly, this internal action program is a prerequisite for successful external marketing. Finally, internal marketing usually starts as a project but it must become a continuous process. Internal marketing demands the active support of top management and a service-oriented organization which provides a strategic base for decision making.

AN INCOMPLETE BIBLIOGRAPHY OF INTERNAL MARKETING

Berry, Leonard L. (1981), "The Employee as Consumer," Journal of Bank Marketing, v. 3, #1 (March) 33-40.

George, William R. (1984), "Internal Marketing for Retailers: The Junior Executive Employee", Developments in Marketing Science, v. VII (Academy of Marketing Science) 322-325.

George, William R. and Fran Compton (1985), "How to Initiate a Marketing Perspective In a Health Services Organization," Journal of Health Care Marketing, v. 5 #1 (Winter) 29-37.

George, William R. (1986), "Internal Communications Programs As a Mechanism For Doing Internal Marketing," in Creativity in Services Marketing: What's New, What Works, What's Developing, M. Venkatesan, Diane M. Schmalensee and Claudia Marshall, eds. (Chicago: American Marketing Association) 83-84.

Grongroos, Christian (1981), "Internal Marketing - An Integral Part of Marketing Theory" in Marketing of Services, James H. Donnelly and William R. George, eds. (Chicago: American Marketing Association) 236-238.

Gronroos, Christian (1985), "Internal Marketing – Theory and Practice," in Services Marketing In a Changing Environment, Thomas M. Bloch, Gregory D. Upah and Valarie A. Zeithaml, eds. (Chicago: American Marketing Association) 41-47.

Gummesson, Evert (1987), "Using Internal Marketing to Develop a New Culture – The Case of Ericsson Quality," in Integrating for Competitive Advantage, Carole A. Congram, John A. Czepiel and James B. Shanahan, eds. (Chicago: American Marketing Association).

Kahn, Anna (1985), "Internal Marketing – The Case of the Swedish Savings Bank," in Service Marketing – Nordic School Perspectives, Christian Gronroos and Evert Gummesson, eds. (University of Stockholm) 25-34.

Martensson, Rita (1985), "Internal Marketing Is Important But Not Sufficient In a Crowded Marketplace" in Services Marketing – Nordic School Perspectives, Christian Gronroos and Evert Gummesson, eds. (Stockholm University) 35-43.

Murray, James G. (1979), "The Importance of Internal Marketing," Bankers Magazine (July/August) 38-40.

Murray, Richard M. and Willian R. George (1979), "Managing CPA Personnel – A Marketing Perspective," The CPA Journal (July) 17-22.

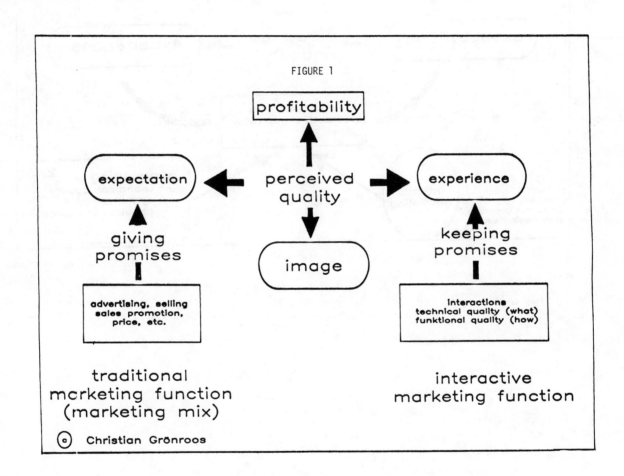

FIGURE 1

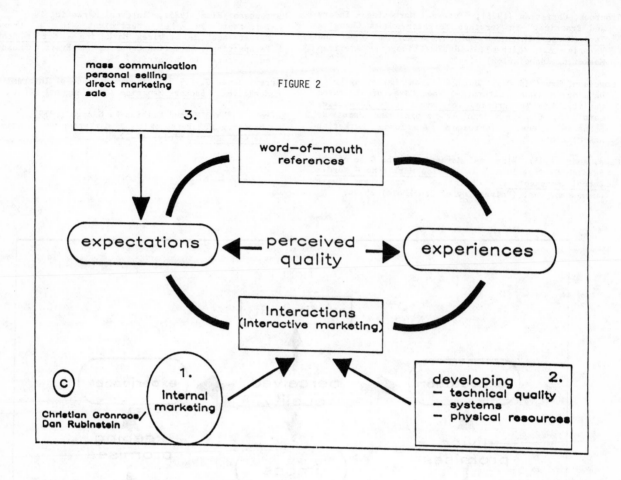

FIGURE 2

USING INTERNAL MARKETING TO DEVELOP A NEW CULTURE - THE
CASE OF ERICSSON QUALITY

Evert Gummesson, Stockholm Consulting Group AB and
University of Stockholm, Sweden

ABSTRACT

Can internal marketing be used in changing a corporate culture? Can approaches and know-how developed in services marketing be of help to an industrial firm producing and marketing to business customers? This paper is about an on-going effort at Ericsson, a major international firm in telecommunications equipment, to change its "quality culture" by means of the Ericsson Quality (EQ) internal marketing program. The presentation stresses two particularly essential issues. The first issue is the actual implementation of the ideas supplied by the internal marketing program. The second is broadening the internal marketing concept to include the notion of the "internal customer".

ON INTERNAL MARKETING AND CORPORATE CULTURE

Internal marketing as a concept has, along with its concommitant techniques, become increasingly established. The concept has received particular attention in Northern Europe and in the research carried out by the "Nordic School of Services" (Grönroos, 1983; Grönroos and Gummesson, 1985). It has emerged out of services marketing. Internal marketing emphasizes the necessity for service firms, where the interface with the customers is particularly broad and intense, to make sure that all contact personnel is well attuned to the mission, goals, strategies, and systems of the company. Otherwise they cannot represent their firm well and successfully handle all those crucial contacts, known as "the moments of truth", that occur in the interaction with customers. It stresses that human resourses are a key factor in developing and maintaining a successful service business.

The idea behind internal marketing is to apply the marketing concept, originally developed for the company's external marketing, to the "internal market" as well. The know-how developed over the years as to how the market is successfully approached is thought to be applicable, with some modification, also to the internal market.

However, the interface between a firm's employees and its customers can be extensive even if the firm is not traditionally thought of as a service firm as such. This is particularly true of firms that market complex equipment or systems, be it to consumers or to businesses. But even if the interface is limited, companies desperately look for better ways of preparing their employees for organizational changes, the introduction of new products and services, new technologies, new routines, etc. Traditional ways of reaching out, using internal memos and magazines, meetings, training courses, and recently to a greater extent video and computer techniques, leave a lot to be desired. Changing a culture is more than "shooting off" a communications program.

In recent years the interest in corporate culture has increased. "In Search of Excellence", Peters and Waterman's unprecedented success, and the spate of management literature that followed in its wake, are basically about the culture of companies and how a culture of excellence is created and maintained. Despite the flood of such recipies for success, many of them both intellectually and emotionally exciting, the more mundane reality of having to implement these grand ideas on a daily basis soon becomes a more difficult proposition than at first meets the eye. In other words: conceiving new ideas may be a great feat but their actual implementation is an even greater one.

THE ERICSSON GROUP

This paper presents a case of internal marketing on a large scale in a business-to-business setting. It is the case of developing a new "quality culture" at Ericsson.

With its headquarters in Stockholm, Sweden, it is a truly international corporation; its home market can only absorb some 20 % of its output, the rest is being sold and partly manufactured globally. In 1985 its sales were US $ 4,5 billion. Ericsson is organized into seven business areas and the total number of subsidiaries and partly owned operations number almost 200.

Since Ericsson was founded 110 years ago it has a stable record of growth, healthy financial status and above all of being at the forefront of applied telcommunications technology. During the past few years, however, it has suffered some financial setbacks.

With the exception of one business area, the customers are few and large, consisting primarily of telecommunications administrations which are state monopolies. The obvious exception to a monopoly situation is the U.S. where, since the recent deregulation, the market consists of seven large, privately owned Bell companies, plus a host of large and small independent operating companies. With a limited number of key customers on one hand and 75,000 employees in 70 countries on the other one can ask where the biggest marketing problem rests: in the external market or in the internal market?

WHY QUALITY?

It is difficult to separate the content of a program from its form (cf. McLuhan's statement that "the medium is the message"). Although this paper is on internal marketing rather than on quality, some aspects of quality have particular relevance for the proper understanding and broadening of the concept of internal marketing.

In 1983 a quality program was triggered by the CEO of Ericsson. The rationale behind the program was a strong conviction that quality was to become the most important weapon in the marketing warfare. Quality has always been a major ingredient in Ericsson's strategy but the situation is a new one. Alternative approaches to quality have emerged. In manufacturing, quality has a long standing tradition. But this is not enough to create overall quality where contributions are needed from all functions of the firm. From a management perspective the focus of quality on manufacturing issues was suboptimal. The traditional manufacturing-oriented approach to quality has been challenged by U.S. thinkers of which J. Edwards Deming, J. M. Juran and Philip B. Crosby are best known. The quality concept has been further developed by the Japanese who could certainly be candidates for the Guinness Book of Records as world champions in combining the roles of quality thinkers and quality doers. The PIMS results (Luchs, 1986) show a correlation between high profits and high quality although the cause and effect relationship is not fully evident. A recent issue of Fortune (Hutton, 1986, p.38) points in the same direction: "As in the past, respondents to FORTUNE's survey point to quality of management and quality of products and services as by far the most important attributes in judging corporate reputations".

Basic differences between the old and the new approaches to quality are reflected in the following statements:

from a product and manufacturing quality concept
to a total quality concept where every function contributes to quality;

from quality being a production management issue
to quality being a top management issue;

from quality being assessed by technicians
to the customer being the judge of quality;

from focus on errors and their appraisal and remedy
to focus on prevention: doing right from the start;

from accepting a certain error ratio as being "normal"
to aiming at zero defects;

from the notion that high quality leads to high costs
to the notion that high quality leads to increased
productivity, increased customer satisfaction and
increased profits.

In conclusion, a change of mindsets coupled with a
change in behavior as concerns quality would be likely
to have positive effects on Ericsson's future.

THE EQ PROGRAM

Thus, as can be seen, many new ideas were waiting to be
brought into the Ericsson culture. How was it, then,
brought about?

The decision was taken to launch the extensive EQ Program. A three year budget of US $ 4 million and a full
time staff of seven was allocated. The task of the staff
was to stimulate line managers to initiate quality activities. Advice was asked from many consultants, both
from the U.S., Japan and Sweden, on quality thinking as
well as on the planning and execution of activities.

To initiate EQ "The EQ 16-Step Program" was presented.
At its core was a list of measures that would be necessary in order to change the quality culture. Here is
a sample of these:

* Analyse customer perceptions of Ericsson and its
  products and services.

* Assess the quality systems at Ericsson and improve
  them.

* Develop more precise quality goals, goal-setting
  procedures and reporting procedures.

* Develop better quality cost definitions and procedures for measuring and reporting quality costs.

* Create an annual Quality Report (an equivalent to
  the annual financial report).

These and other activities were primarily aimed at
creating an environment receptive to quality improvements. This "setting of the stage" is a must if new
ideas are to thrive. My experience of change programs
in organizations, if the programs are limited to communication activities, is that even if the communication is professional, it does not lead to any substantial changes in behavior.

The achievements expected from EQ are summed up in
Figure 1.

FIGURE 1

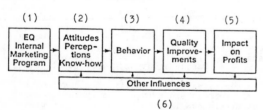

The figure states that EQ (1) could influence attitudes,
perceptions and know-how (2). But even if we have been
successful so far, what guarantees are there that behavior will change (3), that quality will improve (4) and
finally that profits will increase (5)? None, of course,
but one has to be persistent, show stamina, and aim at
success in the long term. Changing a culture is never a
one shot activity. Also, one must not forget other influences (6) that may speed up or delay this process:
the business cycle, activities of the competition, tech-
nological advances etc., and the operational units' own
initiatives, taken independantly of EQ.

The first goal of EQ was to move to square 2 and change
the mindsets of people. This was a move in which communication skills were important and a program based on
established marketing and educational techniques was set
up.

But even in such communication there are pitfalls and
traps. The sequential description in Figure 1 is decep-
tive. Although it is logically neat to postulate that
attitudes and know-how come first and action and results later, it could just as well be the other way
around: that square 3, and even 4 and 5, must be enter-
ed before 2 is reached. Mao once used the expression
that "if you want to know what a pear tastes like, you
have to change the pear by eating it". Until you have
yourself been directly involved in a change you may not
be able to understand what it is all about (Gummesson,
in press). It is very basic, it is "learning by doing".

The remaining part of the paper will concentrate on a
few issues that are of particular significance for the
implementation of changes and the achievement of concrete results. A more complete overview of EQ may be
found in Larsson and Nylander (1986).

ON IMPLEMENTATION AND THE INTERNAL CUSTOMER

Throughout this paper I have stressed the necessity of
getting past the mere communication activities and
getting down to direct action. Arriving at squares 3
to 5 of Figure 1 can be a long and arduous process, a
fact that academic researchers largely ignore (Gummesson, 1974, 1984). Recent work by Bonoma eloquently
spells this out (1985, p. 3): "The preoccupation (of
managers) with implementation problems came as a great
surprise to me, because I was eminently well prepared
to help management find its way out of strategic dark-
ness but blind as a bat about the factors important in
actually getting a strategy executed".

The concept most often referred to as a powerful tool
for implementation is the Japanese QC Circle (or "quality circle"). It is well-known everywhere today. It is
also used by Ericsson but in a slightly amended form and
then called EQ Teams. This is a way of engaging everyone
in quality improvement work and letting them "taste the
pear".

A concept which is less well known but which goes well
both with quality circles and internal marketing is the
internal customer. In the light of this concept we ad-
vocate that everyone at Ericsson has customers inside
the firm and that everyone should act as a supplier to
these. It then becomes just as important to deliver high
quality products and services to the internal customer
as it is to deliver high quality to the external customer. Eventually, quality is a satisfied external customer, the road to which is paved by satisfied internal
customers.

This concept was not fully clear when EQ started but its
significance has grown during the project. We doubt that
it is a new concept and we do not know its origin, but
we know it to be used in Japan, for example by Nissan
Motor Company.

In my experience, the larger problem of corporations,
especially in those of large size, is often integration,
not specialization. For example, a design problem is
just as often an interface problem with marketing, manufacturing, finance etc. as it is a problem which can be
solved inside the design department. The internal customer concept then becomes an "integrator" helping to make
every function, individual and activity a stronger link
in the chain of events which leads to greater customer
satisfaction.

The practical use of the concept requires everyone to
interview his internal customers and find out what he
does well and what could be done better - from the internal customer's point of view. Interviews can be
person-to-person or group-to-group.

Where does this concept take us? It fulfils three essential criteria: it is simple, it involves everyone, and
it is implementable. It is certainly not a high tech
concept of the space age, it involves no fancy statis-
tical formulas and computer programming, it is back to

basics. It is back to the need for understanding one's contribution to the success of the firm. In a complex industrial environment few people, even in high tiers of the hierarchy, fully see their role in the firm's total operations. It creates a natural feedback situation: people get to know if their performance is appreciated or not.

The effect of internal marketing is strongly reinforced by the concept of the internal customer. The concept brings communication down to face-to-face interaction where the actual implementation takes place: on the shopfloor, in the office of designers, planners, clerks and others.

EQ RESULTS

EQ is followed up carefully. On two occasions an external consultant has been brought in to evaluate certain aspects of the acceptance of EQ. Quality activities and results are reported regularly by operational units. It is too early to assess the overall effect of EQ but two examples will illustrate the types of concrete quality results which are within the spirit of EQ.

The first example is from an Ericsson factory which produces printed circuit boards for telephone switching systems. Letting everybody take part in the EQ training sessions and introducing the concept of the internal customer has had a dramatic effect on operations. It has resulted in a 40 % increase of productivity (thus lowering costs), from a 50 to 90 % rate of on-schedule deliveries (thus increasing customer satisfaction), reductions of "error points" (an internal measure of defects) from 100 to 30 (thus reducing future service costs), when comparing the first six months of 1985 to the previous six months.

The second example concerns the product and service quality of computers. A change of focus from appraisal and remedy to prevention initiated field quality task forces to investigate defects in the assembly and delivery to local markets. This has led to eliminating the need for receiving inspection at the local subsidiary (thus lowering costs) and a damatic reduction in defects, for example an improvement of keyboard quality from being only 70 % to being 98 % perfect (perfect including also such things as being completely clean) six months later (thus increasing customer satisfaction and lowering service costs).

These are just two examples of results from individual Ericsson units. The role of EQ in this is not clear cut. One cannot say that EQ caused this to happen even if this would reinforce the egos of those who run the program. In all honesty, we do not know what had happened had EQ not existed. But we can say that EQ has spotlighted the issue of quality, helped to support quality thinking, and introduced new techniques for practical application thereby increasing the likelihood that line managers give priority to quality improvements.

After three years EQ will now enter into its "second wave" and concentrate on certain quality issues. Planing is in full progress when this is written.

CONCLUSIONS

My experience of this and other projects is that internal marketing is a potent concept not only for service firms but for industrial firms as well. It must not be limited to a superficial communications program but should stress action and profits. The notion of the internal customer is a useful contribution for making internal marketing more efficient.

REFERENCES

Bonoma, Thomas V. (1985), The Marketing Edge, New York: The Free Press.

Grönroos, Christian (1983), Strategic Marketing and Management in the Service Sector, Cambridge, MA: Marketing Science Institute.

_____and Gummesson, Evert, eds. (1985), Service Marketing - Nordic School Perspectives, Stockholm, Sweden: University of Stockholm, Dept. of Business Administration, Research Report R 1985:2.

Gummesson, Evert (1974), "Organizing for Strategic Management - A Conceptual Model", Long Range Planning, Vol. 7, No. 2 (April), 13-18.

_____(1984), Resultatinriktad marknadsföring (Result-Oriented Marketing), Stockholm, Sweden: Norstedts.

_____(1986), Quality - The Ericsson Approach, Stockholm, Sweden: Ericsson.

_____(in press), Academic Researcher and/or Management Consultant, London: Chartwell-Bratt.

Hutton, Cynthia (1986), "America's Most Admired Corporations", Fortune (Jan. 6), 32-43.

Larsson, Carl-Göran and Nylander, Per (1986), "Ericsson Quality", Ericsson Review, No. 1, 2-10.

Luchs, Robert (1986), "Successful Businesses Compete on Quality - Not Costs", Long Range Planning, Vol. 19, No. 1, 12-17.

INTERNAL MARKETING OF MARKETING

Fran Compton, American Red Cross, Columbus

ABSTRACT

To help prepare all employees for the implementation of internal and external marketing efforts, this health related agency conducts a simple orientation to the basic concepts of marketing. In the process a matrix is developed which serves as both a training tool and service program analysis tool for management.

INTRODUCTION

Trying to integrate sophisticated business techniques and practices into the not-for-profit and/or health care organization can create unanticipated, negative consequences. Neglect to do so can have even worse ramifications. Marketing is not yet home free. For example, in the November 8 issue of MARKETING NEWS, there is an article citing the hostility of physicians to the concept of patients as "customers" of health service. The American Medical Association has reminded physicians (and marketing persons) that medicine is a "profession, calling and not a business". However, even to practice medicine there needs to be an exchange between the person with a need (patient or 'horror!' customer) and the person with the means to satisfy that need (the physician). Unless the physician is Doc Holliday sitting in the Longbranch Saloon ready to deliver his services on the spot to the next victim of the cowboy in the black hat, there are many others involved in this exchange process. But when we in health services attempt to integrate marketing into our organizations, two possible hazards can present themselves: first, considerable internal hostility, disassociation and barrier erection, and/or secondly, an endowment of the new approach with almost mystical powers that become the special province of one group within the organization - probably the marketing department. (You may soon be expected to solve all problems.) New language and new approaches to old problems, identification of new problems, or changes in the "tried and true way" may seem too strange and threatening to be considered by the rest of the organization. Marketing, with its lexicon of terms from; bundle of benefits, differential advantage and competitive edge, to targeting, etc., with our focus on specific groups rather than on the community as a whole, and most of all our concentration of attention on the user rather than ourselves as the provider. This can all create barriers that make the best of marketing broaden the commitment to success (need I say, to excellence?) an internal marketing of marketing is suggested. Of marketing as a concept, not your finely designed marketing plan as a specific - that comes later. We have used it successfully at our Blood Center in Central Ohio and also field tested it with a hospital and with a divergent group of American Red Cross volunteers.

PROGRAM AND MATRIX

We feel it has been successful, the hostility headed off, the learning was retained, the appreciation enhanced. Additionally, we developed a matrix that lends itself to a variety of managerial uses, as well as an educational tool. We first began this program several years ago after I became inspired by a training course taught by Dr. William George. Recent readings indicate a growing sensitivity to the internal market of our employees. In the spring issue of SERVICES MARKETING Newsletter, James H. Donnelly, Jr., Professor of Business Administration, University of Kentucky, referred to the now well known "moments of truth" in a service encounter. He emphasized that those of us interested in effective service delivery must learn how and why employee performance occurs if we are going to effectively manage

moments of truth. His article very well delineated the connection between employee motivation, behavior, performance and results. My experience has been that one effective way to affect employee motivation is to bring employees on board, developing their awareness of their roles. When employees can buy-in on the marketing or exchange process, their sense of team membership is enhanced and they have a clearer vision of how they are a real part of the mission of the service organization which by definition is to provide (deliver) service.

Let me give you a little background. The American Red Cross organizes its blood collections regionally through the Blood Services division. Within Blood Services it is the Donor Resources Development department which has the responsibility for planning and implementing growth strategies for blood collection. In the past, we were not actively pursuing a marketing approach. However, it was no longer working to hold a bloodmobile and wait for the eager donors to flock in. We could not simply say "we need you" and the donors would respond. Then the needs of the donor were not paramont. Our need was our focus. With the realization that across the nation, we needed to improve our performances, the National American Red Cross began offering training in marketing to Donor Resurces Development directors. They acquired the expertise of Dr. William George. He became our early guru and he pushed us into learning and using marketing skills. He brought us into the more sophisticated arenas of services marketing.

In those early years, DRD was starting to use marketing skills but there were still other areas of the organization that had not been so enlightened. And our DRD departments in many Centers did not necessarily comfortably set the pace for the rest of the organization. In some centers barriers to DRD existed, including a perceived prima donna status (the fact that the women all wore suits seemed to loom large in those days.) Our schedules permitted us to come and go, etc., while others were stuck at their desks and so forth. Could this prima donna status now be ascribed to the marketing departments of health care organizations? You all with the MBA degrees, the charts and graphs, the perceived big budgets, the ear of management...your newness alone? In any case, it seemed to me that if marketing were to work for DRD and blood collections, everyone had to be on board, it has to permeate our organization and I did not want the usual barriers to DRD activities to be raised again.

Fortunately, I work in a very team oriented Center. Also, we did not have a marketing director at the time I began this program so I wasn't on anyone's turf. So, with the approval of management, I was given the opportunity to practice marketing of marketing. We have offered this orientation/training to public relations, volunteers, nursing, technical and management as well as to donor resources staff. To date, all post-training responses have been very positive.

Now to the point. A simple training presentation was developed to communicate the essense of marketing to staff that for the most part do not see themselves as part of the marketing process.

The presentation is designed to last one hour, with 30 minutes of discussion and participation built in. I don't want this to be just another "talking at me" experience. The participation helps build acceptance and enhances retention.

The five specific goals of the orientation are:

1. To clarify the basics of marketing in order to dispel myths about the marketing mystery.

2. To illustrate how marketing concepts include everyone in an organization in everyday activities.

3. To present basic marketing terms to those who are unfamiliar with them.

4. To provide exercise materials concerning basic marketing techniques.

5. To build awareness/acceptance/appreciation.

In a recent mini-workshop at the National convention of the American Red Cross, we used this format with a group of volunteers that had had no previous exposure to marketing terms and were skeptical. We helped a Chairman of Volunteers learn to segment the 100,000 residents of her community. She was needing to recruit some clerical volunteers. We talked her through a simple version of the process to look for women with high school education, clerical skills, not now employed, with children in school at least three hours, and with access to transportation to get them to the Red Cross. It was exciting to see how this volunteer now felt she could be more efficient in her recruitment efforts. She was learning and using marketing skills of the most basic nature and was no longer uncomfortable with the fact that the "American Red Cross is into marketing".

We begin with the clarification that marketing is more than just:

* Buzz words (remember communications about 10 years ago?)

* PR/advertising, although it does include activities from these disciplines.

* Sales/donor resources development, although of course these disciplines are heavily committed to it.

* A management tool, although of course it takes management commitment to marketing orientation for this all to work.

Marketing is defined and simplified to terms of the most fundamental ingredients: Marketing is a way of thinking and acting about what we do based on the concept of exchange. Although this is a gross simplification of the most sophisticated inclusive definitions, it is understandable by the initiates and acceptable to the more experienced.

On to the exchange process. We use a worksheet with five headings: they/want/exchange/we/have.

Of course, we start with the "they" category. We list publics, markets, consumers, research and actual potential. This use of marketing terms under an easily recognized neutral heading adds to their comfort level.

In talking about the "they" category, I talk a group through a segmentation experience. To go from the public of 2.1 million people in Central Ohio to a market of female donors, age 21 - 35 who are not employed outside the home and who live in communities of 1,000 to 5,000 people. Obviously, I indicate that research is what usually gets us to our specific markets, but just to get them thinking in these terms seems to catch their interest. We also talk about the particular wants this group might have. Again, unscientific but illustrative of what marketing is about. The group participation adds zest and already the group is "into" marketing.

We move on to the "we" component. After a few minutes of discussion, participants readily agree that "we" is the entire organization as well as each department and eventually each employee. The fact that everyone is included will be re-emphasized later.

Next we consider what we "have". Perhaps this is the first time many of the participants realize that we are not just taking blood from donors but that we have many "benefits" for them...indeed even a bundle of benefits. Exchanges are being made even if the benefits are usually intangible and subtle. Some of these benefits might include a good feeling about helping others, a mini-physical, cookies in the canteen, time off work, a safe unit of blood at the hospital whenever its needed by anyone.

On to the "exchange". Here we talk about competition, differential advantages, delivery of benefits; marketing mix of the variables including product or service, price, place and promotion and ultimately, the need for a marketing plan to put all this together. At first, most feel that our Blood Center does not have competition since we are a total supply to all our hospitals. To their surprise they are able to identify a number of competitive distractions such as apathy, company picnics on the same day as a bloodmobile, employee lay-offs, a poor economy, and so forth.

Once they identify competition, we talk about how to overcome this competition. This transition to differential advantages is smooth and logical and leads directly into the consideration of benefits and once again, the participants recognize that everyone is involved...from the greeter at the door to the delivery volunteer who rushes the blood to the hospital to treat an injured child.

It takes some stretching of minds to reach a consensus that our product or service is the opportunity to share life, to "feel good about yourself", as well as a safe unit of blood. But there is an easier understanding of price...its the cost to the donor in time, inconvenience, fear, etc. For example donating blood cannot take much less than 30 minutes under optimum conditions. This is the base price (time equals cost), however, inefficient collections that cost two or three hours is a price that is too high for the benefits offered. And many of the participants have a role in controlling this price. This can apply to almost any service - but most employees would see price only in dollars exchanged.

By the end of the discussion on the marketing exchange process, participants understand why a marketing plan is important. They are now supportive of the need to specify how the entire organization plans to manage these exchanges.

A final exercise involves matching features of the blood services program to benefits sought by potential donors. Obviously, the most appropriate method for establishing the benefits sought is to conduct carefully designed marketing research studies of donors, potential donors and non-donors. We have done some of this research ourselves and we use others', especially with feedback from our customers and intuition. One test we compiled included benefits sought such as self-esteem, convenience, time away from work, belongingness, affirmation of health, semi-intangible items such as pins, snacks, etc. We even include psychosecurity, sense of importance, relief from guilt by a fulfillment of a social obligation based on the idea that most people know they should give blood and often feel guilty about not doing so. "Absolution" is a relevant program feature to communicate that "you don't need to feel guilty now" and even for those who were deferred, at least they tried.

The first part of the matrix facilitates analysis of the relationship between benefits sought and program features. It has a broader significance than just this training and can be used as a management or marketing tool in itself. It focuses management consideration on issues such as benefits which may require more attention or features which provide the most and the fewest benefits sought, etc. A grid is used with the list of benefits/features noted across the top and the benefits sought down the left side of the grid. A check is made where the two elements meet. Rows or columns with many notations highlight items of current significance. For example, the effectiveness of the program's recognition component may warrant further study. Those rows or columns with few notations may indicate items of greater potential or of possible elimination. For example, what additional features can be added by the Blood Center to meet the donor's need of "importance"? It enables participants to see more easily the relationship between the features offered by Blood Services and the benefits sought by donors. It is a good tool to evaluate proposed new services. Will we have anything anyone wants?

The second grid extends the analysis by examing who delivers these promised features/benefits of the Blood Services program. Usually it is the DRD department personnel or sales who make the promises, but others within the Blood Center are expected to deliver them. This grid highlights all of those persons directly involved in the exchange process. The impact of the quality and quantity of their delivery greatly affects DRD's ability to mobilize and extend the donor base. The more those who "deliver" the promises of the Blood Services program understand and acknowledge their roles in the exchange process, the more likely it is that the Blood Center will attract more donors, and more units per donor, during a specified time period.

The "delivery of benefits" part of the matrix highlights many of the essential marketing factors that must be considered in developing, or revising, the marketing mix. For example, based on the analysis, blood drive coordinators are a vital force in delivering the benefits of the Blood Center's program. Coordinators are group organizers who do the actual donor recruitment. Management may decide to audit the entire exchange process between coordinators and the Blood Center. More effective exchanges with this target group (Coordinators) should enhance the level of donor satisfaction because of their better delivery of the organization's benefits. Since health education benefits can be delivered by every one of the organization's communicators, an audit here could determine which communicator groups need additional training to become more motivated to deliver the Blood Center's health education services. Focused management scrutiny of the most important marketing factors is facilitated by the "delivery of benefits" part of the matrix. This matrix provides direction for initiating quality control check points and systems within the delivery process. (Copies of the grid or matrix are available through me by sending your request to: Fran Compton, Director, Donor Resources Development, American Red Cross, 995 E. Broad St., Columbus, OH 43205.)

By this point in the presentation, nearly everyone acknowledges his/her role in marketing the Blood Services program. They recognize the validity of a customer-consciousness approach for all Blood Services personnel and the great importance of their own role in achieving it. The marketing mystique is dispelled; it is not seen as the prerogative of only one department. Agreement is established that good marketing in a service organization directly involves all personnel.

Throughout, the presentation is built on group involvement, simple terms and familiar ingredients. It is not an abstract, academic or obtuse lecture on marketing theory, and it exemplifies good marketing in that it is developed around the needs of the internal audience.

ANOTHER SETTING

The benefits analysis exercise, or using the matrix, was undertaken by the planning staff at Medical Center Hospital, Chillicothe, Ohio, a 284 bed general community hospital. Empirical data available from earlier marketing surveys were helpful in determining the benefits sought which were then compared to the features offered by the hospital. Their matrix shows an example of an overall analysis of general

community benefits sought and features offered. It is not a comprehensive illustration because of the wide array of services available. When focusing on specific areas of service delivery to specific target markets, the entries are selected for the relevant needs of the particular group under consideration. According to Roberta Stewart, Director of Planning at Medical Center Hospital, hospital in-patient surgery consumers seek different benefits than do patient visitor consumers in the hospital. She believes, however, that the overall analysis of the general community is useful because the needs and wants of the total hospital environment must be attended to by the entire hospital staff. Their matrix illustrates the great variety of hospital personnel involved in communicating and delivering the benefits and features of the hospital. Clearly, all staff play a part in marketing a hospital's services. Analysis of benefits via these two matrices increase the likelihood of more efficient and effective marketing of the hospital's services. I'm sure the Board of Trustees was surprised at its inclusive responsibility.

EVALUATION

This training evokes positive feedback to the presentation; but is this a perception based on the "excitement of the moment"? Six months after the first training, a brief survey is conducted on a sample of the participants to measure their perceptions about marketing and the training they received. Responses from the various groups to the 15 Likert-type statements indicated the existence of a very positive feeling on the part of the participants to the marketing training and to the usefulness of the marketing ideas they have been exposed to. Most felt they were now using the marketing concepts and understood their role in the marketing process. Yet, in the key marketing areas of all personnel as deliverers of the service, the donor as consumer and recognition of competitors, a higher level of uncertainty points to an on-going need for additional marketing training. Indeed, the uncertain responses on these last three statements may confirm Kotler's "law of fast forgetting" and his warning that managers must always fight a strong tendency to forget basic marketing principles.

The participants were asked, in an open ended question, to describe briefly at least one way they had used the marketing concepts gained from the training. All but one were able to do so, with the responses from the nurses being especially noteworthy of their shift in thinking to that of customer consciousness. The response to the open-ended question on whether to recommend this marketing training to other Blood Centers was very positive, with more than three-fourths giving specific comments as to why they felt it would be good for others to undertake such training. The results of the evaluation are covered in more detail in an article published in the Journal of Health Care Marketing, Winter, 1985.

CONCLUSIONS

Internal marketing, especially in its emphasis on customer consciousness, the "they wants", asserts that to serve the needs of the market, the organization must first serve the needs of its own personnel. This is especially true for service firms because for customers who are purchasing services, the personnel are the service. Dr. George has explained the crucial role of staff in a service firm in this way:

> First, public contact personnel are a key element in an image development program. Second, they can provide vital service differentiation for the firm. Third, since visible and tangible reinforcement is missing in a service offering (as compared to a good), the customer's uncertainty can be most effectively reduced by public contact personnel. They can reassure

customers that the best choice was made and
stimulate them to buy or use or come again
and to tell others of their satisfaction.
In addition to reducing cognitive dissonance,
such human and personal dimensions of the
service will add materially to its perceived
value (and) will encourage repeat sales...

Thus, managers of health care organizations must explicitly
and continuously reinforce a marketing perspective to all
internal personnel.

The training presentation described above is an easy, effective way to initiate a marketing perspective within the
health care organization. It can help head off hostility or
unreal expectations. It can be adapted easily to any health
care setting for training purposes. It is essentially time-
less and can be used as an orientation program for new staff
as well as for initial training when a market approach is
adopted. A matrix with another delivery system could readily be made to reflect an entirely different set of benefits
sought and features offered. Similarly, another set of de-
liverers/communicators could be substituted in the second
matrix. What will remain the same, however, is that all
personnel from the various departments will be able to understand that good marketing includes everyone within the health
care organization.

PRESIDENT'S CLUB:
SUCCESSFUL INTERNAL MARKETING AT BANCOHIO

Clare Balombin, BancOhio National Bank, Columbus

ABSTRACT

In 1985 BancOhio decided to increase its asset (loan) portfolio by setting steep goals. The success enjoyed by the
bank was due to an integrated marketing plan which responded to the needs of those employees responsible for "selling" the loans, as well as to the general public.

INTRODUCTION

BancOhio National Bank in Columbus, Ohio conducted a very
successful loan marketing campaign in 1985. The story of
how we pulled it together involved the integration of several aspects of marketing, particularly internal marketing.
We demonstrated excellence in internal marketing in two
ways, 1) in using the President's Club for Installment
Lenders to communicate to and motivate those employees who
were the primary customer contact persons, and 2) in managing the Loan Promotion Task Force which implemented a
full-scale, integrated promotional campaign as well as
hammering out the details of the President's Club.

BACKGROUND

In early 1985 Retail Line Management at BancOhio National
Bank decided that the overriding priority for the year
would be the generation of quality assets (installment
loans). An in-depth examination of our lending situation,
however, revealed serious problems. In the previous four
years there had been no consistency in lending practices.
The faucet had been turned off and on for dealer loans, as
well as for consumer loans. A large percentage of our own
customers went elsewhere for personal loans.

On the internal side our associates did not feel that they
were adequately recognized for their efforts; they also
felt isolated from management interest, despite their willingness to work hard. This feeling of isolation reflected
the uncertainty evident in our 124-branch network after
several branch closings and our merger with another bank.

Based on the need to generate assets, a 17% increase in
total installment loans booked was established as the goal
for 1985. Raising that much money in loans was more than
a summer project. This idea dovetailed with an examination
of lending patterns over a several year period. For the
first time we realized that there were two peak lending
seasons, and that it was possible to support both with
advertising and promotional campaigns. The traditional
eight-week summer schedule of promotional lending activities, however, could not be extended into a full-year effort without changing the way platform associates were
directed, motivated and rewarded for their efforts. The
usual branch and district level goals were too far removed
from the individual; they could not provide individual rewards and recognition, nor could they incite individual
responsibility for results.

PRESIDENT'S CLUB

We decided to leverage the platform associates' loyalty
and willingness to work hard by formulating goals for 400
individuals. These goals would reflect the effort which
went into "selling" a loan, i.e., the customer contact and
advice on financing options, as well as closing the loan.
(Credit approvals, the former standard, are still used when
tracking problem loans.) Rewarding loan "sales" was a
radical concept for senior management, as well as for those
associates who had previously thought of themselves as
front-office processors of loan documents.

Once the decision was made to provide individual goals -
at the end of March - we had very little time to effect the
necessary changes: Retail line management had to recast
and communicate the lending goals within six weeks of our
go-ahead. Our manual and computer reporting systems had
to be adjusted within six weeks of that occurrence, and
enthusiasm had to be maintained over a year of effort,
rather than over the traditional eight-week summer promotional blitz.

To provide a framework for these tasks, we established a
President's Club for Installment Lenders to honor everyone who reached 100% of his or her goals. The idea for
this "club" arose from the stated desire of the installment lenders for recognition in addition to financial rewards for their hard work. How could they be honored for
their efforts? The insurance industry had its "million
dollar roundtables" which provide plaques, trips, bonuses
and photographs in the local newspapers. Some lenders had
mentioned the positive effects and conversational uses for
handsome desk accessories with their names and their
achievements. BancOhio also had recently appointed a new
president.

The result was the proposal and acceptance of the President's Club as a mechanism to recognize top lenders, with
the proviso that it would have the flexibility to be extended to other product lines if it were successful in
motivating the lending associates and in creating a sales
atmosphere in the banking offices.

Components of the recognition and sales process were:

1) a major kick-off dinner for 360 lending associates
from the three regions to present all elements of both
the internal and external campaigns to everyone involved in selling loans.
2) follow-up sales rallies two months later (in July
and August) in each of the three regions.
3) a "half-way" to the end of the year luncheon with
senior management in September to honor those who had
made 75% of their goals. The purpose was to shorten
the waiting period for recognition.
4) monthly/weekly incentive rewards designed and administered on a regional and district basis by those units
as in previous years.
5) five grand prize trips for two (travel and lodging)
to Hawaii with an additional week of vacation added to
cover the time. These trips were awarded to the one
lending associate in each region with the highest percentage over goal, as well as to the two lenders with
the highest dollar volume overall.
6) an engravable desk accessory (a walnut base with a
pen, calculator and note pad) which would be awarded to
those who achieved 100% of their lending goals by the
end of December.
7) bi-weekly motivational and informational/procedural
newsletters sent under a specially designed "President's Club" letterhead.
8) a final sales rally in January of 1986 with announce-
ment of the grand prize winners and awarding of the
engraved desk accessories by BancOhio's president.
Sales plans for 1986 were also presented.

LOAN PROMOTION TASK FORCE

Immediately following senior management approval of the
marketing plan in late March, a list was drawn up of all
the groups which would be immediately helpful to an integrated marketing plan. These were: market planning
(chair), advertising, consumer credit administration, installment loan systems and operations, retail line management and product management. Telemarketing and market
administration were added as the campaign progressed because of their involvement in the field. Representatives
were invited to an initial planning meeting where responsibilities were explained and divided. Weekly meetings
were held for three months until the first wave of advertising was over and all reporting changes had been made.

Monthly meetings were held until the second flight of advertising approached when weekly meetings were held again.

A wide range of marketing ideas flowed from all members of the group as they took the outline of the external and internal marketing plans and added their own experience and expertise to the solutions. Particular help was provided by the representatives of the installment loan operations department and the consumer credit department. These persons had the "street smarts" to report on both operational quirks and human nature which could change the impact of a proposed program. They provided input on which ideas would go over better with the branches and the public and designed the details of the tracking system which provided feedback to our lenders.

Any problems requiring input from senior management were quickly resolved through the efforts of the various members of the group because of the major role played by all in the design of the final programs. Shared ownership of both the President's Club program and the advertising efforts ensured that all points of view were considered and that the best program possible was implemented.

ADVERTISING

We called our campaign, "We're Lending a $1,000,000 a Day," because we wanted to communicate to both our internal and external markets that BancOhio was back in the business of consumer lending. A wide range of regular media coverage and targeted marketing projects was designed to support our lenders' efforts. We also personalized the lending process in some non-metropolitan areas by using lenders' pictures and newspaper advertisements.

RESULTS

The results of our coordinated efforts to support the sales of installment loans and establish an effective, ongoing internal marketing program at BancOhio during 1985 can be looked at as both qualitative and quantitative successes. In terms of loan volume, BancOhio achieved a 32% increase in year-end new business outstandings for 1985 over 1984. This was 15 percentage points above the original, aggressive plan. These results were achieved without raising the override percentages (percentage of applications which can be approved in spite of being rated below desirable levels by our credit scoring system). Forty-six percent of our lenders reached the 100% mark in terms of their individual goals. These 192 lenders included regional and district managers whose banking offices, as a group, reached 100% of their goals.

BancOhio also increased its installment loan penetration of households claiming at least one account relationship with BancOhio. With a change from 1.33 loans per household to 1.50 loans per household in this group, BancOhio's share of their installment loans increased 40%. Our penetration of all households in the market increased by 12%.

In qualitative terms, the provision of a feedback mechanism and expected rewards improved morale and increased enthusiasm for the job of selling the bank's credit services. The monthly progress reports provided a review of where each lender stood versus his or her annual goals. These also communicated to the lending associates management's expectations for superior performance. In the end a solid feeling of competence and achievement was felt by all in attendance at our final "victory" rally which was "chaired" by the president of the bank. The notation of President's Club achievement on lenders' annual reviews rounded out the bank's efforts to recognize their work.

Several other outcomes resulted from the success of the 1985 President's Club/Installment Loan program. First, the President's Club has been extended in 1986 to include goals for equity lines of credit, new checking and new savings accounts. An appropriate mix of goals has been assigned to each platform associate. This mix reflects individual responsibilities and banking office business patterns. Second, within our new corporate family reporting to National City Corporation, the other major bank affiliate has decided to implement its own President's Club, while a second medium-sized member is considering implementation.

CONCLUSION

An integrated approach which included internal marketing programs helped us to exceed our lending goals at BancOhio in 1985. Our particular successes in internal marketing resulted from a combination of shared ownership and design, the support given by our advertising campaign, the local sales rallies and an incentive program which provided recognition and rewards, as well as an ongoing structure for communicating the bank's priorities.

RESTRUCTURING A MULTIPLE DIVISION SERVICE COMPANY
FOR MARKETING EFFECTIVENESS

James S. Hensel, Univ. of South Florida, Tampa

ABSTRACT

The Peninsula Motor Club is a large multiple division service operation whose operations were extensively audited in an attempt to identify marketing restructuring improvement opportunities. It was management's opinion that their two most critical marketing organization needs were to develop a formal marketing planning department and more expertise in direct mail, media advertising, and sales management. The interesting conclusion of the study was that a more critical marketing restructuring need was to build a marketing infrastructure to help overcome customer satisfaction inhibitors associated with the current service delivery mechanism.

INTRODUCTION

The Peninsula Motor Club is a large multiple division service operation that includes an American Automobile Association motor club membership program, insurance bureau, travel agency, and a special services division. It is the fifth largest AAA operation nationally, with branch offices geographically dispersed across 46 counties in Florida.

The 1980's has been a period of rapid growth for the Peninsula Motor Club in terms of number of automobile club memberships and revenues generated from all operating divisions. Additionally, during this time period the company has been busy evolving toward a more sophisticated and professional management system as well as computerization of its internal operations. As a result, the management team and organization structure has been focused extensively on internal operating matters. A major concern of top management has been that external market opportunities are not being fully cultivated, or totally overlooked altogether.

Senior level management was convinced that most of the organization's revenue growth was being automatically fueled by the accelerated growth of Florida's population base, rather than the result of their own marketing expertise and planned marketing effort. In fact, the lack of a formalized marketing planning approach and functional expertise in the areas of direct mail, media advertising, and professional sales management was perceived as a major deficiency and barrier to future growth, particularly in the face of increasing competition. It was management's opinion that in order to take full advantage of existing market opportunities and continue to maintain an acceptable growth rate they needed to restructure for improved marketing effectiveness. Management's bias was that their two most vital marketing restructuring needs were to:

- Create a senior level corporate marketing position with appropriate staff to concentrate on marketing planning for all divisions.

- Develop and/or acquire necessary functional skill and expertise to overcome external communication deficiencies.

THE SERVICE OPERATIONS AUDIT

A traditional marketing audit procedure was initiated to evaluate the existing state of marketing effectiveness and isolate restructuring improvement opportunities. As a part of the marketing audit procedure a service operations audit was also implemented to focus more specifically on the efficiency and effectiveness of the service delivery mechanism, customer-contact personnel, and support staff.

The Peninsula Motor Club's operations were studied over a six-month time period. Interviews were conducted with senior executives, middle management personnel, and staff in each of the operating divisions, and at the corporate, regional, and branch management levels. Service delivery customer contact and support personnel were also interviewed as to the existing service delivery mechanism, its advantages and disadvantages, perceived levels of customer satisfaction, and suggestions for improvement. Policies, procedures, and rules of operation were also studied, and customers were extensively observed while accessing the service delivery mechanism. An attempt was made to analyze the quality and consistency with which services were presently being delivered, and to isolate customer satisfaction inhibitors.

Problem: An Exclusive Internal Operations and Control Orientation

The study results revealed that the Peninsula Motor Club's service delivery mechanism and customer contact personnel were disproportionately internally and operations oriented, and becoming increasingly inflexible in serving customers. Evidently, the challenges of managing and controlling operations in the face of growth across an expanding number of geographically dispersed branch offices, and the simultaneous demands of system automation and management systems development had led to a more rigid set of policies, procedures, a bureaucratic management structure, and an exclusively internal, control-oriented focus. The very policies, procedures, management systems, and supervisory techniques designed to improve internal efficiency and control during a period of dramatic growth appeared to also be the greatest inhibitors to consistent high quality service delivery and customer satisfaction.

Customer Satisfaction Inhibitors

Since many of the evolved changes were made without customer viewpoint input and were designed solely for internal control and convenience reasons they often created unnecessary customer inconveniences in accessing the service delivery mechanism. And, in the attempt to adhere to many of the new control procedures and satisfy the demands of an automated data processing system customer contact personnel complained that it was difficult to allocate adequate time and effort to providing high levels of personalized service. The focus was becoming more one of following procedures properly rather than serving the customer.

More specifically, the study revealed the following inhibitors to delivering high quality customer experiences:

- A degree of inconsistency and confusion in the interpretation and implementation of policies and procedures.

- A growing inability to respond quickly and accurately to customer problems and inquiries, particularly when they were unique and/or required a creative response.

- A perception on the part of customer-contact and support staff that growth had led to a difficult situation with respect to delivering high quality service in a timely fashion. This was particularly true for peak seasonal situations.

- A feeling of isolation from corporate decision-making and planning on the part of branch management and staff.

- A declining morale and motivation level on the part of customer contact personnel that was based on the feeling that their job was overwhelming.

The end result was an erratic service delivery quality level as experienced by customers and a deteriorating ability to be responsive to customers at the point of customer contact. This was a particularly severe problem given the past reputation of the Peninsula Motor Club and high expectations of its members with respect to reliability, quality, and responsiveness.

THE NEED FOR A MARKETING INFRASTRUCTURE

The interesting conclusion of the recommendation phase of the audit procedure was that the single most critical restructuring need was one of building a marketing infrastructure that stresses a clear understanding of customer viewpoints and needs as a vital input to planning and decision-making, an orientation of all employees and operations to understanding, serving, and satisfying customers, the need for consistency in delivering high quality customer experiences through the service delivery mechanism, and the establishment of long-term customer satisfaction as the most important corporate goal. The study did support senior management's contention that the Peninsula Motor Club was deficient in developing a formalized approach to marketing planning and in acquiring the previously mentioned functional marketing skill/expertise areas. However, it was clear that the development of marketing plans and acquisition of needed functional expertise and skills would have little overall ability to improve marketing effectiveness. A first and more important step would be to induce internal changes that would help transform the Peninsula Motor Club from an operations, internal control, and growth management oriented service organization to more of a marketing oriented one.

Organizational Level Priority Changes

In order to build a marketing infrastructure the following organizational changes with respect to priorities across senior corporate management, division operating management, and branch management would be required:

- Demonstrated support and commitment to marketing as a corporate wide philosophy with its emphasis on understanding and satisfying customers would need to be designated as a high priority by senior corporate management.

- Demonstrated support would involve a funding requirement, performance evaluation emphasis change, and an active internal marketing program.

- Senior level division operating management would need to establish customer-oriented service delivery system design and quality control as a top priority objective.

- Branch management would need to realize that service delivery implementation and customer

satisfaction, responsiveness, and relationship management at the point of customer contact is their most important responsibility.

- Branch managers would be required to shift their existing emphasis on facility management, administration, and selling to more effective management of the customer service encounter for high levels of customer satisfaction.

Infrastructure Definition

The infrastructure itself would involve management system, program content, organization structure, budget procedural, compensation and performance evaluation system, training program, internal communication, operating policy, and supervisory and motivational style changes that support marketing oriented priorities. These changes would center around the characteristics of a marketing-oriented service firm, and would require that the Peninsula Motor Club:

- Design programs for systematic and frequent solicitation of input from customers, and develop effective listening and interpretation capabilities.

- Allocate sufficient resources to training, motivating, and supervising customer contact personnel in customer sensitivity and satisfaction techniques.

- Understand customer expectations, redesign the service delivery mechanism to meet those standards, and ensure that rules, procedures, and policies are rewritten with the customer's viewpoint clearly in mind.

- Design a service quality level and customer satisfaction control system to increase the chances that service quality will be maintained.

- Learn to resolve customer problems quickly and efficiently at first contact.

- Take frequent customer satisfaction measurements with all aspects of the service delivery mechanism, and tie them to the evaluation and reward system.

- Develop an internal marketing program to actively project management's commitment to marketing.

Immediate Action Recommendations

From the standpoint of understanding the customer's viewpoint and more systematic solicitation of their input, it was recommended that the Peninsula Motor Club immediately:

- Initiate a series of focus group discussions and surveys to determine customer likes, dislikes and suggestions for improvement.

- Actively solicit and systematically review customer complaints, inquiries, and suggestions for improvement at all levels of the organization.

- Establish a program of "mystery shopping" and exit interviews to gain direct feedback as to the quality of the customer's experience with the service delivery mechanism.

- Attempt to understand the impact of all service programs and operating procedures on customer perceptions and satisfaction, isolate those contributing to unacceptable levels of satisfaction, and prioritize for redesign.

- Audit the existing branch format and non-personal communication system from the customer's perspective with respect to improvements. Isolate inefficiency and customer satisfaction inhibitors based on the impressions of customers and redesign the physical layout and non-personal communications program accordingly.

With respect to projecting top management commitment to the marketing philosophy with its emphasis on customer orientation and satisfaction it was recommended that:

- A set of written, measurable customer oriented goals be established.

- Marketing be established as a high priority consideration and driving force in the company. Organizationally all departments need to practice marketing, and marketing's authority must come from the office of the Executive Vice President and President of the Peninsula Motor Club.

- A company mission statement and written set of strategic values that communicate a customer orientation be developed. These documents should become the basis for the Peninsula Motor Club's identity, internally for employees and externally for image purposes.

- Management talk enthusiastically about customer satisfaction and quality service in both formal presentations and informal settings.

- Management actively solicit employees' opinions and ideas regarding customer-oriented changes, and involve them in plans to make the company more customer-oriented.

- Employees at all levels, including management, be required to hear directly from customers.

With respect to providing high quality service on a more consistent basis the following recommendations were made:

- Keep open a two-way flow of communication regarding service and quality. Everyone should be held responsible for initiating improvements in service level quality and gathering information on customers' opinions regarding quality.

- A policy of overreacting to complaints about service quality be established and enforced.

- Management should take customer satisfaction and service performance measurements to the degree possible for individuals, teams, branches, and departments and offer incentives that are tied to attainable customer satisfaction goals to motivate and create awareness that they are being measured and evaluated on this basis. Outstanding performance in delivering high levels of customer satisfaction should be recognized on employee review forms, in newsletters, and at meetings.

- Management establish a routine of getting employees together from all levels, divisions, and locations for informal and/or formal sharing of customer-satisfying ideas and experiences.

CONCLUSION

The Peninsula Motor Club's senior management team held a not so uncommon preconceived notion among service company executives as to the most important factors involved in becoming a marketing oriented service organization. They placed exclusive emphasis on the ability of marketing planning and external communications expertise, especially advertising and direct mail, to drive marketing effectiveness. And, they were prepared to allocate significant resources to improving their marketing planning and external promotional capabilities in the pursuit of revenue growth.

A marketing/service audit of their operations supported management's contention that there was a need for a formalized marketing planning approach and greater skill and expertise in the areas of media advertising, direct mail, and professional sales management. However, it also uncovered some service delivery deficiencies and alerted management to the fallacy of prematurely allocating significant resources to these areas prior to making sure that the internal service delivery mechanism is properly in place and capable of providing high quality customer experiences and satisfaction levels. It is important to realize that the effectiveness of external marketing efforts is greatly diluted to the extent that the quality of the customer's experience with the service delivery mechanism is inadequate. External marketing efforts can create awareness, favorable attitudes, and for the Peninsula Motor Club increase memberships and motivate more consumers to access their services and visit their branch offices. However, the critical marketing success factor is the nature and quality of customer experiences and their level of satisfaction with the Peninsula Motor Club each time they visit a branch office and/or access the service delivery mechanism.

From a marketing effectiveness improvement standpoint the requirement was to design a marketing infrastructure that would increase the chances that the Peninsula Motor Club's customers would consistently experience high quality service levels and satisfaction. This would:

- Stimulate positive "word-of-mouth" recommendations.

- Encourage repeat usage patterns.

- Build a large base of consumers with favorable attitudes toward the Peninsula Motor Club against which external marketing efforts could be more productively leveraged.

Senior management at the Peninsula Motor Club concluded that external marketing expenditures would be more wisely spent once a proper marketing infrastructure was put in place. The chances of positive customer experiences would be greatly enhanced and thus maximum impact from marketing expenditures generated. On the other hand, large external marketing expenditures prior to getting "the internal house in order" could backfire by driving more consumers to experience mediocre to good service levels, when very good service was the expectation.

SERVICE QUALITY SURVEYS IN A TELECOMMUNICATIONS ENVIRONMENT: AN INTEGRATING FORCE

John F. Andrews, General Telephone of the Northwest, Everett, WA
James H. Drew, GTE Laboratories, Waltham, MA
Michael J. English, GTE Service Corporation, Stamford, CT
Melanie Rys, Total Research Corporation, Princeton, NJ

ABSTRACT

We describe the role of service quality surveys for the telephone operations of GTE Corporation, show how these surveys can be used for a variety of different purposes, and discuss how features of these surveys have a unifying effect on several different GTE business groups.

We discuss a theoretical framework for the use of customer surveys in this business environment, in which we draw heavily on the model of Parasuraman, Zeithaml, and Berry (1985). Then, we consider the particular challenges faced by a service measurement program in the telecommunications industry, paying special attention to peculiarities in the GTE environment, including its position in a previously regulated, but now increasingly competitive market. In this context we show how these features are used by several operations, marketing and other groups within the corporation, and how they act as organizational integrators.

INTRODUCTION

In a deregulated, competitive environment, quality means satisfying the customer, eliminating his service problems, anticipating his needs, and doing all this better than the competition. From the business's point of view, the focus is always on the customer. Thus, it is crucial to understand how company activities are affected by customer input, and how the company in turn affects the customer's perception of service quality. We believe that customer surveys are the most valuable source of insight into customer perceptions, and we argue here that such surveys have a competitively advantageous unifying effect on company structure.

The model of Parasuraman, Zeithaml, and Berry (1985) conceptualizes one way in which corporate activities and perception interact with customer service perceptions. They suggest that customer satisfaction is a function of the complete transfer of customer expectations through service design, service delivery, and customer service perception without losing any important elements of the initial customer expectation.

Potential gaps or points where transfer might be incomplete include:

1. the gap between what customers actually expect, and what management believes they expect,

2. the gap between what management believes about customer expectations, and what it considers feasible and designs into specifications and delivery mechanisms,

3. the gap between what the company specifies, and what it actually delivers, and

4. the gap between what the company actually delivers, and what it communicates to the customer, affecting what customers expected they were to receive or their perception of what was delivered.

Customer opinion surveys are an extremely powerful tool in reducing these gaps. They directly identify failures to perform against service delivery specification as well as provide the starting point for identification of inadequate service specifications. By providing a pipeline to the customer's perception, these surveys also provide a means to keep management strategies in line with customer needs as well as providing a data source for addressing those needs through sophisticated analysis. In these ways, customer opinion surveys can have a clear effect on the operation of the organization, which in turn has a great deal to do with the competitive position of the company.

While the proper use of customer surveys among one's own customers can be sufficient to avoid certain gaps in the service quality model, it does not address the final quality requirement — competitive advantage. It is vital that service quality be benchmarked against all major competitors. The emergence from a monopolistic environment has created in telecommunications and other industries a fuzzily dichotomized scenario of partial regulation and partial fierce, open competition. Customer surveys must then also provide information on service quality perception among competitors' customers and the determinants of choice among competing products and services. Already vital, this perspective should become an accepted view as the telecommunications industry emerges to inevitable complete open market status.

Integration among distinct organizational entities is the key to customer survey value and is almost solely responsible for establishing the link between customer needs, service delivery, and the perception of quality by customers as measured by surveys. This linkage ultimately leads to customer base retention and expansion. Within the context of customer surveys, we identify three forces for integration.

a) First, the set of corporate customer opinion surveys are a focal point for the separate business purposes of a vast variety of corporate and company organizations. All or some of these surveys are thus used by groups within these organizations.

b) Second, through the contributions of these many groups, the surveys themselves have many design features which ensure their ease of use for all the user groups.

c) Third, in the course of using these surveys, the organizational groups have ample occasion to interact with each other, so that diverse viewpoint viewpoints are exchanged and common purposes developed. Furthermore, the other surveys sponsored by these groups (e.g., of customer contact employees) provide vehicles for group interaction, through inter-group survey design and linked results.

Corresponding to these integrating concepts, there are three concepts of the survey process itself which may be used to structure the integration of diverse organizational purposes.

1. Integration fostered by the concept of a survey (survey as a whole): This includes the role of a survey as a single focal point for diverse functional areas, as a core data base for strategic planning, as an unbiased arbitrator, and as a cross-company common resource.

2. Integration though survey design and specifications (within a survey): This includes the use of specific survey design specification such as rating scale choices and specification

of reporting conventions to engender widespread survey usage, understanding, applicability, and acceptance.

3. Integration across multiple surveys: This includes the integrated design and analysis of several parallel surveys to foster functional integration, provide information on specific issues from multiple perspectives, and support cross-functional strategies and cooperation.

It is apparent that the first two corresponding forces mentioned in each list, namely surveys as a focal point and survey design as an integrator, are virtually equivalent. However, the corresponding third points are slightly different, the former involving group interactions in the course of using the customer surveys, and the latter involving joint usage of different surveys. Thus, there are four integrating forces which we discuss below.

Before considering the specific forms of this integration in more detail, we briefly describe the business environment in which these surveys work, and the general goals of the service quality measurement program in which the surveys reside.

ENVIRONMENT

A major part of GTE Corporation's business consists of the provision of local telephone service, as provided by a number of regional telephone operating companies whose franchises extend over significant parts of the United States, Canada, and Puerto Rico. Within GTE telephone operations, there is a headquarters staff which studies and formulates programs of common concern to the operating companies. Many of the franchises are geographically adjacent to Bell Operating Company territories. Customers, or accounts, are divided into two major classes: business customers and residential customers.

Local telephone service to the customer (both business and residential) comprises a number of interrelated factors, including intra-LATA calling, connection to long-distance carriers, billing, repair, installation, operator service, custom calling features, provision of premises equipment, and sales and consultation to answer unique needs. The basic architecture of the survey program reflects the structure of the customer base and its varied telecommunications activities. Customers in small, medium, and large companies are surveyed by the business customer opinion survey, while residential customers are surveyed by a different instrument. For some telephone services, such as repair or installation, the survey population is defined by the customer's recent experience of that activity.

GOALS OF SERVICE QUALITY MEASUREMENT

We believe that since the very definition of quality resides with the end user's judgement, the first goal of a service measurement system is the estimation of the level of satisfaction in the customer base (i.e., what is the mean rating for general or particular services among each segment of the customer base?). In addition, operating company managers at a sufficiently high level can be associated with delivering these satisfaction rates or rate trends, so it is possible to hold these people accountable for "their" ratings and thus use the survey results as one personnel evaluation device, on a limited basis.

This latter usage naturally leads to a desire to identify the network sources of dissatisfaction among customers, and to assess their relative impact. More generally, it is useful to develop models of customer behavior which reflect the mechanism by which an individual's evaluation is formed. Bettman's (1979) information processing models are a useful guide in this activity, as are Duncan's (1984) models. Related to this desire, one may have an interest in measuring the perceptual impact of service modifications, such as the installation of new switches or a new format for billing.

Because we also believe that a customer's definition of quality depends on the other service providers in the market, it is vital that service quality be measured not just for one's own company but benchmarked against all the major competitors in a given market. It is possible then to use this competitive intelligence in two related ways: as an indicator of a competitor's relative strengths and weaknesses to identify target markets and target customers, and as a new way of interpreting one's own satisfaction ratings. Occasionally, too, the survey respondent will request further information or a sales call, despite the fact that the survey is (and must ethically be) intended only as an intelligence tool, so the process also becomes a sales generator. (Of course, to preserve the integrity of the survey, survey sponsorship and sales information are divulged only at the respondent's request.) Finally, insofar as the survey convinces the customer that the operating company is serious about obtaining and using his opinion, it also generates good-will.

Thus, service quality surveys are not only quality assessment devices and evaluation trend indicators, but also personnel evaluators, consumer research devices, operations planners, and market intelligence tools.

INTEGRATING FEATURES OF THE SURVEYS

There are several general ways in which these surveys tend to unify different organizational entities within the telecommunications corporation. First, several different kinds of functional groups make use of the survey results, for a variety of purposes within the overall goal of responding to the customer's needs. Furthermore, that usage may be part of a chain of actions, in which several such groups interact in interpreting and acting on survey results. Some survey-using groups may themselves be teams comprising diverse corporate groups. This usage naturally leads to an interest in the methods by which the surveys are implemented, and thus to an active role in the ongoing planning of the surveys. It follows that certain features are designed into the surveys which facilitate their simultaneous use by many groups, and help group representatives "buy-in" to the survey process.

Survey Usage by Different Entities

We have outlined the major objectives of our surveys in preceding sections, and have indicated that the survey program is used by the staff and line operations groups of the GTE operating units (the various local telephone companies), by corporate headquarters staff, and by various integrated teams. (The latter consist of combinations of corporate and operating unit function VP's, who address multi-organization strategic issues.) Figure 1 identifies these groups, and shows their relative use of the surveys: a group with a longer bar will generally make more use of the surveys than one with a shorter bar.

Figure 2 shows the relative use of the surveys for each of several purposes, which are specifications of the survey goals abstracted in the previous section. As examples of these uses, we offer the following:

1. Strategic planners use the aggregate results of these surveys to probe the minds of GTE and competitor customers to identify their key needs and dissatisfaction sources, and to find gaps and competitive opportunities regarding perceptions of competitors.

2. The staffs of the telephone companies use the surveys to assess quality and its trends over time, and to evaluate service office and other organizations' performances. These groups also effectively act as customer advocates in the sense

that they use survey evidence to bring other groups to focus on customer-reported weak areas.

3. Marketing groups are primarily interested in the surveys' probing of consumer behavior, its information on potential competitors, its indication of new or restructured services/products to meet customer needs, and the sales leads it generates.

4. Network engineers, and other telco operating personnel, use the surveys as indicators of unreported physical system problems, and as indicators of the effectiveness of improvements in the physical plant.

Types/Categories of Survey Usage

Figure 1.

5. Marketing planners and network planners use the surveys to respectively develop marketing strategies and network technology deployment plans. Operations planners use detailed survey results to guide the priority of placement of the new technologies, and to guide other capital and service programs. Service operations personnel develop and implement the latter programs.

6. In addition, public affairs departments are interested in the customer concerns voiced by survey responses, and in perceptual changes wrought by changes in communications efforts.

The seriousness with which these survey results are viewed also plays a role in extending their use. At the direction of headquarters staff, the operating companies use these results to set long-term strategic performance objectives, for which telco upper management (e.g., the company president) is held responsible. Furthermore, reports are monitored monthly and narratives required for any business unit whose ratings do not fall within specified vicinities of those objectives. It follows that nearly all personnel in the operating units have at least an indirect interest in the survey results. These entities are thus inspired to "buy-in" to the survey process and thereby integrate their aims with other survey users.

Relative Survey Usage

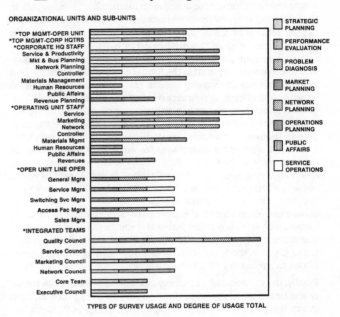

Figure 2.

Group Interactions in Using Survey Data

In the preceding section, we described the unification of the goals of various groups by their common, but individually distinct, interest in the customer survey results. Many of these groups also integrate through their interaction in processing survey results. We give some instances in the following list.

1. During September 1985, after three successive months of declining residential satisfaction rates with direct distance dialing, the corporate Service and Network departments formed a joint task force to diagnose and correct the problem. The transmission problems which were identified as a primary contributor to the rate declines were attacked by interfunctional teams which created noise mitigation programs. In addition, one operating unit created an inter-company team with exchange and interexchange carriers. As a result of these programs, direct distance dialing survey results have shown steady improvements for the last nine months.

2. In early 1986, a substantial decline in customer satisfaction with billing services was traced to decreased clarity of the customer's monthly bills. Integrated interfunctional teams comprising representatives from customer service, business relations, finance, and information management systems were created at the corporate level to propose solutions. Operating units simultaneously worked with these teams as well as with customer focus groups. Since some proposed bill format changes affected interexchange carriers, they were brought into the discussions as well.

3. In the past year, GTE network planners needed to make certain watershed decisions in deploying new technology to meet customer needs. From the survey-identified priority of customers for transmission and call completion quality, strategy setting corporate teams from service, network, and marketing groups worked with operating unit staff to set new standards on the implementation of switching and transmission technology. Subsequent surveys have confirmed

favorable customer reaction to this new equipment, in places where it has been used.

A more general format for intergroup interaction, then, occurs in the following way: Many organizational groups need information beyond what is routinely produced in the survey reports, the first step of which is often the production of more detailed, or more statistically sophisticated, data from the surveys. Since the Service and Productivity staff is the formal client of the research firm which produces the survey results, the organizational group in question will engage in frequent consultations with that staff. This general interaction occurs in many ways, such as when an Operations group needs further survey details (e.g., What do customers give as the reason for their dissatisfaction with billing service?), or when a Marketing group asks for some new analysis of the existing survey data (e.g., What dissatisfiers are most highly related to a customer's overall evaluation?). Another way in which these interactions occur is when a standard survey occasionally suggests the need for some special study. Because of the widespread use of the customer surveys, the Service and Productivity department is widely regarded as the source of survey expertise and experience within the Corporation. Therefore, that organizational group is the focal point for any other group which contemplates the planning of a special survey.

Finally, direct consumers of survey results occasionally note trends or anomalies which point to some service delivery problem. That group then works with the the operating group (e.g., transmission or switching engineers) to localize the problem, and test for its correction. The group fixing the problem may itself be a cross section of functional groups and may not even be totally internal to the Corporation.

Integrating by Survey Design

The interest these and other business groups have in survey results leads them to help design the survey procedures and their instruments. It follows that there are many features of these surveys which are simultaneously useful to many of these groups, those features therefore serving as a uniting force for the groups. They thus tend to purposely act to satisfy customer needs and expectation, whereas historically they generally worked independently without common purpose. We now list ways in which the survey design has exploited and reinforced that unification.

1. First, the sampling design of the surveys (i.e., the process by which population units are selected for interviewing) reflects the needs of several business groups. Customers are sampled periodically to ensure that the appropriate telco managers have continual performance feedback. This is true even for very small serving areas.
2. Occasionally, certain serving areas are sampled more heavily than usual, at the behest of engineering groups, to assess the effect of some new piece of equipment.
3. Marketing groups recommended the total sampling of "large" business customers, and the interviewing of the business's telecommunications decision makers.

The survey instruments also reflect specific group needs incorporated in a general interest setting.

1. Both the residential and business surveys contain an item by which customers rate the quality of their telephone service. The rating scales for these questions were designed to be straightforward, intrinsically meaningful, and easy to present to upper management: this ease of use has been vital in gaining cooperation from all survey users.
2. Since marketing groups are also interested in the loyalty of the customer base, a second general rating question is couched

in terms of whether the respondent would recommend his service to an acquaintance who did have a choice of services. This question is of intrinsic interest to marketing groups, and is also a useful probe of general satisfaction.

3. Operations groups are interested in ratings of specific service offerings (repair, billing, etc.), and such questions are asked both for operational use and for detailed analysis by corporate strategists. Thus, this question block simultaneously serves two distinct business groups.

Survey results are reported at several different levels of detail and of aggregation to satisfy the needs of different business groups. Corporate strategists, for example, need results summarized at the Corporate level primarily, while telco operations groups need results at the service or central office level. The latter groups also need customers' descriptions of specific service problems (e.g., a rude repairman). These kinds of information can be routinely produced from both the business and residential surveys.

Several operational aspects of the interviewing process also help unify business group support for the surveys.

1. In the business survey, the sponsor of the survey is identified as GTE—the entire Corporation—and the independent research firm conducting the interviews is seen as a member of the GTE team.
2. Action comments are often given by the customer during the course of the interview, to be passed on to one of several possible GTE groups for a response. The comments range from
requests for telephone repair to requests for sales calls; in this regard, they are an obvious link from the survey to several business groups.
3. Finally, several different telco organizations cooperate to furnish interviewing information and to send advance letters to business customers to secure their cooperation.

Integrating Across Multiple Surveys

In previous sections, we have discussed the effect of GTE's customer survey program in integrating the goals, approaches, and operations of diverse organizational groups. Here we consider the motivation for, and integrating effect of, other quality surveys in their relation to customer surveys.

We extend the concepts of cross-group and cross-functional integration described earlier by formally recognizing the nonindependence of the survey efforts as tools for competitive advantage. Internal and external survey processes are seen as intrinsically related. Cross-design and analysis of several parallel surveys fosters functional integration, provides information on specific issues from multiple perspectives, and supports cross-functional strategies and cooperation.

This third level of integration is also important in extending the usefulness of surveys as aids in minimizing the service quality gaps of the Parasuraman, Zeithaml, and Berry model we sketched in the Introduction. We have described the impact of the customer survey program in closing the gaps between customer expectations and management perceptions (gap 1) and between customer expectations and customer perceptions (gap 5). These two are directly addressed by the single survey program. However, extension of the quality measurement program to measuring other gaps requires the integrated use of multiple surveys.

A specific example of such a survey is the following. GTE's employee opinion survey periodically gauges the perceived work climate by interviewing employees in each division. A link can be discerned between our customer surveys and the employee survey by focusing on employees who have considerable customer contact such as repairers and installers. It has been suggested that such employees personify the service offered (See Shostack, 1977) and that their actions have a disproportionate effect on customer opinion. These employees are also viewed as most capable of assessing customer satisfaction directly, and the current employee survey asks them to project in this manner. By concentrating on employee effectiveness and customer knowledge, we can minimize the gaps between specification and delivery of service (gap 3) and communications to customers (gap 4). See Schneider and Bowen (1985) for a discussion of these concepts in use in a banking environment. Solomon et al. (1986) provide a theoretical outline for the role of customer contacts.

Other formal surveys and internal measurements are also linked to the customer survey. Modeling of relationships between customer and employee survey responses and internal, operational quality measures such as installation time helps to avoid gaps in translating expectations into specifications. Thus this final level of integration introduces the customer perspective into all facets of operations and encourages cross-utilization of information by multiple groups and from many sources.

SUMMARY AND CONCLUSIONS

We have described many of the features of the GTE telephone operations customer surveys, and the environment in which they exist. The architecture of the survey program parallels the structure of the Corporation's customer base, and provides a vehicle Corporate and operating company management use for focusing on the customer's needs and expectations. Indeed, service quality is defined in terms of customer satisfaction within the Corporation, and these surveys therefore play an irreplaceable role in GTE business operations and planning.

As a result of the preeminent position of customer surveys within the Corporation, the surveys provide a powerful force unifying otherwise disparate units of the Corporation. That unifying force is exhibited in three different ways. First, the surveys themselves are used by a wide variety of groups in the Corporation. Second, many of these groups are directly involved in survey program design so that elements of the surveys are simultaneously and continually useable and valuable to each group. Third, in disseminating and analyzing the survey results, otherwise isolated groups take the opportunity to diagnose and solve problems together. These unifying forces lead to the following classification of unifiers: the survey program unifies by the design of particular surveys, by the very existence of each survey, and by interactive usage of multiple surveys.

We have found, then, that customer opinion surveys play a central role in Corporate thinking and that their conception and use foster a number of types of integration among business groups.

REFERENCES

Bettman, J.R. (1979), *An Information Processing Theory of Consumer Choice,* Reading, MA: Addison-Wesley.

Duncan, O.D. (1984), "Measurement and Structure: Strategies for the Design and Analysis of Subjective Survey Data," in *Surveying Subjective Phenomena,* C.F. Turner and E. Martin, eds. New York: Russell Sage Foundation.

Parasuraman, A., V. Zeithaml, and L. Berry (1985), "A Conceptual Model of Service Quality and Its Implications for Future Research," *Journal of Marketing, 49, 4* (Fall 1985), 41-50.

Schneider, B. and D.E. Bowen (1985), "Employee and Customer Perceptions of Service in Banks: Replication and Extension," *Journal of Applied Psychology, 70,* 423-433.

Shostack, G.L (1977), "Breaking Free from Product Marketing," *Journal of Marketing* (April 1977), 73-80.

Solomon, M.R., C. Suprenant, J.A. Czepiel, and E.G. Gutman (1985), "A Role Theory Perspective on Dyadic Interactions: The Service Encounter," *Journal of Marketing* (Winter 1985), 99-111.

THE MEASUREMENT OF GAPS IN SERVICE QUALITY

Robert C. Lewis, University of Massachusetts, Amherst
David M. Klein, Florida Atlantic University, Boca Raton

The definition and measurement of "quality" in any arena is no small matter. These factors have been found to be particularly elusive with regard to services. If quality, per se, is an "elusive and indistinct construct," "often mistaken for imprecise adjectives," and "not easily articulated by consumers," (Parasuraman, Zeithaml & Berry 1985), then the added intangibility of services certainly compounds the difficulty of definition and measurement. Yet, as quality measurement has become so vital to manufacturers and marketers in the commercial goods sector and if, as Rabin (1983) has pointed out, quality is the single most important consumer trend of the 1980's then it becomes imperative, both theoretically and empirically, for service marketers to provide for its application in the service sector.

This factor has prompted some researchers to begin to develop various definitions of service quality and subsequently to develop service quality models. A basic consistency and consensus rests among these numerous attempts. Essentially, consensus rests on largely abstract dimensions such as perceptions, expectations and satisfaction. This commonality leaves little apparent need, at least at this stage, to quarrel with such a framework. Rather it provides an opportunity to test these dimensions and to seek empirical confirmation.

Empirical confirmation of abstractions, however, is no less elusive than the definition of quality itself. It seems, in fact, that the frustrating attempts at definition may be preventing, rather than facilitating, successful efforts toward empirical confirmation. This problem, such as it is, may be a long time in resolution.

Similarly, however, what can be measured are the differences between the abstractions. For example, if quality is defined vis-a-vis expectations, and perception is the level of satisfaction derived, then it seems only logical that if we can measure the difference between the two we will have, not a definition of quality, but a measurement of its existence or non-existence, regardless of what "quality" may be. This measurement, in fact, may be just a more significant marketing tool. It also has the advantage of being somewhat less of an abstraction, although not totally, to deal with and this considerably eases our task.

Some researchers, notable Parasuraman, Zeithaml and Berry (1985), have called these differences between abstractions as gaps. Others, such as Blake, Dexheimer and Mercuri (1986) have referred to the measurement of these differences as disparity analysis. The work presented here rests on the service quality model developed by Parasuraman, Zeithaml and Berry. After a brief review of the conceptual foundations of our research, already familiar to service marketing researchers, we present the findings from two studies of gap analysis in widely divergent service areas -- hotel services and medical services.

CONCEPTUAL FOUNDATIONS

Service Quality

Gronroos (1984) developed a model to explain what he calls the "missing service quality concept." The model rests

largely on the construct "image" which represents perceived service quality which, in turn, represents the gap between expected service and perceived service. Gronroos deplores the use of the term quality as if it were variable itself rather than "a function of a range of resources and activities." He argues that this range includes what customers are looking for, what they are evaluating, how service quality is perceived, and in what way service quality is influenced. Gronroos defines "perceived quality of the service" as dependent on two variables -- expected service and perceived service, or collectively, the outcome of the evaluation process. Gronroos then argues, as did Swan and Combs (1976) before him, that service quality can be divided into two dimensions.

One dimension, technical quality, lends itself to somewhat objective measurement by the consumer. It is "what the consumer receives as a result of his interactions with a service firm." This could be a hotel bed, a restaurant meal, or a doctor's prescription. The second dimension, functional quality, represents the service process, or the expressive performance of the service. This quality is perceived by the consumer in a very subjective manner. Together, technical quality and functional quality of a service represent a bundle of service dimensions and, in Gronroos' view, create image, a third quality dimension.

Consumer expectations are influenced by image. In fact, image may be a quality dimension capable of overriding substandard technical and functional service quality delivery. We interpret this to mean that consumers may be satisfied in spite of absence of technical and functional quality in the service. Conversely, they may be dissatisfied in spite of their presence. Image is a difficult construct to measure. We can, however, measure satisfaction as a surrogate for image. We could assume that this is a reasonable assumption if we find disparity between satisfaction, and technical and functional delivery.

Service Delivery

Gronroos' contentions have considerable support in the literature. Sasser, Olsen and Wyckoff (1978) choose to confine their measurement of service quality to the three dimensions of materials, facilities and personnel. Lehtinen and Lehtinen (1982) also conceive of three dimensions which parallel those of Gronroos: physical quality, corporate quality (image) and interactive quality. It is the contention of Lewis and Booms (1983) that "Service quality (however broken down into its focal elements) is a measure of how well the service level delivered matches customer expectations."

Thus, it would seem that we should not really be measuring service quality, per se, but rather the quality in the delivery of the service on at least two, and very possibly three, dimensions. This may appear, at first glance, to be a fine distinction but, in fact, it is a very important one because it eases our task considerably. The elusive quality now becomes a somewhat less elusive delivery, perhaps still intangible but less abstract.

THE COMPLEXITY OF SERVICE DIMENSIONS

Nightingale (1986) classifies services along three

dimensions: person-related services, product-related services, and information-related services. For example, he contends that although the hospitality industry provides a number of product-related services, e.g., car parking and laundry, more importantly it provides person-related services such as rooms and meals for individuals. Person-related services are geared toward a main objective "to bring about some change of state in the customer, or to maintain an existing state, which for one reason or another he is unable to do for himself, or chooses not to." Accordingly, a hotel provides rest and refreshment. Nightingale has chosen the term "person-related" in preference to "personal" to emphasize that these services are oriented towards people rather than exclusively provided by people. Consumption of these services generally involves four elements:

* direct consumption of physical goods (such as food)
* use of physical facilities (such as buildings and furniture)
* interactions with persons providing the service
* information about the service.

The key characteristic, says Nightingale, "is that the customer is inextricably involved in the process of providing them. Indeed, the process is frequently as much a part of the service as its outcome."

Nightingale adopts a similar yet slightly different approach in defining quality in the service context. He attributes two meanings to the word quality. The first relates to the particular attributes which serve to define the nature of the service. The second usage is as a qualifier in assessing or measuring such an attributes. The two meanings combine to give a particular value or level which Nightingale calls a service characteristic. As an illustration, the menu is an attribute of a restaurant meal: wide choice of menu is a service characteristic.

We are in agreement with Nightingale's view and would contend that, as such, service quality, per se, is so confounded in many cases that it is extremely difficult if not impossible to measure. The consumer of a particular service seeks to satisfy a somewhat hierarchical set of needs and wants, partly related to the essential service and partly to subsidiary attributes. An essential purpose might be an overnight stay at a hotel. Subsidiary attributes may include accessibility, convenience of location, availability, timing and flexibility as well as interaction with those providing the service and with other customers. Customers will have expectations as to how all these needs should be met, which may in themselves be rather hazy and imprecise.

When presented with the actual offering of these multiple variables, the consumer forms an impression which is almost immediately compared with expectations, and the resultant level of satisfaction is determined. Each consumer will regard various service attributes as more or less important, and various service characteristics as more or less desirable. For many there may be a minimum threshold of accessibility, such as the availability of car parking, which Czepiel (1980) calls the "maintainer" characteristics: "those basic physical/functional features that underlie the use of the service." All together, the consumer obtains a service experience comprised of a multitude of service transactions which he selects from an offering. Each transaction contributes to the service experience and has characteristics relating to the whole set of transactions which is more than the sum of the individual elements. We might call this sum an overall feeling and liken it to Gronroos' concept of image.

SERVICE GAPS

Nightingale has conducted a number of studies of service quality using the repertory grid technique. He discovered considerable differences in perceptions between customers and providers which, he states, usually came as a surprise to management. Nightingale found very strong evidence that "management perceptions of quality of service frequently differ from the perceptions of customers, colleagues and staff."

The differences in perception noted by Nightingale are what Parasuraman, Zeithaml and Berry (1985) call "service gaps." These researchers undertook an exploratory qualitative study to investigate the concept of service quality. Focus group interviews with consumers and in-depth interviews with executives were conducted. Parasuraman, Zeithaml and Berry researched four different service categories to gain insights into what managers perceive to be the key attributes of service quality, what consumers perceive to be the key attributes, whether discrepancies exist between these two perceptions, and whether these results can be utilized to establish a general model to more efficiently explain service quality from the consumer's standpoint. What they found were "gaps." These gaps were incorporated to create the service quality model reproduced in Figure 1 where various gaps identified by Parasuraman, Zeithaml and Berry are shown on the left hand side of the model. (For ease of illustration, Gap 4 is not shown in Figure 1 because it was not relevant to the present study. See Parasuraman, Zeithaml and Berry 1985, p. 44 for the full model.)

Figure 1. Service Quality Model

CONSUMER

Word of Mouth   Personal Needs   Past Experience
Communications

                        (D) Expected Service

        GAP 5
                                                GAP 7
                        (C) Perceived Service

                                        GAP 5
MARKETER
                        (B) Service Delivery

        GAP 3
GAP 1

                        Service Quality
                        Specs
                                        GAP 8

        GAP 2

                        (A) Management
                        Perceptions of
                        Consumer
                        Expectations

Adapted from Parasuraman, Zeithaml and Berry (1985)

The gaps identified in the model are self explanatory and a full explication is contained in the original article, so further discussion will not ensue here. What is pertinent to our research is that Parasuraman, Zeithaml and Berry have determined from their research, labeled as propositions one through five, that these gaps have a definite impact on the consumer's evaluation of service quality.

It is Parasuraman, Zeithaml and Berry's model and their concluding challenge for future research that forms the basis for the empirical research findings presented here.

Our research, however, identified three additional gaps not included in the model. These gaps we have labeled Gap 6, Gap 7, and Gap 8 and can be seen on the right hand side of the model in Figure 1. Each will be discussed and elaborated upon in the research findings.

GAP MEASUREMENT

Two divergent service classifications were explored in our gap research. Lovelock (1983) identified hotel and restaurant services as involving tangible actions directed at people, discrete transactions with no formal relationship, and services low in contact personnel judgement but high in customization of service delivery. Medical services, on the other hand, are described by Lovelock as tangible actions directed at people, (continuous delivery services with a formal relationship), high in contact personnel judgement, and high in customization of service delivery. The key differences then are in the formality of relationships between transactions and the extent of contact personnel judgement. Findings from the two studies follow.

Gaps in Hotel Service Quality

Twenty-three upper management persons (administrative and department heads) of a 400 room hotel in a large eastern metropolis were surveyed as to what they believe are customer expectations in selecting a hotel, their perception of their own hotel's service delivery, what customers particularly like and dislike about their hotel, and the overall fulfillment of expectations and satisfaction with their hotel in the view of customers who had stayed there. The same questions were directed at 116 randomly selected customers staying at the same hotel over a two week period.

Both management and customers were asked to evaluate 44 hotel attributes on a 1 to 5 scale, where 5 represents a high rating. T-tests were used between each pair of attributes that represented a potential for service quality "gaps." Mean scores and significance levels are shown in Table 1.

Table 1. Gap Mean Differences and Their Significance in the
Service Quality Model

Hotel Attributes	Mean[1]				Gaps[2]				
	A	B	C	D	1 AD	5 CD	6 BC	7 BD	8 AB
1. Actual price	3.90	4.00	3.20	2.67	*	***	**	*	
2. Price/value	4.05	4.19	3.25	3.50			*	*	
3. Good reputation	4.43	4.91	4.10	4.06	***		*	*	*
4. Prestige of property/chain	4.38	4.30	4.10	2.80	*	*		*	
5. Location	4.33	4.33	4.20	3.97					
6. Nearness to safe parking	3.67	4.14	3.45	2.83	***		**	*	
7. Cleanliness of room/bath	4.00	4.30	4.05	4.78	*	*		*	
8. Size of room/bath	3.32	4.10	3.25	3.77	***		**		*
9. Quality TV/radio	2.68	3.90	3.36	2.68		**	**	**	*
10. Comfort of bed	3.36	4.25	3.60	4.23	*	**	**		*
11. Decor, furnishings of room/bath	3.32	4.50	3.25	3.58			*	*	*
12. Exterior aesthetics	3.14	4.70	4.25	3.40		*	***	*	*
13. Public rooms aesthetics	3.36	4.70	4.15	3.70			**	*	*
14. Modern, contemporary	3.05	3.40	2.74	2.37	**		***	*	
15. Historic, traditionality of hotel	2.95	4.75	4.45	3.30		*		*	*
16. VIP rooms, sections	3.32	4.60	3.82	2.53	**	*	*	*	*
17. Physical condition of rooms/baths	3.82	4.39	3.55	3.97			**		***
18. Variety of services offered	4.09	4.16	4.21	3.65	***	**			
19. Promptness of all services	3.43	4.00	3.58	4.00	***				***
20. Professionalism of staff	4.30	4.58	3.89	4.48		**	**		
21 Quick check-in/check out	3.39	4.11	3.89	4.39	*				**
22. Reservation system convenience	4.17	4.15	3.78	3.81					
23. Staff friendliness	3.55	4.47	4.26	4.31	*				*
24. VIP treatment	2.96	4.26	3.75	3.43			***	*	*
25. Rooms made up promptly	2.91	4.16	3.94	3.48				**	*
26. Eating/drinking options	4.32	4.74	4.21	3.94	***		**	*	**

[1] Attribute means on scale of 1 (low) to 5 (high).
    A. Management's perception of consumer's expectations;
    B. Management's perception of hotel's service delivery;
    C. Consumers' perceived service.
    D. Consumers' expectations.

[2] *t-test two-tail probability .01
   **t-test two-tail probability .05
  ***t-test two-tail probability .10

No.	Attribute									
27.	Restaurant food quality	4.23	4.84	3.83	4.07			*	*	*
28.	Room service availability	3.86	4.47	4.38	2.58	*	*		*	**
29.	Drinks quality	3.64	4.63	3.88	2.50	*	*	**	*	*
30.	Wine list quality	3.36	4.79	3.87	2.50	**	*	*	*	*
31.	Restaurant/bar price varieties	3.82	4.21	3.31	3.00	*		*	*	
32.	Late night food service available	3.36	4.37	4.07	2.33	*	*		*	*
33.	Elegant dining available	3.77	4.19	2.93	**	*	*	*	*	*
34.	Restaurant service quality	4.23	4.74	3.83	3.84			*	*	*
35.	Year around pool	3.35	.na	.na	1.93	*				
36.	Sauna, steam bath, exercise	3.10	.na	.na	1.81	*				
37.	Management attention	4.05	4.26	3.67	3.29	**		**	*	
38.	Shops in hotel	2.77	3.18	2.95	2.19	***	**		*	
39.	Night life, enter.	3.36	4.53	3.44	2.22	*	*	*	*	*
40.	Small amenities, e.g., mints, soaps	2.52	3.89	3.00	3.10	***		*	*	*
41.	Quietness of room	3.91	4.25	3.74	4.38	**	**	***		
42.	Quietness of hotel	3.82	4.39	3.68	3.75			**	**	**
43.	Security of hotel	4.45	4.33	3.89	4.42		**	***		
44.	Security of area	4.45	4.22	3.63	4.30		*	**		

Gaps:
1. Between A, management's perception of consumer expectations and D, consumer's expectation;
5. Between C, consumers' perceived service and D, consumers' expectations;
6. Between B, management's perception of hotel's service delivery and C, consumers' perceived service;
7. Between B, management's perception of hotel's service delivery and D, consumers' expectations.
8. Between A, management's perception of consumer expectations and B, management's perception of hotel's service delivery.

Gap 1

Gap 1 is the gap between management perceptions of guest expectations and the expectations of the guests to determine if management actually knows what guests expect. Our study shows that, for the most part, management believes that guests expect more than the guests themselves expect.

In the 27 cases where the gap is significant at .10, guest expectations were higher than management's in only eighth cases. Five of these eight cases, however, might be considered extremely critical ones where management does not realize their importance: cleanliness, comfort of bed, quick check-in/check-out, staff friendliness (all .01), and quiet (.05). It is of note that, with the exception of comfort of bed, the other four critical areas are clearly intangible (functional qualities). These four areas also show up repeatedly in surveys as high on the list of features that travelers look for in a hotel, and which encourage them to return. It should also be noted that many of the attributes which management perceives as eliciting higher consumer expectations are tangible in nature (technical qualities).

Gap 5

Gap 5 is the gap between consumer expectations and their perceptions of services received - effectually, what they actually get. In this case the respondents expectations were exceeded on 14 of 20 attributes at a significance level .10. They were not exceeded, however, on cleanliness, comfort of bed, staff professionalism, quiet and security, all at .05 significance and primarily, once again, intangible functional qualities and critical attributes.

Gap 6

Gap 6 measures the difference between consumer perceptions of delivery and what management believes they deliver, i.e., management's success in carrying out what they perceive to be customer expectations. It is not too surprising to learn that management perceives their service delivery as being more successful than customers perceive it to be in all cases, 29 of 44 at .10 significance level. We might conclude that the management of this hotel is very self-assured and somewhat oblivious to their failings.

A subjective measurement was also taken of Gap 6. Respondents of both samples were asked open-ended questions such as: What do you find (think people find) particularly satisfying and dissatisfying about this hotel? As multiple responses were permitted there are no significance tests, however the most frequent responses and their percentage of total responses are shown in Table 2. These findings show that intangibles are not as outstanding at this hotel as management believes them to be. They also show that it is the intangibles at this hotel which upset customers more and not the technical qualities that management believes are upsetting.

Table 2. Attributes that Particularly Satisfy/Dissatisfy Customers at this Hotel

Attributes	Percent Mentioning			
	Satisfies		Dissatisfies	
	Mgmt	Custmrs	Mgmt	Custmrs
Location	38%	39%		
Room quality	38	31	19%	4%
Staff attitude	67	25		
Atmosphere/ambience	57	15		
F & B quality	52	10		
F & B facilities	24	6		
Service	24	25	14	9
Parking			62	15
Room Size			33	17
Price/value			24	17
Noise			24	9
Maintenance			19	24
Check=in/check-out			0	9
Restrictive policies			0	13

Gap 7

Gap 7 reflects a comparison of management's delivery to consumers' expectations. The Gap 6 pattern persists. Management perceives their services delivery as lower than customer expectation in only two cases. In only one of these, cleanliness is the different significant (.01). This clearly indicates a very high guest expectation in this area.

Gap 8

Gap 8 measures an internal situation: Does management believe they deliver as much as they believe customers expect? In this case they clearly do believe it, with no significant exceptions.

Gross Measures

Customer and management respondents were also asked to indicate, again on a 1 to 5 scale, whether the hotel experience was (was believed to be) satisfying to them (their customers). They were also asked whether it met (believed it met) their expectations. Customers only were asked to rate the hotel in terms of overall quality. The results shown in Table 3 show that management, once again, believes it is doing a better job of meeting customer expectation and satisfaction than the customers actually feel, clearly a major gap in service quality.

Table 3. Measures of Satisfaction Expectation and Quality

	Mgmt	Custmrs	Signifnce
Expectations	4.00	3.42	.014
Satisfaction	4.13	3.43	.013
Quality		3.95	

The quality rating by the customers, however, is quite high and does not indicate any real lack of quality. From management's point of view, however, this is no reason for complacency; in fact, it may be that management is too complacent already. The assumption might be made that while the customers of this hotel are not really dissatisfied with it, they are vulnerable to competition in the industry, especially in the event of new construction in a nearby location. In fact, that is exactly what has occurred since this study was conducted.

Does quality predict satisfaction? One would naturally assume so. We regressed satisfaction with quality in this study to test the assumption. The correlation coefficient between the two variables is .69 (p .01) with a resulting R^2 of .48 at .001 significance. This finding leads us to believe that there is another gap that needs to be researched. Clearly, quality does not explain all the variance in customer satisfaction. The unexplained variance may be what Gronroos calls "image," the gap between expected service and perceived service. The correlation between expectation and perception (measured here as quality) in this study is .63 (p .01). In Gronroos' sense we could construe the missing .37 as the "image gap."

Gaps in Medical Service Quality

Toward further identification and at least face validation of the relationships between perceptions, expectations and satisfactions, in service, a qualitative pilot study was conducted of health care service quality. What follows is a compilation of observations derived from eight different medical practices. The direction of this investigation was mapped in coordination with the hospitality study reported above, using the same theoretical justifications as well as epistemic biases. Although the practices involved vary according to specialty, certain commonalities in terms of "gaps" have been identified.

An ongoing program of attitude surveys was implemented into each of the health care offices as part of their ongoing internal marketing plan. Additionally, doctors and their staffs were administered "audits" which qualitatively assessed critical areas of potential conflict as well as other information found to be relevant by one of the authors in prior research and consulting.

The findings indicate that although doctors easily recognize the need for offering proper health care treatment (the "essential service"), they are somewhat hazy, if not altogether unaware, of the impact of offering appropriate collateral services. In keeping with Nightingale's four elements of service, it was found that these doctors are also relatively unaware of the importance of their physical facilities and personal interactions between staff and patients, (i.e., internal marketing) and surprisingly unaware of the negative impact of poor or incomplete communication of critical health information by them, as practitioners, to their patients. These lapses in service delivery may appropriately be construed as Gap 5 and Gap 6, respectively, in the service quality model of Figure 1. Clearly, both of these gaps also represent elements of Gap 1, the gap between customer expectations and management perception of expectations, and elements of Gap 7, the gap between expected service and service delivery.

A pronounced gap was found to exist between practitioner and patient with regard to the office environment. The two major complaints of patients in this regard were the poor selection of reading materials (usually a lack of variety or materials not properly oriented to the market segment being served) and the inadequacy of seating conditions in the reception area. Doctors stressed the overall aesthetics of the office design to the neglect of specific attributes, a Gap 2 failing.

Between the practitioners and their staffs, the greatest source of perceptual gaps are in regard to specific office operations. While each doctor in this pilot study seemed to have a good feeling for the overall operational effectiveness of his office, they are often oblivious to particular functions or occurrences. For example, the staff at one dental office had an established periodic client recall system. However, in a personal interview, the dentist indicated that a recall system should be designed and implemented into his practice.

The final area of perceptual gaps in health care services, and perhaps the most critical, exists as the triangle between the practitioner, the staff, and the patient. In direct response to a question regarding the doctor's explanation of the patient's problem and treatment in an area provided for open comments on the patient surveys, as well as the results of a telephone survey program implemented by one practice for a telephone survey program implemented by one practice to patients who had failed to return for follow-up care, a major criticism of the doctor was his inadequate follow-through regarding his treatment and recommendations. The patients felt that the treatment had not been adequately explained or sufficiently elaborated upon.

The practitioner falls into Gap 7 when he does not take the extra time required for, and seldom recognizes the value of, patient follow-through as a marketing tool toward ensuring patient return, product loyalty.

Unexpectedly, the staff at almost any practice will whole-heartedly (yet often blindly) support the doctor in feeling that the treatment plan is sufficiently explained to their patients. Thus, the fourth element described by Nightingale, information about the service, was found to be the most complex and most critical, in the health care services field.

SUMMARY

Two diverse service categories, hospitality and health services, were examined in relation to the service quality model suggested by Parasuraman, Zeithaml, and Berry to describe the quality gaps in service delivery and the service experience. Previous works by Gronroos, Nightingale, Czepiel, and others were utilized to establish the parameters for fit to the model. Rather than another attempt to define service quality, the authors have approached the issue from the null perspective, the perspective that quality can be measured more effectively and efficiently by its non-existence, i.e., the gaps in service quality. These are embryonic studies with considerable impact for service marketers. We recommend replication and extension by the services research community.[1]

REFERENCES

Blake, Brian F., Carl Dexheimer, and Nori Mercuri (1986), "Disparity analysis; a double-edged sword," Marketing News, (Jan. 3), 34-35.

Czepiel, John A. (1980) Managing Customer Satisfaction in Consumer Service Businesses, Cambridge: Marketing Science Institute, Report No. 80-109.

Gronroos, Christian (1984), "A Service Quality Model and its Marketing Implications," European Journal of Marketing, 18 (4), 36-44.

Lehitinen, Uolevi and Jarmo R. Lehtinen (1982), "Service Quality: A Study of Quality Dimensions," unpublished, Helsinki: A Service Management Institute.

Lewis, Robert C. and Bernard H. Booms (1983), "The Marketing Aspects of Service Quality," in Emerging Perspectives on Service Marketing, L. Berry, G. Shostack, and Upah, eds., Chicago, AMA, 99-107.

Lovelock, Christopher H. (1983), "Classifying Services to Gain Strategic Marketing Insights," Journal of Marketing, 47 (Summer), 9-20.

Nightingale, Michael (1986), "Defining Quality for a Quality Assurance Program -- A Study of Perceptions," in the Practice of Hospitality Management II, R. Lewis, et al, eds., Darien, Conn., AVI Publishing

Parasuraman, A., Valerie A. Zeithaml, and Leonard L. Berry (1985), "A Conceptual Model of Service Quality and Its Implications for Future Research," Journal of Marketing, 49 (Fall), 41-50.

Rabin, Joseph H. (1983), "Accent is on Quality in Consumer Services This Decade," Marketing News, 17, (March 4), 12.

Sasser, W. Earl, R. Paul Olsen, and Daryl Wycoff (1978), Management of Service Operations, Boston: Allyn & Bacon.

Swan, J. E. and Combs, L. J. (1976), "Product Performance and Customer Satisfaction: A New Concept," Journal of Marketing, (April).

---

[1] Special thanks to L. Jean McCracken for editorial suggestions.

HAVE WE DEFINED SERVICES AS AN INTANGIBLE GOOD TO FIND A USE FOR EXISTING MARKETING TOOLS?

Frank W. Davis, Jr., University of Tennessee
James R. McMillan, University of Tennessee

ABSTRACT

Definitions, to be valuable, must facilitate understanding of the topic. This paper suggests that the intangible product definition of service not only inhibits a clear understanding of services but actually creates many myths. After addressing several common myths it presents an alternative definition of services and suggests an economic framework for analyzing service industries.

INTRODUCTION

Services have now become the glamor issue of academics. They are being widely written about in journals and frequently discussed in the media. They are being identified as the primary source of new employment and the basis of the post industrial society. The ever-widening discussion, however, seems to be based on the faulty premise that services are intangible products in which production and consumption are inseparable (Zeithaml, Parasuraman & Berry 1985, p. 33). Only a few dissenting voices are heard, such as Dixon and Smith who suggest that the intangible definition of services is "tautological at best." They continue, "It is logically impossible to determine the characteristics of something which has not been identified, and then utilize these characteristics to identify the object of study." (1983, p. 77)

The problem with this tautological (intangible product) definition is that it distracts our attention from fundamental methods[1] of defining an industry. Thus, the purpose of this paper, after first addressing other common myths about services is to present a non-tautological definition of services and then to suggest an approach for developing an economic framework for service industries.

THE SERVICE MYTHS

Although many people believe that they know what the word "service" means, upon closer examination it appears that each discipline and occupation develops a different definition for the word. A scan of the Oxford English Dictionary will yield definitions ranging from the activity of a servant or slave, to the activity of a physician tending to the welfare or advantage of another, to the supplying of electricity, water or gas to a building, to advice or assistance given to customers after the sales to employment in the military. The many diverse definitions of services lead to potentially harmful misconceptions about them. These misconceptions typically have root in fact, but are often based upon a misinterpretation of these facts.

The Services are Servants Myth

One of the most common stereotypes of services is that they are the activity of servants such as maids, valets, chauffeurs, gardeners, bootblacks, cooks and butlers. This stereotype is rooted in the binary neo-classical microeconomics classification of the economic system into entrepreneurs and consumers. When entrepreneurs hired people,

these individuals were considered to be "factors of production" used to create products and were thus called employees. On the other hand, consumers by definition, do not produce but only consume products and services. Therefore, services became another name to describe the functions provided by individuals who worked for consumers. It was perceived that since these individuals did not supply products they must provide services. This definition of services was extrapolated to include servant type activities even if provided by a business such as a fast food restaurant.

In reality, persons providing personal services are employees in the same way workers in manufacturing are employees of the entrepreneur. Corpus Juris Secundum, a definitive legal reference, introduces the concept of Employer-Employee law with the following statement:

> "The relationship of employer and employee is substantially the same as that of master and servant, but it has been said that the terms "employer" and "employee" make a better designation of the relation in this industrial age, particularly in view of the fact that Americans as a rule do not like the word "servant" .... Generally speaking a "servant" or "employee" is a person who renders service to another, usually for wages, salary, or other financial consideration, and who in the performance of such service is entirely subject to the direction and control of the other, such other being respectively the "master" or "employer." He is deemed to be a master who has the superior choice, control, and direction of the servant, and whose will the servant represents not merely in the ultimate result of the work but in the details." (Emphasis added) (1948, p. 24)

Whenever an individual works under the direction and control of an employer (or master), he/she is an employee whether he/she is a physician working in a hospital, an autoworker assembling automobiles, an accountant working for a CPA firm, a social worker employed by government, a soldier working for the military, or a domestic working in the home. Thus every employee provides service to their employer but no employee is a service. In like manner, fast food restaurants are not services even if the employees perform functions normally provided by domestic servants such as cooking.

The Services Are A New Phenomenon Myth:

One of the recurring themes of recent literature has been that services are a new type of product. Marvin Harris (1981, p. 179) suggests that "as productivity in manufacturing and mining rose, surplus labor was drawn off into the production of information and services." Others stressed the shift from a pre-industrial to industrial to a postindustrial economy to emphasize the shift from agriculture to manufacturing to services.

The implication of such statements is that first there was agriculture, next the Industrial Revolution brought manufacturing to its height, and then followed a third wave or revolution which we call services. This is a misleading orientation based on the emphasis and/or hype of the business disciplines and their literature rather than reality.

---

[1]"Industries" include firms with common production functions and firms with high cross elasticities of demand for their outputs. (Pegrum 1973, p. 121).

A different perspective can be obtained by turning attention from economic and business literature to an historical work such as The Rise of Modern Industry by J. L. and Barbara Hammond. The Hammonds (1937, pp. 66-80) describe the changes that had to occur before the Industrial Revolution and "Modern Industry" could flourish. First, the age of mercantilism evolved to stimulate regional trade. Second, transportation and communications improvements were necessary to permit regional acquisition of resources and the development of large markets necessary to support mass production. Third, educational institutions had to evolve to conceptualize and to disseminate the knowledge and skills that made mass production technology possible. Fourth, the development of a legal system was necessary to resolve conflicts and to provide the security necessary for people to be willing to invest. Fifth, a banking and financial system had to be in place to facilitate trade and investment. Sixth, various jobshops had to be available to produce specialized machines, make parts for new inventions and otherwise be supportive to the needs of new manufacturers which were not large enough to have their in-house facilities already in place. The needed support services were provided by the guild system which made a large number of broadly trained craftsmen available. Each of these developments so necessary to the advent of modern industry were nothing but what are today called services.

Since James Watt invented the steam engine, cited by many as a major catalyst for the Industrial Revolution, he should be a prime example of a product oriented age. In reality, however, Watt was totally service oriented. His father was a "housewright, shipwright, carpenter, and undertaker as well as a builder and contractor". James' first job was as an instrument repairman. He also designed and produced quadrants and other mathematical instruments for a professor of Natural Philosophy at the University. He moonlighted by repairing musical instruments. While further experimenting with his engine, he worked as a land surveyor and planned and directed the construction of the Monkland Canal. His first engine was a failure, primarily because of leaks. Consequently he engaged an ironmaster, John Wilkinson, to custom fabricate a cast iron cylinder that did not leak and thus his second engine was successful. After hiring an attorney to lobby Parliament to extend his patent, Watt outsourced the manufacture of virtually all components. The main parts were obtained from John Wilkinson's custom fabrication works. Other parts were bought elsewhere. In fact, Watt even had the purchasers of his engines pay the custom fabricators for the components directly. Watts' employees only assembled the engines at the customer's site once all the parts had arrived and then Watt leased, not sold, the engine. The annual lease fee was to be one-third of the fuel savings between the Watt engine and the preceding power source (Hammond 1937, p. 110-130).

This case is but one illustration of the fact that far from services being a post industrial phenomenon, they were in fact a preindustrial development essential before the industrial era could begin. Unfortunately, the belief that services are a new development directs our efforts away from understanding the interaction of products and services to heralding their newness and looking for explosive new growth opportunities that may be illusionary.

The Extraordinary Growth Of Services Myth:

The first chapter of current books on services typically devotes at least one paragraph to chronicling the phenomenal growth in services. One book, for example, citing the Monthly Labor Review and Survey of Current Business, states that 72 percent of all U.S. employment is currently in the services sector and that "between 1953 and 1984, nearly 9 out of every 10 of the 48 million nonfarm jobs added to U.S. payrolls were provided by services." (Heskett 1986, p. 3) This widely accepted belief, although totally accurate according to U. S. Census data, is misleading. A closer

study of the data collection process used by the Census Bureau reveals that the data may not indicate a change in economic activity or function so much as a change in organizational structure.

Congress passed legislation on May 1, 1810 authorizing the Federal marshals to take "an account of the several manufacturing establishments and manufacturers within their several districts, territories, and divisions." Total responsibility for questions and methods were left to the discretion of the Secretary of the Treasury. The Treasury Department developed 27 broad categories of products and assigned the marshals responsibility for contacting the manufacturing establishments in their territories to gather the required information. This established the Census practice of collecting data by establishment (Langham 1973, p. 2). "The establishment - based coding system classified each establishment once. Thus the entire economic activity of the operating unit is classified into the industry of the primary activity, at the expense of clouding over detailed data on secondary and support activity." (Marcus 1986, p. 2) The establishment approach worked well when firms were small or when large manufacturing facilities produced everything under one roof.

The shift to mass production of products during the second part (post 1850) of the Industrial Revolution solidified this approach. The mass production factory was based upon large scale manufacturing typically with a centralized steam power plant, large production equipment, and specialized labor organized by narrowly defined work task. During this period work was no longer organized by general skill areas, but rather by employees who specialized in doing a specific task producing a specific product. The establishment was the Bethlehem Steel Plant in Bethlehem, Pa. or the Ford River Rouge Auto plant in Michigan. If the primary output of the plant was steel, then Census classified the establishment as a steel plant and total employment as employees of the steel plant.

As manufacturing management matured and sought better cost control, they looked for methods to better accomplish the same functions with less investment and greater flexibility. Products were distributed through independent wholesale and retail firms rather than directly from the factory. It was often less expensive to purchase parts rather than to produce them in-house. Legal service was often under retainer rather than maintained as an in-house staff. Temporary employees were used for peak time needs rather than hiring permanent in-house staff. CPA firms and service bureaus were an attractive alternative to buying computers and continuing to hire in-house accounting and bookkeeping staffs. Maintenance and janitorial service were likewise contracted for.

As soon as the establishment begins to contract for the function rather than hire its own in-house staff, then this is perceived as a growth in services since the function is now provided by a different establishment and the new establishment is a service. A recent magazine article used the term "hollow corporation" to describe organizations that no longer produce for themselves but rather obtain them through contract manufacturing. To better understand the shift toward services, consider the one person entrepreneurial firm that decides that there is now an opportunity to sell a microcomputer with particular attributes. To reduce the time required to get the product to market, the firm contacts with a custom R & D firm to design the unit, with a custom assembler in Korea or Taiwan to assemble it (outsourcing), with an air cargo service to bring it to the U.S., with an advertising agency to promote it, a distribution center to warehouse it and pick orders, an insurance service to insure it, a bank to finance it, a telemarketing service to sell it, rental trucks driven by temporary employment service drivers to deliver it, and a financial services firm to process all accounts receivable and payable. By using services to perform each of these functions rather than do them in house, the firm is able to avoid the time delay, effort and expense of having to develop each function and without residual commitment once the product life cycle is over.

If all of these functions were performed in-house at the marketing firm's facility, then a large increase in computer manufacturing employment would be reported. However, when the functions are performed outside the firm as described above, virtually all of the jobs are seen as being in the service industry. Table 1 indicates that this example is far from theoretical, but is actually indicative of what is happening in practice.

TABLE 1

Hollow Corporations

Company	Products	Revenue (millions)	Employees	Manu- facturing Employees
Nike	Athletic shoes	1000	3500	100
Esprit	Apparel	800	3000	500
Emerson Radio	Electronic	500	700	150
Sun Micro- systems	Computers	150	1400	200
Ocean Pacific	Apparel	15	67	0

Source: Business Week, March 3, 1986, p. 66.

Public pressures to reduce government employment have also created a decline in public employment and a "growth in services." Consider the theoretical agency that formerly hired 1000 employees: under administrative guidelines to reduce public employment the agency does not replace 100 retiring employees but instead relies on the services of 300 new workers obtained under contract with a temporary employment service. Under current Census data collection procedures, this would represent a decline of 10% in public employment and a growth in private sector service employment of 300 new jobs. Marcus (1986, p. 7-8) describes the Census Bureau's concern about the data collecting process as follows:

> It is felt that some of the growth in services showing up in economic statistics is due to the shift towards contracting out for services previously performed in-house... It would be interesting to know the impact of the growth due to contracting out for services. Unfortunately, the Bureau has no conclusive data.

Thus, there has not actually been the large growth in services chronicled in the media. Instead, activities that have been a major part of the economy for a long time are just now being "discovered." This discovery is not caused so much by the development of new service functions, but by a change in the way services are obtained and by increased effectiveness of the Census in disaggregating the data. This disaggregating of data has tended to mislead writers into implying more than they should from the Census data. The Census Bureau understands the limitations of the data but users often do not.

Myth That Services Are Products (Although Intangible)

Our nation uses product management concepts to manage a service oriented society. To understand this orientation, one must realize that business disciplines did not develop until mass production of products began. The impact of the mass production was so great that capitalists and managers were not the only ones totally involved: academics became keenly interested in the industries that were able to raise the standard of living of the masses in a way that government, charities, and other groups never had. The academic interest in mass production was complemented by the growth in public education and new developments in communications. Thus business academic disciplines began to develop. They had a well defined research lab (the factory), an audience (students and aspiring managers), and the tools (inexpensive books and reports) needed to broadly chronicle the focus of their research.

Neo-classical economics developed first with the concepts of marginalism by Jevons (1871) and Menger (1871). Marx had suggested that labor created value (1867); now Bohm-Bawerk (1889) wrote that capital also created value. Marshall (1890) developed "partial equilibrium analysis" using both supply and demand curves and Walras (1874) developed modern microeconomics with demand and supply functions creating an equilibrium point.

With this theoretical framework, other disciplines began to evolve to address specific production line problems. Garcke and Fells (1887), Norton (1889), and Lewis (1896) introduced the concepts of cost accounting to help the factory manager determine the unit cost of producing the product by combining fixed factory cost and variable material and labor cost. Scientific management evolved with Taylor and the Gilbreths in the early 1900's, followed by organizational behavior in 1924 with Mayo's Hawthorne experiments. Marketing began with Scott (1911), Hagerty (1913), Shaw (1915) and Nystrom in 1915 leading to the 1920's which Bartels has labeled the "Golden Decade". Physical Distribution did not evolve until the famous Drucker comment in 1962, "We know little more about distribution today than Napoleon's contemporaries knew about the interior of Africa. We know it is there, and we know it is big; and that's about all."

The reason for recounting this brief history is to establish that the current disciplines of economics, accounting, management, marketing and distribution are not fundamental business disciplines but are merely the ones developed during a time when academia as well as a large part of society were enamored with and focused on conceptualizing management problems facing the mass production sector. Thus products became the given, the base on which all marketing concepts were constructed.

It is the contention of this paper that little progress has been made in developing a theoretical basis for services because of the near universal acceptance of a faulty premise. We have assumed that since services are intangible products, service concepts will grow out of product concepts.

DEVELOPING A DEFINITIONAL FRAMEWORK FOR SERVICES

If services are not the role of household servants, not intangible products; if services are not a rapidly growing new phenomenon, what are they? To define services it will be necessary to reexamine some of the most fundamental definitions and principles used in economics and management as their conceptualists originally did. However, there is one change -- the problem to be solved is now different. The problem is no longer the market mechanism for setting price, Malthus' concern about population growth and poverty, Keynes' concerns about business cycles, Robinson's concern about competition nor even Williamson's concern for transaction cost analysis (1985). The concern of this work is identifying the difference between product producing organizations and service rendering organizations. To address this problem, it is necessary to reexamine the fundamental purpose of an economic system.

Economic Systems Produce Benefits:

The purpose of an economic system is to produce utility. For this reason, micro economic texts begin with utility analysis and suggest that the price of an item is determined by its marginal utility. Implicit in this analysis is the assumption that products when consumed provide the individual with a stream of benefits. Products, however, are simply one method of providing utility or benefits to the purchaser.

Pre Defined And Pre Produced Benefits Are Called Products

If the purpose of an economic system is to provide benefits ("utility" to the economist), then it becomes obvious that there are two types of benefits: benefit packages that are defined and produced in advance of sale (products), and benefits that cannot be predefined and prefabricated (services).

This simple definition of services raises a question - Why does one organization elect to produce a service while the second chooses to produce a product? The answer is simply that it depends upon the nature of the benefits the user desires.

Five characteristics need to be present for the benefit package to take the form of a product: 1) The benefits desired must be able to be totally defined in advance allowing the product to be produced without further definition. 2) The standard package of benefits (product) must be acceptable to a large market. Unless there is a large market for the product it will not justify the erection of production lines to produce it. 3) The benefit package must be able to be produced in advance, without interaction with the ultimate user. 4) The value of the product must be able to be maintained in inventory. Inventory is the process that allows the disconnecting of production and consumption. 5) Title to the benefit package must be able to be transferred instantaneously.

Other Benefits Are Services

If the firm is able to develop a package of benefits which meets all five of these conditions, it typically produces a product which it then offers for sale in the marketplace. If one or more of these conditions cannot be satisfied, however, then the organization produces a service. For example, if an individual is physically able to wear a standard size suit, then the product can be defined in advance adequately to allow preproduction. If an individual cannot wear a standard size, then custom tailors evolve to fabricate made-to-orders clothes that can be defined only when the customer arrives. Likewise, medical procedures cannot be produced in advance since the patient's presence is necessary for the delivery (production) process to begin. These conditions are well recognized in the literature (Zeithaml, Parasuraman & Berry, 1985) but are typically viewed as product attributes rather than environmental constraints on the firm's production function. By specifically addressing these environmental conditions, service management decision making becomes three dimensional rather than two dimensional as it is in products.

AN ECONOMIC FRAMEWORK FOR SERVICES

Decision Making For Product Managers

When a product is produced there are two temporal dimensions for decision making. In Economics these dimensions are called the Long Run and the Short Run. In the long run, management must ask 2 basic questions: Should we produce the product? What level of production should we organize for? The major driving force for the decision is the concept of economies of scale. By increasing the size of the investment in the specialized equipment, the per unit production cost can be reduced, but if the predicted level of demand is not realized the capital investment may be lost. Therefore, the major issues are how will the production cost vary with production line volume, and what is the probability of achieving the sales volume necessary to realize the lower costs? Once these issues are resolved, managerial decisions shift to the short run, and long run costs become irrelevant or "sunk."

In the short run (defined as the accounting period since that is when sales and production data are available) the emphasis is on the level of production that should be scheduled. As sales increase or decrease, the production manager attempts to adjust production schedules so that marginal cost and marginal revenue are equalized. If sales are low, production is reduced; if the costs of layoffs and rehiring is high, then inventories are built in anticipation of seasonal or other increased sales during future periods. The ever present decision rule is to equate marginal cost and marginal revenue. The cost of the production line is irrelevant because that decision cannot be remade. The role of management is to make the most profit possible for the given level of production facility. The long run decision is only made once, but short run management decisions are made continually each and every accounting period.

Decision Making For Service Managers

Service managers likewise have long run and short run decisions just as product managers do, only they produce the capacity to serve, not a product that they can put into inventory. In the long run a hospital constructs buildings and equips operating and therapy rooms. The airline buys planes and contracts for facilities with airports. The attorney and physician select a university and the type of training they will acquire. As with products, these long run decisions are based upon expected demand. In the short run, they obtain the resources needed to schedule the facilities they decided to build in the long run. The hospital will decide on the number of wings and operating rooms to schedule and commit the personnel necessary to staff them. The airline will decide on the number of flights between each city pair, allocate planes to each run, schedule arrivals and departures, and schedule employees necessary to offer this level of capacity. The attorney and physician will decide on their office hours, the number of support personnel (nurses, secretaries, bookkeepers, aides) and establish work schedules. The short run decisions will be based, like product decisions, on expected marginal revenues and expected marginal costs.

It is here that the economics of services differ substantially from the economics of products. The majority of product decisions are made in the short run. If no customer arrives to purchase the product on day one it will simply be kept in inventory to be sold when a customer arrives on day two, three, or four to buy it. The exact timing of the sale does not matter since all sales for the accounting period are aggregated and a distinction is generally not made between sales on day one vs. day two, three or four. Services, on the other hand, do not have the luxury of producing prior to the sale and maintaining value in inventory. The hospital incurs the cost of scheduling hospital beds, but unless the patient arrives when the capacity is available the capacity is wasted. The airline incurs the cost of providing transportation, but unless the seats are full when the plane takes off the capacity is wasted. Since services cannot inventory unused capacity for later sale, most service decisions must be made in the immediate run just as most product decisions must be made in the short run. Whereas the short run decisions are based on the organization's scheduling horizon (typically the accounting period), the immediate run is determined by the capacity life of the service. In the case of hospital or hotel room, the immediate run is typically that day. For an airline flight it is the booking period prior to takeoff. For the physician or attorney it is minute by minute since the capacity perishes every minute it is not used.

Just as most product decisions are make in the short run rather than the long run, most service decisions are made in the immediate run rather than the short run. Decision making in the immediate run is likewise made on the basis of marginal revenue and marginal costs, but these are different in the immediate run than in the short run. Whereas the product firm thinks in terms of aggregate demand during the accounting period, in the immediate run the demand curve is often limited to the potential customer standing before you at the moment. Although the law of large numbers and traditional demand curve analysis applies in the long and short run, in the immediate run the service provider frequently has only one customer asking for a service with only the probability that another may appear within a given time period. Thus the decision whether to accept the customer, the price to be charged and many other decisions must be based purely on a one point demand curve with only future probabilities for the other points.

Immediate run costs are also totally different from short run costs. Just as costs that were variable in the long run are fixed and outside of the decision making process in the short run, so variable costs in the short run are fixed and outside of the decision making process in the immediate run. Thus immediate run decisions must be based upon immediate run marginal revenue and immediate run marginal costs. Instead of fixed and variable costs, there will be fixed capacity costs (costs that are variable in the long run but fixed in the short run), variable capacity costs (costs variable in the short run but fixed in the immediate run), and variable service delivery costs (costs that are variable in the immediate run). For example, fixed capacity costs for a airline will include the costs of the planes, reservation software and computer, maintenance facilities, etc. Variable capacity costs will include the cost of the flight crews, fuel, maintenance, etc. The variable service delivery costs will be the travel agent's commission and the cost of the meals and beverages consumed by the passengers with a very slight additional cost in fuel due to the weight of the passenger and their baggage. The variable capacity costs vary according to the capacity actually scheduled, while the service delivery cost is the incremental cost of allowing each additional passenger to use an otherwise empty seat.

SUMMARY AND IMPLICATIONS

The length of this paper does not allow the full development of the three dimensional service model and all of its implications for service management. It does suggest, however, that just as the various product disciplines developed around the two dimensional economic model, so the study of services will develop around the three dimensional service economic model with primary emphasis on immediate run analysis. The implication of this approach are far reaching and will imply non product oriented concepts such as: 1) traditional demand curve assumptions do not hold for services. 2) the role of the market place is different for services. 3) service users buy benefits on faith, not arms length examination of attributes. 4) competitive bidding increases the price paid for services. 5) traditional market segmentation principles increase the cost of service delivery and make them non competitive. 6) price discrimination in services is essential to reduce delivery cost. 7) economies of utilization not economies of scale are the primary managerial concern. 8) the separation of the entrepreneurial and capitalist functions are turning agricultural, mining, and manufacturing industries into services.

These unsubstantiated statements are not listed as proven but simply to suggest a range of potential mindset changes implied by this definition and the three dimensional economic model.

REFERENCES

Blum, Alan I. (1985), "Auxiliary Establishments As a Source of Information on Secondary Services." Working paper presented to the Census Joint Advisory Committee, Arlington, Va., November 14.

Corpus Juris Secundum (1948), Brooklyn, NY: The American Law Book Company and West Publishing Company.

Dixon, Donald F. and Michael F. Smith (1983), "Theoretical Foundations For Services Marketing Strategy," Emerging Perspectives on Services Marketing, Leonard L. Berry, G. Lynn Shostack, Gregory D. Upah, eds, Chicago: American Marketing.

Hammond, J. L. and Barbara (1937), The Rise of Modern Industry, New York: Harcourt, Brace & Company.

Harris, Marvin (1981), America Now: The Anthropology of a Changing Culture, New York: Simon and Schuster.

Heskett, James L. (1986), Managing in the Service Economy, Boston: Harvard Business School Press.

Langham, Charles G. "Economic Censuses of the United States: Historical Development." Working paper #38, Washington, DC: U.S. Government Printing Office (June).

Mantoux, Paul (1961), The Industrial Revolution in the Eighteenth Century, London: Jonathon Cape.

Marcus, Sidney O. (1986), "Secondary Services, What are They and How Do You Measure Them." Presented to Census Advisory Committee of American Marketing Association at the Joint Advisory Committee Meeting, Arlington, Va., April 10.

Pegrum, Dudley F. (1973), Transportation: Economics and Public Policy, Homewood: Richard D. Irwin.

"The Hollow Corporation," (1986), Business Week (March 3), p. 57-81.

The Shorter Oxford English Dictionary on Historical Principles (1973), Oxford: The Clarendon Press.

Wright, Carrol D. and William C. Hunt (1900), The History and Growth of the United States Census, Washington, D.C.: U.S. Government Printing Office.

Zeithaml, Valarie A., and A. Parasuraman, & Leonard L. Berry (1985), "Problems and Strategies in Services Marketing," Journal of Marketing, 49 (Spring) 33-46.

QUESTIONING THE UNQUESTIONED IMPORTANCE OF PERSONAL SERVICE IN SERVICES
MARKETING: DISCUSSION AND IMPLICATIONS

Morry Ghingold and Kurt C. Maier, University of Cincinnati

ABSTRACT

This paper offers a counterargument to the generalized
assumption of personal service maximization in services
marketing. Analyses are presented which demonstrate the
weakness of this assumption from three perspectives:
customer preferences/perceptions, marketing strategy,
and the Service Life Cycle. A preliminary paradigm is
offered using these factors, which proposes a dynamic
and situational view of the role of personal service in
the service marketer's marketing strategy.

INTRODUCTION

With a shrinking industrial base and new
information/communication technologies, the United
States continues to move towards an increasingly
service-based economy. Consistent with this shift has
been the growing interest of marketing researchers and
practitioners in examining the nature of services
marketing, services marketing techniques, and, to a
lesser extent, the structure of services markets (e.g.,
Leavitt 1976, Shostack 1977, Lovelock 1981, Upah et al.
1983). A recent theme in services marketing research
has been the importance of personal contact/service for
the customer in evaluating service quality, presumably a
critical dimension of success in services marketing
(e.g., Wyckham et al. 1975, Zeithaml 1981, Fisk 1981,
Parasuraman et al. 1985). It is the contention of this
paper that the attention given to the personal service
dimensions of services marketing, while warranted, needs
to be more fully developed. Specifically, the
generalized (though not unequivocal) assumption
regarding the importance of personal service in the
services marketing literature, and the subsequent
implication that practitioners should therefore seek to
maximize these factors, is not universally correct.
Rather, a more pragmatic view is advocated, which
hypothesizes a decreasing role for personal service in
service delivery, given certain strategic and/or market
conditions. As explained below, three variables are
viewed to mediate the importance of personal
service/contact: 1. customer preferences/perceptions of
personal service; 2. the strategic merit of personal
service investment for the service marketer; and 3. the
parallel concepts of the Service Life Cycle and customer
sophistication/familiarity with a service class (see
Wasson's 1978 conceptualization of learning requirements
and the Product Life Cycle). The literature review and
theoretical development supporting this view are
presented below.

Before going further, we must address the problem of
what exactly is meant by "personal service" in the
service encounter. Intuitively, it would seem that
personal service is a multidimensional perceptual
phenomenon, occurring in the mind of the consumer.
Consequently, truly objective definitions of "personal
service" will prove elusive, since a customer's view of
the personal service factors in any given service
encounter is idiosyncratic.

For the purposes of this paper, though, it is useful to
think of "friendly, courteous personal service" by
viewing employees as information/assistance dispensers,
giving customers aid, technical information, and
impressions about themselves, as well as the firm.

Surrogate measures of personal service may then be
constructed (though we avoid that here), based on, for
example:

- amount of personal contact between parties;

- amount of information dissemmation by
employees to customers (i.e., expertise);

- perceived helpfulness of employees by
customers;

- other customer perceptions, e.g., "perceived
salesperson friendliness," etc.

Clearly, each of the above dimensions of personal
service applies differentially to differing forms of
services (e.g., tax preparation services versus ice
cream shops). As such, the individual service marketer
or marketing researcher must specify the domain of
personal service for the service encounters he/she is
interested in since "personal service" per se is likely
to be specific to each business/target market, hence our
use of the term personal service in this paper will be
general rather than specific. In any case, though, it
is clear that the dimensions of, and subsequent
measurement of personal service factors requires further
research. Moderating effects must also be delineated.
For example, the mutual expectations and role of the
service encounter participants appears to affect
eventual customer judgments of service quality (Grove
and Fisk, 1983; Solomon, et al., 1985). Purchaser
confidence and/or experience with the service would also
seem to affect customer perceptions. Again, the need
for further research is illustrated.

THE IMPORTANCE OF PERSONAL SERVICE IN
SERVICES MARKETING: A LITERATURE REVIEW

Although the marketing literature remains somewhat
ambiguous as to whether services marketing need be
conceptually different from traditional product
marketing (see Enis and Roering 1981, Lovelock 1981),
there does appear to be substantial agreement that
services marketing varies from product marketing along
certain dimensions that warrant particular attention
(Shostack 1977, Upah et al. 1983). Some of the more
commonly cited areas of difference are (from Stanton
1975, Bateson 1977, Shostack 1977):

1. The intangible nature of services;

2. perishability of services;

3. labor intensiveness;

4. inseparable nature of service production and
consumption;

5. heterogeneity of service quality;

6. the experiential nature of services.

Many of these factors make services relatively difficult
for consumers to evaluate, in contrast to physical
(i.e., observable) products, which can be inspected
and/or experienced for quality judgments prior to
purchase (Fisk 1981, Zeithaml 1981, Parasuraman et al.
1985). Services are not generally subject to similar

discriminating tests, making pre-purchase quality judgments difficult.

This difficulty in evaluating service quality evaluations has led to an increasing belief among marketing researchers in the importance of personal and experiential dimensions of services, holding the view that the service consumer must seek out other attributes to judge the service. Besson (1973) and Eiglier et al. (1977) point out the importance of the physical surroundings where the service is rendered on quality judgments, as does Kotler (1984) in his reference to "atmospherics." Grove and Fisk (1983), in a dramaturgical analysis of service exchanges, made note of the fact that interpersonal influences are crucial to customer evaluations of services. Fisk (1981), Wyckham et al. (1975), Zeithaml (1981) and Parasuraman et al. (1985) all echo similar sentiments, each in some form suggesting that consumers seek tangible cues, especially interpersonal experiences (i.e., whether the saleshelp is friendly, courteous, etc.) to judge service quality levels. This theme is reinforced by Solomon et al. (1985) in their presentation of a role-theoretic framework for analyzing service encounters, using the customer-service representative dyad as the unit of analysis. The implication drawn by the authors is that the customer contact point is a critical determinant of the customer's global satisfaction and quality assessment of the service.

The above would tend to suggest that most services marketing researchers are in general agreement that the level of "friendly, courteous and responsive" attention given to the customer is a critical determinant of the customer's service quality judgment and satisfaction. This would appear to dictate that purveyors of services should strive to offer the most helpful, expert, friendly, and courteous personnel available, to ensure that the customer's view of the "service experience" positively brims with quality and satisfaction.

The generalization should be revised, however. Services marketers may be misapplying (marketing) resources by blindly pursuing strategies of personal service improvement and/or service quality maximization. Clearly, service marketers must respond to competitive and market structure forces. As well, the unique dynamics of the service provider-customer relationship and customer preferences also tend to shape the marketing environment for the services marketer. Individually, each of these factors may affect on the appropriate level of personal service investment for the services marketer. Collectively, they may define several marketing environments which may mandate disinvestment in the personal service dimension. The relationship between each of these factors and the role of personal service/contact in the service marketer's marketing mix are elaborated upon below.

Customer Preferences/Perceptions

The situational relevance of personal service is intuitively illustrated by benefit segmentation. Applying a benefit segmentation paradigm would suggest that not all consumers desire or value similar levels of friendly, expert, courteous, helpful service. Some consumers may be willing to trade off personal service for other attributes, (e.g., lower price, greater convenience, etc.) or may simply not attach much relevance to it. The relative size of the personal service-insensitive segment in a given service market may, in some cases, be significant. Prime examples are the proliferation of low-service fast-food restaurants, no-frills airlines, and "zero-level personal service" automated teller machines for banking transactions.

The role-theoretic perspective advocated by Solomon et al. (1985) is consistent with this argument. By defining quality as the correspondence between customer expectations of what will occur and customer perceptions of what does occur in the service encounter (see also Parasuraman et al. 1985), it is possible for the same behavior by servicepersons to be perceived and/or valued differently by various customers. As such, subsequent evaluations of service quality and/or satisfaction would then also be expected to vary. This view is supported by Booms' and Nyquist's (1981) demonstration of the variability in customer perceptions of service "friendliness," and subsequent quality and satisfaction judgments, building on the notion of the customer as a participant in "defining" the service encounter. Should the customer not expect much in the way of personal service, nor place much utility on it, the personal service dimension will be of little consequence in the customer's subsequent evaluation of the service experience and future purchasing behavior.

This intuitive relationship between consumer utilities or preferences for personal service has been represented in Figure 1 (albeit oversimplified). Although Figure 1 purports to represent a linear relationship between consumer preferences/sensitivity (or elasticity) to the service marketer's investments in personal service (improvement), it is likely that this relationship will be non-linear and vary dramatically between market segments and service categories. Nonetheless, the underlying assumption does tend to suggest numerous scenarios in which (segments of) consumers would be indifferent to, or not value, personal service, suggesting that investments in personal service level maximization may be poorly allocated.

Figure 1

Generalized Relationship Between Customer Sensitivity to Personal Service Dimensions and the Service Marketer's Investment in Personal Service (Improvement)

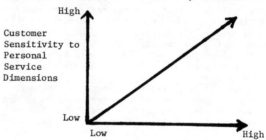

Service Marketer's Investment
in Personal Service (Improvement)

Service Marketing Strategy in a Dynamic Competitive Environment

From a service delivery marketing strategy perspective, the role of personal service must also be questioned. Marketers of services have long had to wrangle with the trade-off of providing individualized service against the need to provide efficient, standardized, cost-effective levels of personal service (Solomon et al. 1985). Moreover, service quality need not depend heavily on personal dimensions where the service rendered may be thought of as a generic (e.g., window washing). In such cases personal service will not constitute a sustainable competitive advantage for the service firm. And, for those firms seeking to maintain high quality images based on customer exchanges with personnel in non-generic service categories, the nature of the differentiating feature is such (i.e., personal service) that it can be easily duplicated by competitors, thus negating the original firm's advantage. Porter (1985) has noted that one requirement of firms seeking to obtain a competitive advantage over others is that the differentiating factor must be difficult/impossible to duplicate by competitors, or it will cease to be a differentiating factor as it is adopted by competitors. Kotler's (1984) discussion of the "friendly banks" evolution serves as an excellent illustration. As financial institutions began to compete for customers, several banks initiated "friendly" behavior, stressing "personal service." As these banks began drawing more customers, the competition countered with their own versions of the personal service theme until all banks were seen as "friendly," thus negating the usefulness of personal service as a differentiating advantage. In the often fragmented and highly competitive environments faced by many service marketers one might expect the emulation process (to the personal service bandwagon) to occur relatively quickly, forcing firms to compete on other bases.

Aside from the issue of sustainability one must also consider the applicability of personal service as a strategic variable. Personal contact/service may be irrelevant in a variety of service encounters (e.g., after hours commerical janitorial services, self-park and pay parking garages/lots, etc.). Or, even when relevant, personal service may not be a useful differentiating variable when the costs of personal service improvements are likely to outweigh marginal contribution returns (e.g., having more flight attendants per flight, recruitment of the best, experienced restaurant personnel at high wage rates for a fast food operation).

In sum, the importance of striving to maximize personal service levels must be viewed as being mediated by the degree to which such efforts: 1. provide a sustainable and relevant differential advantage over competing service firms; and 2. are cost effective in terms of the extent to which marginal revenue gains offset the incremental costs of improved service levels to the customer base. Given this framework it would seem likely that certain service industries would not be candidates for personal service emphasis, as illustrated in Figure 2. As above, this figure oversimplifies the relationship between "applicability and sustainability of personal service as a differential advantage" and the service marketer's investments in personal service (improvement), depicting a linear function. Although the pictorial linear function need not be taken at face value, the essence of the argument, i.e., that personal service investments are not equally relevant in the strategies of all services marketers (e.g., discount brokerage houses, same-day-outpatient-service "batch" cataract clinics, etc.), does seem appropriate.

Figure 2

Generalized Relationship Between the Applicability/Sustainability of Personal Service as a Differential Advantage and the Service Marketer's Investment in Personal Service (Improvement)

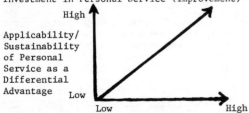

Service Marketer's Investment in Personal Service (Improvement)

The Service Life Cycle and Customers' Information/Learning Requirements

Finally, the personal service/contact--customer satisfaction relationship must be seen in dynamic terms against the backdrop of the Service Life Cycle and increasing customer sophistication. Following from Wasson (1978), customer information/learning requirements will tend to decrease over the stages of the Service Life Cycle. If an important dimension of the service representative's role is related to information provision, either explicitly, as dispensers of service-relevant information, or implicitly, as sources of quality cues (e.g., Zeithaml 1981), the stage of the Service Life Cycle becomes an important mediator of the significance of personal service/contact to customer satisfaction and repeat purchase. For those "new" services where customers have had little (if any) experience and/or possess very limited knowledge of the service (e.g., laser therapy for clearing arterial blockages in lieu of bypass surgery), greater information needs and hence, greater utility of personal service/contact, will likely be exhibited and used as an attribute of service quality. Conversely, for well established service categories, in which consumers are likely to have more extensive usage experience and, possibly, buying sophistication or knowledge, the value of information provision and/or personal service may be far lower (e.g., air travel between two large cities of reasonable proximity, making deposits/withdrawals from a bank, grabbing a fast meal while "on the road," having one's windows washed, etc.). In this scenario the service may be thought of as being in the maturity stage of its life cycle with consumers having greater knowledge of the service and its range of benefits. Attribute salience is likely to change and the service itself may be thought of more as a generic or commodity.

Thus, the Service Life Cycle/customer sophistication paradigm would suggest that initially (introduction and early growth stages) buyers will require (and value) greater amounts of information and reassurance regarding the nature and quality of the service. Service marketers must incur the costs necessary to provide high levels of personal service and often must develop the market" since they are offering something new to new customers. As these customers use the service category more and more, or are at least becoming increasingly familiar with the service category, (i.e., late growth and maturity stages) it is likely they will become more sophisticated and/or knowledgeable in their purchase decision making, requiring less information and possibly decreasing the value or utility attached to extensive personal service (e.g., photocopying services, simple meals outside the home (not to be confused with "dining experiences") etc.). Changes in attribute salience may evolve and brand switching/experimentation will occur. In the extreme, the service may be reduced to a commodity status where price becomes dominant and personal service is seen as an unnecessary cost which increases prices (e.g., photofinishing services for non-hobbyists, long-distance telephone services, etc.).

This paradigm would tend to suggest disinvestment in personal service/contact over the life cycle of the service so that other attributes which may be gaining in importance to customers can be enhanced (e.g., greater convenience, faster service, lower prices, etc.). This proposition can be seen as analogous to the erosion of full-service and department store customer bases by the mass merchandisers and discount/catalog retailers. These latter marketers offered a distinct attribute bundle which emphasized lower prices and lower service levels, consistent with the preferences of more knowledgeable shoppers who felt secure in their own abilities to make good buying decisions and did not, therefore, value personal service. This relationship between stage of the Service Life Cycle and the need for service marketers' investments in personal service (improvement) is portrayed in Figure 3.

Figure 3

Generalized Relationship Between Stages of the Service Life Cycle and the Service Marketer's Investment in Personal Service (Improvement)

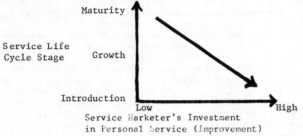

Service Life
Cycle Stage

Service Marketer's Investment
in Personal Service (Improvement)

Discussion

This paper has presented several revisions to the generalized assumption of personal service importance in services marketing. Three factors, consumer preferences/perceptions, marketing strategy considerations, and the Service Life Cycle were all shown to present cases for situational disinvestment in personal service/contact by services marketers. The situational aspect is critical, since no "rules of thumb" can be prescribed. Nonetheless, a pragmatic approach is required to determine the appropriate marketing mix for successful services marketing given the marketers' objectives and the dynamics of marketplace conditions.

Although it is not possible to specify hard and fast decision rules, one may still generalize certain strategic insights from the three analyses presented earlier. These generalizations which are intended only as loose guidelines can be synthesized as follows:

1. Investments in personal service (improvement) should be maximized to the extent that

    a) the service is in the early stages of the life cycle;

    b) sensitivity to personal service (i.e., customer preferences/perceptions/elasticities) in a given market segment is high;

    c) the applicability and sustainability of personal service as a differential advantage in the given market segment is high.

2. Investments in personal service (improvement) should be minimized (or negative) to the extent that

    a) the service is in the later stages of the life cycle;

    b) sensitivity to personal service in the given market segment is low;

    c) the applicability and sustainability of personal service as a differential advantage in the given segment is low.

3. Investments in personal service (improvement) should be closely monitored and tested periodically for those services that fall between 1 and 2.

The role of personal service in the strategy or program of the service marketer must be consistent with the objectives of the specific firm. Thus, high service firms may still succeed under conditions attached to Proposition 2 above if a specialized "niching" strategy is used (e.g., super-luxury air travel, fine dining, etc.). Nonetheless, the broad framework presented offers intuitive appeal and reasonable generalizability. Rather than viewing services marketing as a generic, researchers and practitioners must appreciate the unique requirements of any services marketing effort and the role of all marketing mix elements in successful services marketing. The strategic and market based variables discussed in this paper suggest that personal service contact will not be important or effective in generating customer satisfaction for all services and/or all market segments.

The purpose of this paper has not been to specify hard and fast rules for service marketing management, however. Rather, a marketing orientation or philosophy is advocated to encourage a matching process between actual service delivery (including dimensions of personal service) and the benefits or attributes sought by the desired target market. Our premise is simple: determine what your target customers want, and in light of strategic and economic constraints/opportunities, try to provide a superior version of those wants. As such, personal service may or may not play a pivotal role in customer satisfaction and service marketing strategy. The main issue, however, is to determine the exact role of personal service and all other service attributes or features as a prerequisite to service marketing.

By continuously evaluating the everchanging skills and resources necessary for all service businesses in the firms portfolio, it may be possible to make the conceptual leap to a portfolio management model for multiservice marketers, balancing the financial, physical and human needs of each service business against the pool of available resources and services marketing opportunities. Although this concept of a services portfolio is beyond the scope of the present paper, it is hoped that the more modest framework presented herein serves as the starting point for further discussion and research in the areas of services strategy and success.

REFERENCES

Bateson, J. E. G. (1977), "Do We Need Services Marketing?" in Marketing Consumer Services: New Insights. Cambridge, Mass.: Marketing Science Institute.

Besson, R. (1973), "Unique Aspects of Marketing Services" Arizona Business Bulletin, v. 9, November, pp. 8-15.

_____ and D. Jackson (1975), "Service Retailing: A Strategic Marketing Approach," Journal of Retailing, v. 51, Summer, pp. 75-84.

Booms, B. H., and J. N. Nyquist (1981), "Analyzing the Customer/Firm Communication Component of the Services Marketing Mix," in Proceedings of the AMA Special Conference on Services Marketing, J. Donnelly and W. R. George, eds. Orlando, Florida: AMA.

Eiglier, P., E. Langeard, C. Lovelock, J. Bateson, and R. Young (1977), Marketing Consumer Services: New Insights. Cambridge, Mass: Marketing Science Institute.

Enis, B. and K. Roering (1981), "Services Marketing: Different Products, Similar Strategy" in Proceedings of the AMA Special Conference on Services Marketing, J. Donnelly and W. R. George, eds. Orlando, Florida: AMA.

Fisk, R. (1981), "Toward a Consumption/Evaluation Process Model for Services," in Proceedings of the AMA Special Conference on Services Marketing, L. Berry, C. L. Shostack, G. Upah, eds. Chicago, Ill: AMA.

Grove, S., and R. Fisk (1983), "The Dramaturgy of Service Exchange: An Analytical Framework for Services Marketing" in Proceedings of the AMA Special Conference on Services Marketing, L. Berry, G. Shostack, G. Upan, eds. Chicago, Ill: AMA.

Kotler, P. (1984), Marketing Management, Englewood Cliffs, N.J.: Prentice-Hall.

Leavitt, T. (1976), "The Industrialization of Services," Harvard Business Review, Fall, pp. 63-74.

Lovelock, Chris (1981), "Why Marketing Management Needs To Be Different for Services," in Proceedings of the AMA Special Conference on Services Marketing, J. Donnelley and W. R. George, eds. Orlando, Florida: AMA.

Parasuraman, A., Zeithaml, V., and L. Berry (1985), "A Conceptual Model of Service Quality and Its Implications for Future Research," Journal of Marketing, v. 49, n. 4, pp. 41-50.

Porter, M. (1985), Competitive Advantage New York: Free Press.

Rathmell, J. M. (1966), "What Is Meant By Services," Journal of Marketing, October, pp. 32-36.

_____ (1974), Marketing In The Service Sector, Cambridge, Mass.: Winthrop Publishing Co.

Shostack, G. Lynn (1977), "Breaking Free of Product Marketing," Journal of Marketing, v. 41, April, pp. 73-80.

Solomon, M., C. Suprenant, J. Czepiel, and E. Gutman (1985), "A Role Theory Perspective of Dyadic Interactions: The Service Encounter" Journal of Marketing, v. 49, n. 1, pp. 99-111.

Stanton, W. (1975), Fundamentals of Marketing 4th ed., New York: McGraw Hill.

Upah, G., L. Berry, and G. Lynn Shostack (1983), "Emerging Themes and Directions For Services Marketing," in Proceedings of the AMA Special Conference on Services Marketing, L. Berry, G. Shostack, G. Upan, eds., Chicago, Ill: AMA.

Wasson, C. (1978), Dynamic Competitive Strategy and Product Life Cycles, 3rd ed. Austin, Texas: Austin Press.

Wyckham, R., P. Fitzroy, and G. Mandry (1975), "Marketing of Services: An Evaluation of the Theory" European Journal of Marketing, v. 9, n. 1, pp. 59-67.

Zeithaml, V. (1981), "How Consumer Evaluation Processes Differ Between Goods and Services," in Proceedings of the AMA Special Conference on Services Marketing, L. Berry, G. Shostack, G. Upan, eds. Chicago, Ill: AMA.).

ISOLATING TANGIBLE REPRESENTATIONS OF INTANGIBLE SERVICE DIMENSIONS: AN EXTENSION OF THE REPERTORY GRID METHODOLOGY

Cliff Scott, Old Dominion University
John B. Ford, Old Dominion University
William Lundstrom, Old Dominion University

ABSTRACT

The authors discuss and demonstrate a procedure for identifying the intangible dimensions of services, then "tagging" those dimensions with tangible service attributes. Both questionnaire development and data analysis are discussed, yielding an integrated procedure. The example survey and analysis provided leads to suggestions for promotional themes.

INTRODUCTION

One of the most important, and troublesome, aspects of services is their intangibility (Berry, 1980; Upah, 1980; Booms and Bintner, 1982). This aspect is of central importance because, as Berry's (1980) exposition on the topic demonstrates, the concept of intangibility is the key to comprehending the essences of services marketing. When purchasing a service, Berry explains, the consumer does experience a cash outlay, however, s/he has nothing tangible to show for it, i.e., "services are consumed but not possessed" (pp 24).

The problems of intangibility are particularly troublesome because that which one cannot "put in a box" is more difficult to quantify, comprehend, and of course, market. Ergo, the intangibility problem causes confusion at two levels. First, services are more difficult for the consumer to understand, evalu- ate and compare. Secondly, they are more difficult for the marketer to describe, bene-fitize, or demonstrate. All of these problems stem, in whole or in part, from the intangibility of services.

If the marketer was able to make his/her service more tangible for the consumer, this would be a major step towards the effective marketing of that service. This paper attempts to explain and demonstrate a research procedure designed to allow the marketer to take just such a step.

Recent theoretical developments have begun to evolve a conceptual as well as procedural basis for dealing with the problem of intangibility. These procedures allow for the isolation of tangible aspects which represent the intangible service attributes to the consumer (Lewis and Klein, 1986). As such, these pro-cedures allow the market researcher to "crack the code" which links the consumer's image of the service provider with observable and events in the real world.

Lewis and Klein's use of Kelly's (1955) repertory test procedure represents a major advance for the services marketer. They have described a research sequence which allows the marketer to isolate those tangible items which may spell service quality to the consumer. The present paper extends Lewis and Klein's work in three ways. First, it is an actual application of the technique—the reader may see the procedure in action. Second, it "broadens" the technique by adding a second exploratory research technique—the critical incident approach—which is particularly useful when the customer may be relatively unfamiliar with the service in question. Last, it adds the technique of factor analysis, allowing the following three research questions to be answered:

1) What are the major intangible dimensions (themes) consumers use when evaluating this service?

2) Which tangibles are associated with which dimensions?

3) How strong is the connection between any theme and any tangible items?

The data used for this demonstration deal with the field of health care. The data were drawn from a convenience sample, and no attempt to make inferences concerning the field of health care should be attempted from current results. The purpose is solely the demonstration of research technique.

PRE-TEST TECHNIQUES

Subjects from two populations were interviewed during the pretesting phase of this project. A seperate interview procedure was used for each population. The first population consisted of hospital staff members, who were interviewed using the repertory grid technique. Hospital patients formed the second population, and were interviewed using the critical incident technique.

Hospital patients were interviewed for the obvious reason that it is their perceptions which are in question. Despite this fact, patients do not make ideal subjects due to their overall lack of exposure to hospitals, and the field of health care in general. It is entirely possible that the patients could have some concerns which they lack the vocabulary to express adequately. In order to address this content validity issue, hospital staff members were included in the pretesting procedure. Simply stated, the researchers were more concerned about some important item being excluded than about some irrelevant item being included. An omitted item could substantially reduce the worth of the analysis. An included, irrelevant item would not be expected to correlate with other items on the questionnaire, and would therefore be largely removed from the analysis at the factor analysis stage. Both of the interview techniques will now be described.

The rep grid test requires that the researcher is in some way able to represent the objects under investigation to the experimental subjects. The researcher may show the subjects the actual items in question, or if the items are well enough known to the respondents, the researcher may simply use cards on which the names of the items have been printed. In the present example, the class of objects under investigation was hospitals, and the respondents were hospital employees. Therefore a simple representation was deemed appropriate: the name of each area hospital was types on a card, and these cards served as the represen-tations.

A second exploratory research technique was also be employed in the current study. It was the critical inci-dent technique. This approach "consists of a set of proce-dures for collecting direct observations of human behavior in such a way as to facilitate their potential usefulness on solving practical problems and developing board psycho-logical principles" (Flanagan, 1954, p. 327).

Stated most simply, the critical incident technique calls upon the individual subject to report events within their own experience. These events, or incidents, should be both the best and the worst examples from some defined domain.

For example, let us assume that one wishes to gather information on the topic of "What makes a teacher effective?". The researcher would use the following line of questioning in the interview: "Could you please describe an incident for me which you feel is an example of particularly effective (ineffective) teaching?" By proceeding in this fashion, the researcher will gather a set of "incidents" which typify both effective and ineffective performance.

PROCEDURE

The procedure used for these interviews was as follows. The researcher informed the respondent as to the purpose of the survey. The researcher then selected three of the cards, in a random fashion, and presented them to the respondent. The respondent was then asked, "Please tell me how two of these hospitals are alike and the third is different". It should be apparent that this situation is designed to elicit constructs: two similar objects forming a concept, and the third forming the contrast pole. The subject responses were recorded on three-by-five cards for subsequent taxonification. The researcher repeated this procedure until either 1) the respondent's pool of personal constructs was exhausted, or, 2) a thirty-minute time limit was reached.

Fifteen staff RN's and individuals associated with the marketing function at a 300-bed hospital were interviewed via the repertory grid procedure. Such individuals may be seen as analogous to corporate service reps or salespersons in that they are the interface between the customer and the corporation. As such, these individuals, due to their daily contact with the patients, are a rich source of information on the topic of customer concerns. For purposes of the current exposition, these rep grid interviews represent the "heart and soul" of the Lewis/Klein procedure.

The stimuli placed before these individuals were cards representing each of the twelve hospitals within the surrounding grater metropolitan area. In accord with the repertory grid procedure, the respondents were repeatedly presented with sets of three randomly selected cards and asked to state how two of the hospitals were the same and the third was different. The total response set was then categorized by the researchers.

Fifteen current hospital patients were interviewed using the critical incident technique. These individuals were asked to relate examples of particularly good and particularly bad events which they experienced during their hospital stay. These interviews were augmented with ten additional critical incident interviews with individuals who had been hospital patients during the last two years. Again, the responses were categorized by the researchers.

Once the interviews had been carried out and the responses categorized, development of the final questionnaire was a simple and straightforward matter. The same item selection procedure was followed for each set of responses. First, the response categories were placed in sequence according to the number of entries within the category. A cutoff number of entries was then determined via a scree test procedure. All categories above the cutoff were included on the questionnaire. So, for the patient interviews, any item being mentioned by three or more patients was included on the final questionnaire.

The questionnaire was administered to 116 upper level undergraduate business students. The sample was drawn strictly on a convenience basis. As has been discussed, due to the characteristics of the sample, no attempt to draw conclusions concerning the health care industry will be made. The only intent is the demonstration of a research technique.

DATA ANALYSIS

As a result of the pretest procedures, 28 variables were included in the analysis. The results did lend themselves to clear interpretations with high loadings on a few key variables. These high loadings did not overlap across any two or more factors, which improved the clarity of the interpretations. There were 7 loadings in excess of .50 on Factor 1, 5 loadings in excess of .50 on Factor 2, 6 loadings in excess of .50 on Factor 3 and 2 loadings in excess of .50 on Factor 4.

The rotated factor loadings and the corresponding tangible variables for Factor 1 are as follows:

FACTOR 1 - 22.2% of trace

Variable	Loading
Quality of Doctor Care	.75514
Ability of the Staff	.68083
Quality of Nurse Care	.65568
Hospital is Clean	.64853
Advanced Equipment Used	.64306
Good Reputation of Hospital	.56155
Full Range of Services Present	.54611

The tangible variables identified here all appear to deal with elements of competency. The highest loadings were for 1)quality of the doctors, 2) ability of the staff, and 3) quality of the nurses. These aspects of health care justify the naming of this dimension as STAFF COMPETENCY.

Here we see that certain tangible items may be used as "TAGS" to represent COMPETENCY in the consumer's mind. These items refer to cleanliness, equipment and range of services. Such items may be thought of as the concrete represents which denote COMPETENCY to the consumer.

The rotated factor loadings for Factor 2 also were high. The loadings and their corresponding variables were as follows:

FACTOR 2 - 14.7% of trace

Variable	Loading
Large Ad Campaign Used	.74426
Hospital is Large	.67025
Hospital Affiliated with Others	.65462
Community Affairs Involvement	.65157
Hospital is Small	.63466

These variables deal with the awareness of the community or involvement of the health care facility in the community. The three highest loading variables here were; 1) large ad campaign, 2) hospital is large, and 3) hospital is affiliated with other hospitals. This underlying intangible dimension was identified, therefore, as COMMUNITY PRESENCE.

The loadings for Factor 3 are as follows:

FACTOR 3 - 6.6% of trace

Variable	Loading
Atmosphere of Hospital	.74426
Nurses are Friendly	.63135
Family Orientation	.62444
Atmosphere is Positive	.59872
Quality of the Food	.59614
Doctors are Friendly	.54075

These variables deal with the atmospheric elements of health care. The highest loadings were for: 1) atmosphere, 2) nurses are friendly, 3) hospital is family-oriented. This underlying dimension was therefore identified as AMBIENCE.

Again, see that certain tangible items may be used to represent Ambience. Any programs involving family members should be helpful in this instance. Such programs are currently often associated with pre-natal care. Quality of food appears to be a good, and underutilized, option. It is interesting to note that not a single hospital employee mentioned "food" in the pre-test. This fact points out the wisdom of using more than one pre-test procedure.

The last of the four factors had only two variables which loaded over .50, but these variables were very distinctive and allowed a clear interpretation. These two variables and the corresponding factor loadings are as follows:

FACTOR 4 - 5.2% of trace

Variable	Loading
Pediatric Facility Available	.72416
Maternity Facility Available	.70483

These variables both involve specialty services provided by a health care facility. They are 1) pediatric facilities are available and 2) maternity facilities are available. This last underlying dimension was, therefore, identified as SPECIALITY SERVICES. It should be noted paranthetically that the variable "Outpatient Clinic Available" loaded above .49 on this factor which lends further credibility to this factor interpretation.

RESULTS

The procedure followed was able to identify 4 major intangible dimensions employed by the sample population in its perception of health care facilities in particular. The identified dimensions were 1) STAFF COMPETENCY, 2) COMMUNITY PRESENCE, 3) AMBIENCE, 4) SPECIALITY SERVICES. For the purpose of this limited sample population, the first major question posited in the introduction, "What are the major dimensions which the consumer employs in his/her perception of a service?," has, therefore, been answered.

As far as the second posited question, "Which tangibles are associated with which dimensions?," is concerned, the tangible variables associated with these dimensions were also identified. STAFF COMPETENCY was associated with the use of advanced equipment and the presence of a full range of services. COMMUNITY PRESENCE was associated with the amount of advertising done by the health care facility, the involvement of the facility in community affairs, the affiliation of the facility with other facilities, and the size of the facility. AMBIENCE was associated with the family orientation of the facility and the quality of the food. Finally, SPECIALTY SERVICES was associated with the availability of pediatric and maternity facilities.

The last posited question, "How strong is the connection between any given intangible dimension and any given tangible item?," has also been addressed. The associations involved were strong as noted by the high rotated factor loadings. The variables associated with COMPETENCY were all above .50, with 4 above .64 and 1 above .75. The variables associated with COMMUNITY PRESENCE all had factor loadings above .63 with one above .70. The variables associated with the AMBIENCE dimension all load above .50, with two above .60. The two forming the SPECIALITY SERVICES dimension both had rotated factor loadings in excess of .70, which is quite high. All of the questions raised in the introduction have therefore been answered through the use of this procedure.

CONCLUSION

From this research it can be seen that Lewis and Klein have indeed developed a point of view which may prove to be of central import to the services marketer. The problems inherent in the intangibility of services often leave the marketer with an incomplete basis for strategy development. This type of tool makes it possible for the services marketer to develop more actionable plans and strategies, and, therefore, increases the chances for success in the marketplace. While the sample chosen for this research was one of convenience and does not allow for this research was one of convenience and does not allow significant inferences about typical health care consumers or the health care field in general, it does demonstrate the applicability of this useful tool and adds another important option to the service marketer's array of strategic tools.

The study reported demonstrates that this extension of the Repertory Grid Procedure is capable of offering clear and specific suggestions to the marketer. The most obvious application would be in the area of Promotion. These results suggest both WHAT themes should be presented within the advertising, and HOW to make those themes more tangible to the consumer.

For example, the results indicate that the marketer might wish to stress the AMBIENCE of the hospital. Good choices of specifics to stress in such a campaign would include: the quality of the food, personal attention from the nursing staff, and educational, or other, programs which involve the patient's family. The data indicate that these tangibles are intimately related to the samples' perceptions of the ambience of the hospital. As such, they appear to act as "cognitive handles" for the consumer, and are real-world representations of the intangible, "AMBIENCE." For the marketer who wishes to attack this particular attitude in the minds of the public, these items may represent the "points of tangibility" at which the attack should be aimed.

Once again, it must be stated that the data presented were drawn on the convenience basis. The intent is to demonstrate the applicability of that technique. No attempt should be made to draw conclusions concerning the field of health care from current research.

REFERENCES

Bannister, D. (1962), Personal Construct Theory: Summary and Experimental Paradigm", Acta Psychologica 20, 104-120.

Berry, Leonard L. (1980), "Services Marketing is Different", Business, 30 (May/June), pp. 24-29

Booms, B.H. and M.J. Bitner (1982), "Marketing Servises By Managing the Environment", Cornell Hotel and Restaurant Administration Quarterly, 23 (May), pp. 35-39.

Flanagan, John C. (1954), "The Critical Incident Technique" Psychological Bulletin 51, 327-358.

Kaplan, Stephen (1973), "Cognitive Maps in Perception and Thought", in Image and Environment: Cognitive Mapping and Spatial Behavior, Downs and Stea, Eds., Chicago: Aldine Publishing.

Kelly, G.A. (1955), The Psychology of Personal Constructs, New York: W.W. Norton.

_____ (1963), A Theory of Personality, New York: W. W. Norton.

_____ (1970), "A Brief Introduction to Personal Construct Theory", in Perspectives in Personal Construct Theory, D. Bannister, Ed., New York: Academic Press.

Lewis, Rober C. and David M. Klein (1986), "Personal Constructs: Their Use in the Marketing of Intangible Service", Psychology and Marketing, Vol. No. 3.

Sampson, Peter (1972), "Using the Repertory Grid Test", Journal of Marketing Research, 78-81.

Upah, Greg D. (1980), "Mass Marketing in Service Retailing", Journal of Retailing, 56 (Fall), pp. 59-76.

Zaltman, G., C. Pinson and R. Angelmar (1964), Metatheory and Consumer Research, New York: Holt Rinehard and Winston.

ROLE OF THE TRACKING STUDY AS AN INTEGRATING MECHANISM
IN THE SERVICE ORGANIZATION

John Martin, School of Management, Boston University
Anne Bailey Berman, Chadwick Martin Bailey Consultants, Boston

ABSTRACT

This paper addresses the problem of multi-branch and multi-functional service organizations in obtaining timely and actionable information in a manner than can contribute to increasing coordination among operational units. It is proposed that the tracking study can contribute to the solution of this problem.

An approach for developing and maintaining an effective tracking system is summarized, and its use in organizational integration discussed. The authors use their experience in the cable industry to illustrate the main points, but these conditions parallel many other service organizations.

INTRODUCTION

Service organizations in consumer markets by their nature must be close to the consumer. Their relationship to the consumer is often personal and intangible (e.g. see Shostack 1977; Lovelock 1981), represented by such attributes as "speed of service" and "helpfulness." Customer perceptions of a service can change rapidly and may rest on external factors not directly attributable to the service organization itself. For example, use of VCRs affect perceptions of cable television. Perceptual changes may also be due to variations in the organization's actions, such as slower reaction to service calls.

Many service organizations deliver their product to the consumer by multiple interactions using several functions. Thus, a sales representative, repair person, office clerk and computer billing system all interact in the company's impact on the customer. This effort must be coordinated (Zeithaml et al., 1985) to provide both consistency and improvements in service.

The problem a service organization faces is to obtain market information that is both timely and pertinent. This is complicated when there are many geographically-dispersed branches. To build effective strategies or react adequately to market threats, timely assessments must be made of both market conditions and company performance in meeting customer needs for all locations.

The challenge of dealing with complex consumer perceptions and behaviors requires information with multiple capabilities for analysis. Not only is it necessary to gauge movements in market factors (such as consumer behavior), but likely reasons for the movements must be identified. Further, the information flow should be used to enhance organizational coordination so essential for effective strategy implementation.

A major contribution to obtaining timely and pertinent information is the marketing information system. Internal data, such as sales, can be easily updated and made immediately available using standardized measures that enable comparisons over time and across branches. Many companies the conduct periodic market studies to investigate "problems" as they become apparent.

The need for regular inputs of standardized market data is sometimes met by commercial suppliers of "panel" data such as A.C. Nielsen. However, the unique requirements of many service organizations are frequently not met by this panel data, and more, singly or in cooperative groups, are developing tracking studies.

The purpose of this article is to present the tracking method as an effective and cost efficient source of information for strategic decisions that can also contribute to integration. First, the cable television industry is described since it is used to illustrate the paper. Second, the nature of tracking studies is examined, giving some advantages and an overview of available options. Third, the benefits of a tracking study for organization integration are outlined. Finally, an approach to the "varied group" form of tracking study is discussed as a means of enhancing integration.

THE CABLE TELEVISION INDUSTRY

Cable television emerged in rural areas to solve the problem of commercial television reception. Subsequently, it was introduced into urban areas to provide greater television viewing choices; now, about 40% of households nationally have access to cable.

Although the industry originally consisted of small companies servicing single communities, industry growth has resulted in larger companies servicing multiple communities. Further, systems in geographic proximity are being consolidated under common signal transmitters and management. Now, the typical cable company has multiple branches, called systems, widely located and servicing varied publics.

Cable companies face a competitive environment. They have growing competition from alternative technology in the home, such as VCRs and computers. Further, satellite dishes are an immediate threat, the telephone an evolving threat and alternative entertainment a continuous threat.

In this environment, the role of the cable company has evolved notably. Initially just a local technical conduit, cable managers now face complex customer needs. Problems of low subscriber penetration, declining interest and stability in premium services, and competition are raising recognition among cable managers that they must become marketing oriented in all functional areas.

Basic to the future of a cable company, and most service organizations, is information for market decisions. At the corporate level, managers need information for strategic decisions and system control. Further, effective implementation of a strategic market plan requires system integration. System managers need information about their markets to formulate system market plans and provide control. Again, effective plan implementation requires functional unit integration.

THE TRACKING STUDY APPROACH

The procedure of "tracking" involves making repeat market measures over time with "standard" measures for valid comparisons. A well known tracking study is the Consumer Price Index where the regimen is kept as stable as possible. Interestingly, the term "tracking study" is rarely used in the marketing literature although in common use among research practitioners. Terms such as "base line," "longitudinal research design" (Kinnear and Taylor, 1983), "monitors" (e.g. The Yankelovitch Monitor) and "panels" are used to represent forms of tracking studies.

Advantages of Tracking Studies

The tracking study has advantages compared to other alternatives such as using studies only when specific market problems seem to exist. The advantages include:

1. Problems, and often solutions, are identified early.
2. The impact of strategic action can be followed and adjustments made if necessary.
3. Managers can use marketing information more effectively if there are measures with which they are familiar.
4. Personal motivation due to the reduction in uncertainty when making decisions.
5. Although regular studies may be an additional cost for some organizations, their are economies from repetition of the same methodology.
6. Regular flows of standardized information can be used to bring people together to build integration.

The contribution of a tracking study to integration is the focus of this paper, and dealt with in a later section. However, another issue must be dealt with first. This is to delineate the forms that tracking studies can take and suggest one of these for use by service organizations.

Forms of Tracking Studies

Most forms of tracking study are represented by the four sets of conditions. These are the outcome of sample selection options and the alternative types of information sought which are now examined.

Sample Options. In the first sample option, a group of respondents or units such as stores is recruited and maintained for repeat use. This is called a constant group or panel. Here there is agreement to participate in one or more studies, usually for payment. The panel is well documented in the literature and widely used in practice.

Sometimes the panel and tracking study are treated as synonimous. For example, Ruddick et al. (1983) define a tracking study as "an on-going periodic survey of pre-recruited consumers who rate their use of various products and services." However, whether tracking occurs or not depends on the use of the panel. It is the repetition of measurements that represents "tracking" while the panel is the group of respondents used.

A disadvantage of the panel for perceptual measurement is that people are affected by prior exposure, especially when data collection instruments are the same. This is an "instrumentation" effect. Further, panels may not be representative due to problems such as self-selection bias and mortality. Such factors raise questions about the validity of panels (Sudman, 1964; Farley et al. 1978). There is support for some forms of data collection using a panel where respondents regularly record their behavior in diaries (See Sudman, 1964; Parfitt, 1967).

The other sample option is to draw an independent random sample for each iteration of a tracking study so that repeat use of respondents is rare. This means that so long as the population definition and source of respondents is constant, reliable comparisons among samples can be made. The renewed random sample method or varied group form relies on "probability" to ensure that over time samples are equivalent. However, it avoids many of the problems of panels such as instrumentation threat and self-selection.

Information Options. The other factor that characterizes tracking studies is the way the data is used. The measures either describe changes in conditions and performance over time (descriptive) or assess the likely impact of one or more strategies (causal). For descriptive measures, changes are expected to reflect the conditions of factors within or external to the organization unrelated to the study. Thus, descriptive measures for a cable company might indicate a decline in the customer-related performance of personnel (internal) or the impact of a hurricane (external) on cable reception/service.

For causal information, the objective is to "test" a new strategy or concept. Experiments expose selected respondents to "treatments" such as direct mail information or a new product. Changes in the measures are therefore "induced" because the situation has been "contrived" and the treatments may never really be used.

A tracking study, constant or varied group for, can be used for both descriptive and causal purposes. However, experiments introduce artificial changes that "contaminate" the tracking data and limit its use for other purposes. This does not prevent use of a tracking instrument in an experiment. An example is to rotate "treatments" embedded in the instrument to assess such things as price elasticity.

ROLE OF THE TRACKING STUDY IN ORGANIZATIONAL INTEGRATION

Corporate mangers need to integrate at the systems level to achieve strategic plan objectives. Decisions about resource allocation concern not only the role of each system, but that of functional areas, such as field service, across all systems. A decision may be to "grow" an individual system or to upgrade telephone response effectiveness across the entire company.

A system providing services to a local community has a number of operating units including sales; customer service; administration; installation and maintenance; engineering and local programing. Each department has individual functions and goals, and from the customer's perspective has different performance roles. The situation is similar for, say, financial service organizations.

Each unit may carry out it's narrow function in or out of alignment with customer need priorities. For example, the installer interacts with the customer outside the office when there is customer excitement about the potential of cable television. Likewise, a service representative may interact with the customer during time of disagreement over billing or complaints about service delivery.

Due to multiple points of interaction with the consumer, the service organization needs effective interaction among operational units. This requires communication and impetus to encourage the construction of a consistent consumer strategy. The tracking study can provide five major contributions to organizational coordination:

1. Comprehensive corporate overview for integrated service strategy development and control.

2. A targeted focus on individual operating units as interdependent components of service.

3. Timeliness of data directly relate to immediate issues of implementation.

4. Familiarity of measures for confidence and ease of application.

5. Repetition of measurements to provide "rewards" and greater market understanding for subsequent market programs or feedback for adjusting the present program.

6. Ease of implementation.

Comprehensive Overview

The tracking study provides performance measures for each operational unit by system or branch. From the corporate perspective, system performance can be directly compared and action at the system level encouraged. In some instances, it may be necessary to distribute additional resources to overcome imbalances among the systems. Further, systems may be sold under certain conditions.

On one hand, the tracking study places the systems in a competitive situation within the organization, a concept not that familiar in cable. On the other hand, managers see success depending on the resolution of company-wide market performance problems. So there is an incentive for system managers to cooperate in determining how best to improve market performance. One system, having high customer service performance may play a leadership role in this aspect of cable operations by making recommendations to other systems whose performance is less stellar.

Targeted Focus on Operating Units

At the corporate level, the tracking study measures the performance of operational units across the organization. Thus, if office telephone response is seen to be poor in several systems, new telephone systems or more personnel may be allocated. The outcome is a consistent and coordinated corporate level drive for improved performance by service function across the organization.

The tracking study gives the system manager both an overview of performance relative to that of the total organization, and a view of the contribution of each operational unit in system performance in terms of customer perceptions. For example, operational unit performance can be related to outcome measures such as "satisfaction" and "drop intentions" to give the relative contribution of operating units. Thus, managers can determine to what extent subscriber satisfaction is related to the ease of reaching the office by phone, service maintenance, program variety or guides.

Timeliness

A major advantage of the tracking study is the provision of timely information for managers when formulating and implementing strategies. Time consuming but necessary tasks such as exploratory research, setting information objectives and development of valid measures are substantially completed by the first wave of data collection. Data is collected regularly, and rapidly if needed. An example is the purchase of a new system when comparative data is required to evaluate the acquisition.

When using regular tracking studies, management activities can be timed around the study with a precise schedule for plan formulation, implementation and evaluation. Thus, action to improve a cable guide based on information from one tracking study can be evaluated from the subsequent study 6 months later. Further, regular information input leads to more coordination (through meetings) and flexibility in the plan implementation process.

Repetition of Measurements

Central to the tracking study is the repetition of measurement. Managers receive more than a "snap shot" of the market and are able to observe trends. Multiple measurements over time add to manager confidence in data validity, and so they are more secure in acting on the new knowledge: a willingness to accept evaluations and work together to the benefit of all operational units.

Familiarity of Measures

Also due to the repeated nature of the tracking study, managers and staff become more familiar with measures and what they represent. The learning process that accompanies many one time studies is abbreviated because of this familiarity giving cost (time) benefits.

Familiarity also means that more time and thought is given to application of the information rather than trying to just understand it. Constant referral to standard measures means that the information is used more effectively. Again, this enhances coordination among operating units which are all using the same "language" in talking about performance.

System managers are able to meet with staff representing all operational units immediately upon receiving the results of a study wave to discuss future action. This is particularly useful for dealing rapidly with problems that cut across more than one unit.

Ease of Implementation

As already mentioned, a consequence of the tracking study is immediate information flow during plan implementation. This means that greater flexibility in strategy adjustment is possible due to regular information inputs. Implementation affects all units, so coordination is again encouraged. Flexibility increases the likelihood that operational people in the units will enthusiastically carry out requirements of the market plan.

In summary, then, the tracking study has many distinct advantages in comparison to the use of less systematic and regular information collection procedures.

DESIGN OF A VARIED GROUP TRACKING STUDY

Development of a tracking study to meet the decision needs of service managers requires a systematic approach. The one outlined here is based on the authors' experience. It involves development of both a strong interaction among managers and a detailed understanding of the market. In particular, the tracking study process is used as a vehicle to enhance integration. The five stages are now discussed using cable situations for illustrations, however, the issues raised are directly applicable to most other types of service organizations.

Managerial Input Stage

The objectives of this stage are to establish organizational understanding and support and delineate basic conditions or requirements for the study.

The success of a tracking study rests on securing manager confidence in it's relevance to decisions. Thus, in this stage the relationship between management and the tracking study is established. Use of tracking results by managers is especially affected by their initial acceptance. A program that explains and encourages participation in the tracking process enhances coordination and use.

Essentially, managers determine the functional role of the study by providing the decision objectives and guidelines for the information they require. A strategy the authors have successfully used for creating manager understanding and for collecting initial insights into the functional role is to conduct seminars. Here explanations and examples are provided and managers encouraged to present, discuss and agree to decision objectives.

It is also essential to establish clear responsibilities and requirements for the tracking study. Responsibility is usually vested in one individual at the corporate level. Other decisions include the frequency of data collection and reporting, and how to handle the data base. For example, depending on how the information is to be used, the manager may want to create a separate data base or integrate the data into the marketing information system.

Methodology Delineation Stage

Given the establishment of manager support and decision objectives, the market situation must be examined and a research methodology developed that will provide the data to meet the decision objectives. Initial focus is on exploratory research where various techniques are used to gain an understanding of the markets to be tracked. This can be complex when several markets in different parts of the county are involved.

Based on the exploratory research, design of the tracking study is outlined. This includes sample size and structure, data collection techniques and procedures, identification of study sponsor and timing. At this stage, costs play a role in the selection of options. For instance, to track 20 cable television systems, data collected by telephone interview at $15 per response or mail at $4 per return gives a variation of $132,000 where four studies of 3,000 respondents each are conducted.

Now attention is focused on setting information objectives. The information must both match manager decision objectives and anticipate issues which may surface upon initial review of the data. This is a tall order. It is necessary to have some clear "model" in mind which reflects the underlying rationale of the study and meets anticipated analysis. At the least, there must be adequate dependent variables such as satisfaction, independent variables such as beliefs and moderator variables such as location. Table 1 shows examples of categories useful for grouping information objectives.

TABLE 1

EXAMPLES OF MEASURE CATEGORIES

Type of Measure	Example
1.Behaviors	Hours watch Cable per week
2.Attitudes:	
Behavioral Intentions	Likelihood of dropping premium
Beliefs	Quality of cable reception
Satisfaction	Evaluation of overall service.
3.Knowledge	Name of cable company
4.Conscious Reasons	Direct reason for dropping cable
5.Expectations	Anticipated contribution from HBO
6.Psychographics	Price conscious
7.Demographics	Age
8.Situation	Location of system

Following the establishment of information objectives, measures are constructed. Sometimes, previous research can be used. More often, measures are developed from scratch, a difficult task for the multi-item scales used to measure attitudes and psychographics.

Given questionnaire length limitations, only those measures can be included that make a contribution. It is preferable to conduct "pilot" studies to secure sufficient

data for validity tests. Further, techniques such as multiple regression and multiple discriminant analysis can be used to prioritize variables for exclusion. The process of selecting measures needs continual input from managers, which again means coordination.

Data Collection and Analysis Stage

Field application requires careful organization. Random samples are drawn from multiple system customer lists perhaps biannual. Timing is a serious consideration since collecting data at times such as Christmas can adversely affect response. Further, data entry must be coordinated with collection in order to expedite the results.

Data analysis must be planned to meet the requirements of the management structure as well as the operating units. At least reports are needed by the corporate and systems levels and by functional units across the systems.

The corporate level report emphasizes overall performance and potential for revenue expansion. Tracking reports make a notable contribution to these information requirements. For instance, Table 2 illustrates a corporate tracking report showing an aggregate index of performance. It took only two iterations of a tracking study to show a cable system with both extensive customer dissatisfaction and inadequate potential (not shown here) to increase subscriber revenue. The "Station" system was sold in 1985.

TABLE 2

AGGREGATE INDEX OF CUSTOMER PERFORMANCE*

System	Index						System Quotients		
	1984		1985		1986		1984	1985	1986
	P	I	P	I	P	I	Q	Q	Q
Hills	80	100	83	104	85	106	114	115	106
Western	75	100	75	100	77	103	107	104	96
Auther	84	100	90	107	88	105	120	125	110
Manly	63	100	65	103	69	110	90	90	86
Station	50	100	48	96	-	-	71	67	-
Average	70	100	72	103	80	114	100	100	100

* Performance is measured using several measures combined into one indicator. "P" is the performance measure based on a 0 to 100 scale, "I" is the index using 1984 as the based period, and "Q" is calculated by expressing each system performance score as a percent of the average for all systems combined.

The quotients compare each system with the company average and provide impetus for "competition" among the systems. The latest results reveal that "Western" has fallen below average despite an actual performance improvement. The quotient encourages the manager to "keep up."

The system-level report emphasizes operating units and factors that explain the level of and/or variation in performance. Table 3 illustrates functional unit performance for an individual system. Clearly things have deteriorated both in absolute terms, as shown by the index, and relative to other company systems, as shown by the quotients. While the telephone system in particular seems a major problem, the real problem can only be handled by integrated action.

The system manager formulates strategies to improve performance. Required information involves analysis, usually multi-variate, to segment the market and identify factors related to performance outcomes. For example, cluster analysis by attitudes produced the segments shown in Table 4 for a system. Likewise, multiple regression shows that reception and "program variety" better explain customer satisfaction than does field service.

TABLE 3

INDEX OF FUNCTIONAL UNIT CUSTOMER PERFORMANCE

FUNCTION	Index						System Quotients		
	1984		1985		1986		1984	1985	1986
	P	I	P	I	P	I	Q	Q	Q
Telephone busy ratio	35	100	40	114	50	143	87	95	132
Installation Satisfaction	82	100	85	104	75	91	109	109	94
Service call Satisfaction	72	100	72	100	68	94	103	100	92
Billing system	92	100	90	98	85	92	102	97	90

* Performance is measured for each functional area. For example, the busy telephone ratio is the proportion of times people they believe they contacted the system office and the phone was engaged. "P" is the performance measure based on a 1 to 100 scale, "I" is the index using 1984 as the base period, and "Q" is calculated by expressing each system performance as a percent of the average for all company systems combined.

TABLE 4

SUBSCRIBER SEGMENTS FROM CLUSTER ANALYSIS OF TRACKING ATTITUDE (BELIEFS) DATA FOR AN INDIVIDUAL CABLE SYSTEM

Segment Name	Percent of Market
1. Entrenched Cable Lovers	36.8
2. Cost Inhibited Acceptors	20.3
3. The grateful Affluent Outgoers	12.0
4. The Morally Cautious	8.3
5. Limited Contribution Viewers	7.5
6. The Technically Frustrated	6.8
7. Cost Inhibited Moralists	4.5
8. The Cable Adverse	3.8

Managerial Implementation Stage

Reports alone are not adequate to ensure full use of a tracking study. A program is necessary to assist managers at all levels to understand the findings, examine the implications and request additional analysis. This program can include meetings as part of the marketing planning process and special seminars on the tracking study.

The tracking study provides a data base which has major benefits for additional analysis. Indeed, the data can be used to "simulate" the outcomes of possible strategies. Procedures must exist so managers can easily request additional information that is provided rapidly and in an understandable form. Finally, since coordination is a critical purpose for the tracking study, every effort must be made to invite participation across all units. Discussions can be oriented toward the benefits of cooperation and the need for integration of effort.

Evaluation Stage

A tracking study is only as good as its maintenance. This means recognition of changes in management needs and market conditions. Managers must be encouraged to evaluate the value of information so that unnecessary variables can be removed and new information objectives proposed.

Continued investigation of the market, through on-going exploratory work, raises issues which seem important yet not included in the study. This exploratory work, together with analysis of the existing data base, gives input for the improvement of measures, methods and reports.

CONCLUSIONS

Tracking studies have a number of distinct advantages for use in the service sector in comparison to other alternatives of producing market information. A major advantage is that the tracking study process and information output flow can be used as a vehicle to enhancing coordination. The potential of this contribution is notable where so many service organizations have multiple interactions with their customers.

This article presents tracking studies as a vehicle for enhancing integration in service organizations. It is demonstrated that the tracking study can be a basis for bringing together decision levels and functions, including corporate, branches and operational units, to learn from each other and coordinate activities. With interrelated performance, all have a vested interest in cooperation.

In addition to the integration role, the tracking study generally assists decision making throughout the organization, especially in providing continual standard information. Over time, cost economies are gained in comparison to conducting a series of individual studies.

BIBLIOGRAPHY

Farley, J.U., Katz, J.P. and D.R. Lehmann (1978), Impact of Different Comparative Sets on Evaluation of a New Sub-Compact Car Brand," Journal of Consumer Research, 5 (September), 138-42

Kinear, T.C. and J.R. Taylor (1983), Marketing Research, New York: McGraw-Hill, Inc.

Lovelock, C.H. (1981), "Why Marketing Management Needs to be Different for Services", in Marketing of Services, Donnelly, J.H. and W.R. George (eds), Chicago: American Marketing Association

Parfitt, J.H. (1967), "A Comparison of Purchase Recall with Dairy Panel Records", Journal of Advertising Research, 7, (September), 16-31

Ruddick, M.E., P.K. Sherwood and R.E.Stevens (1983), The Marketing Research Handbook, New Jersey: Prentice-Hall, Inc.

Shostack, G.L. (1977), "Breaking Free from Product Marketing", Journal of Marketing, 14 (April), 73-80

Sudman, S. (1964), "On the Accuracy of the Recording of Consumer Panels: II", Journal of Marketing Research, 1, (August) 69-83

Zeithami, V.A., A. Parasuraman and L.L. Berry (1985), "Problems and Strategies in Service Marketing", Journal of Marketing, 49 (Spring), 33-46

RESEARCH FOR COMPETITIVE ADVANTAGE

Robert S. Duboff, Decision Research Corporation

ABSTRACT

This article discusses the importance of objective research in identifying the causes for a company's successes and failures. The success of the research effort depends on effective sampling and following a structured methodology, with planning, development of hypotheses, analysis and implementation. Using this process should provide users with a competitive advantage in marketing and sales.

Most companies are competing -- for clients, for customers, for new business, for repeat business, for new employees, etc. Yet, rarely does a company really know why they lost or won in any individual instance or in the aggregate. While there is always anecdotal evidence, rarely are the true reasons for success or failure known.

If you ask why you have lost a proposal, the potential customer generally says your price was too high. They won't tell you that they didn't like your firm's presentation or the fact that your team was all male. Why should the client bother to give you unpleasant news even though it would prove helpful to you?

Similarly, when you win a proposal or successfully recruit a new staff member, they will rarely tell you their true reasons but instead will tend to say what they hope will serve their goals in dealing with you.

Because any company vitally needs to know its success factors and its true weaknesses, objective market research is required. However, simply doing research does not guarantee that you will learn the actual factors that caused you to win or lose. First, there must be recognition that selection decisions are typically made on two levels: rational and emotional. The buyer needs to feel good about the decision and to have objective reasons to support the choice. In fact, most customer relationships that run into trouble do so because the company or product selected may have only satisfied the buyer on one of these two levels.

Secondly, it must be recognized that many purchase decisions are not made by one person. This is readily evident for products and services sold to businesses but is also true for many consumer items which really must appeal to both adults in a two-adult household or to a child and parent(s). In these cases, the views of all pertinent parties must be elicited for the research to be meaningful.

Third, and equally important, the research must be conducted with two categories of respondents: the successes and the failures. In this way, you can compare responses to understand the relationship between the buyer's values, your company's performance and the competition. For example, maybe the differences between your wins and losses is simply that you win with certain types of buyers who value certain attributes and lose with others. This would mean you have to screen potential customers (better) and/or work to change the values of those who automatically reject you otherwise. Another outcome could be that where you won, the buyers had a far better understanding of what you can do. This would suggest the need for (better) advertising and marketing or more stress on describing your capabilities during the selling process to those not knowledgeable about your company.

Finally, the research must be done so that respondents never recognize who the researcher's client is. Otherwise, the research will be no more effective than your own inquiries as to why you have won or lost.

The process the research follows is as important as the underlying principles. This research - like all research - must follow a structured pattern to produce reliable, valid and credible results. The key ingredients are:

o Upfront planning and interaction between your organization (including all those charged with using the results) and the researchers
o Development of specific hypotheses (regarding both emotional and rational issues) to be tested.

A typical design follows these steps:

1. Planning meeting
2. Review of past research
3. Hypothesis generation session
4. Qualitative research with winners and losers (e.g. - a series of focus groups including some respondents who selected you and some who rejected your company)
5. Survey
6. Implementation

The analysis focuses on identifying the reasons where and why you were successful and why you weren't. In the latter instance, analysis can also focus on specific competitors and an understanding of their tactics.

The implications will address how best to increase the hit rate which could include any or all of these tactics:

o Developing and executing a differentiation strategy
o Sales training
o Improving the quality of performance
o Improving awareness or image of your company/product

While good research is not easy or cheap, the benefits far exceed any risk. If it is done well, the study should answer the basic marketer's need to know, "why do we lose when we lose," and its less asked but equally important cousin, "why do we win when we win?"

THE IMPACT OF OPERATIONS ON CUSTOMERS

Christopher H. Lovelock, Christopher Lovelock & Associates, Cambridge, MA.

Have you ever been in a hotel where the attitude of the management and staff seemed to be that they could do a much better job of running a nice hotel if only the guests would stop cluttering up the lobby, messing up their rooms, and constantly calling for room service? Have you ever been told you couldn't ride a bus because you didn't have exact change? Has the Post Office refused to accept a parcel from you because it wasn't properly wrapped? Or has a restaurant forced you to wait until 8:45 p.m. for that romantic table for two that you had reserved for eight o'clock?

If you answered "yes" to any of these questions, then you have experienced some of the many tedious impacts of operations on customers. However, an operations manager would be entirely justified in claiming that each of these situations also reflects the impact of customers on efficient management of operations.

The operations function creates and assembles the service product, often working under real time conditions. Historically, operations concerns have dominated service management. The introduction of a marketing orientation into service businesses has sometimes met with resistance from operations executives, who see marketing as just an add-on function that should be confined to consumer research and communication efforts. Consequently, when marketers seek to get involved in product design and service delivery, their efforts may be resented by operations managers as an intrusion into the operating domain.

The issue is not merely a matter of turf: it reflects the operations focus on delivering a smooth-running and cost efficient service. Langeard et al (1981) note how a seemingly attractive product innovation, championed by marketing management in a quick service restaurant chain, led to serious operational difficulties. The product in question was a new menu item. As recalled by a senior operations executive:
It was a big mistake. Our stores are small. They didn't have space for the new equipment that was needed. It (the menu item) was really popular with our customers, but started to mess up the rest of our operation.....Marketing people are often very creative but should concentrate more on being total businessmen. Operations people tend to rate the marketing folks on how well they understand the operation.

Despite interfirm and inter-industry differences, there are a number of key operations issues and concepts with which all service marketers ought to be familiar. In this paper, I discuss nine operational topics that are as relevant to marketers as to operations personnel: (1) improving productivity; (2) standardization versus customization; (3) maker versus buy; (4) batch versus unit processing; (5) management of capacity; (6) management of queues; (7) facilities location and design; (8) the learning curve; and (9) quality control.

Marketers need to understand why these topics are of concern to operations managers, and how they impact both operations and marketing strategy. But I'm not proposing a one-way street for learning: it's most important that operations personnel recognize the implications of their strategies for customers.

Many of these topics are, of course, interrelated. For instance, effective management of capacity is very important for improving productivity. Establishing appropriate queuing systems helps to ensure that capacity is used to the best advantage. The actual design of facilities should be given to processing customers (or objects requiring servicing) in batches rather than one by one.

Since this paper deals with the impact of operations on customers, I will focus on high contact services where the customer enters--and remains in--the service factory.

Marketing Implications of Operational Concepts and Strategies

Improving Productivity

At the heart of most operational strategies is the search for productivity improvements, which occur when the volume/value of output improves relative to the volume/value of inputs.

Operational approaches to achieving this goal include working employees harder; recruiting and training more productive employees; reducing employee turnover; investing in more efficient equipment; automating labor tasks; and standardizing both the process and the resulting service output.

At issue for marketers is whether these approaches are positively or negatively received by customers. In recent years, more attention has been paid to ways of involving the customer more actively in service delivery through various forms of self-service. But as Lovelock and Young (1979) point out, such approaches may fail if not planned and managed with customer needs and preferences in mind.

Standardization versus Customization in Delivery System Design

Standardization involves limiting service options and achieving consistency in output by creating a production line approach to service creation and delivery. It entails division of labor, limited discretion for workers, substitution of technology for people, and managing customer behavior to achieve conformance with the operating system (Levitt, 1972). Translated, that means: just like McDonalds.

Led by franchisors, more and more service firms are standardizing their operating procedures. Costs are reduced as a result of economies of scale, and bottlenecks become easier to identify and eliminate. Quality control is aided by increased conformance to clear specifications. And standardization of job tasks allows the organization to recruit relatively unskilled, inexpensive workers who require only limited training to perform highly routinized tasks.

However, standardization has its disadvantages when seen from a marketing perspective: variations in needs tend to be ignored and customers may tire of a uniform, homogenized service output. Further, service may start to deteriorate as employees performing highly repetitive tasks become bored and robot-like in their dealings with customers.

Marketers should understand the forces that drive the search for standardization. Instead of resisting the concept as it applies to the core of the service, they should look for opportunities to personalize the service through use of the customer's name and to customize peripheral elements--such as letting customers choose garnishes, dressings and salad bar items in a fast food restaurant. Marketers should work with operations personnel to identify the relative appeal of alternative service formulations to different market segments, and should promote such advantages as consistency of quality and the sense that "you know what you're getting."

Make versus Buy

Make or buy choices by a service company are simply vertical integration decisions, and usually reflect such criteria as costs, quality control, and availability of capacity. Common "buy" decisions in services include: subcontracting recruitment and training of employees to temporary help firms; using contract food services; and entering into agreements with intermediaries such as travel agencies, 800 number operators, and brokers to supply information, accept reservations, and make sales.

From a marketing perspective, using outside suppliers results in loss of control to a third party who may place a higher priority on serving other clients. It may be harder to be responsive to customers and more difficult to resolve complaints. Further, customers will tend to blame the supplier of the core service, rather than the subcontractor, for any shortcomings.

But there may be important benefits, too, from buying rather than making. Subcontractors who specialize in delivering a particular service can generally do it better. Tapping into national networks and employing agency representation allows a firm to increase its geographic coverage and thus enhance its sales potential. Finally, the use of subcontractors at peak periods allows the firm to be responsive to surges in demand.

An important form of competition for many services comes from do-it-yourself decisions. Current or prospective customers may decide to recruit their own labor and expertise rather than renting, to purchase their own equipment and facilities instead of contracting out, or to self-insure rather than purchasing insurance. Understanding customers' needs, motivations, and resources on the "make versus buy" dimension is central to development of effective marketing strategies.

Batch vs. Unit Processing

Batch processing involves servicing multiple customers or items simultaneously instead of singly. This may yield economies of scale as well as making the most efficient use of capacity. One example would be transporting a group of people in a bus rather than sending each individual separately by taxi.

Among the marketing drawbacks of batch processing are that customers feel they are just one of a crowd. Further, the behavior and demeanor of other customers becomes part of the service experience, service scheduling tends to be less flexible, and sometimes customers have to wait until a large enough group has been assembled to constitute an economically viable batch.

Marketing benefits include the possibility of passing on cost savings as lower prices for consumers, and the fact that other customers may contribute positively to the experience ("meet interesting people").

Management of Capacity

The capacity of a specific service organization can be defined as the highest quantity of output possible in a given time period with a predefined level of staffing, facilities and equipment. In short, the firm cannot serve more customers than it can handle.

Capacity planning is vital in capacity-constrained service organizations. It helps to keep costs down by avoiding wasteful underutilization of people, buildings and machines. It reduces the chance that staff and employees will become bored and sloppy. And it leads to development of queuing and reservation systems to resolve the problem of excess demand.

Creative marketing solutions to imbalances between demand and capacity include managing demand through pricing and promotional strategies, searching for countercyclical services in periods of low demand for the original service, and identifying countercyclical locations where moveable assets (such as rental cars or highly mobile employees) can be more profitably redeployed elsewhere.

Management of queues

Waiting lines occur whenever the number of arrivals at a facility exceeds the capability of the system to process them.

The first task in queue management is to determine the rate of arrivals over time (so that serving capacity may be planned accordingly). Also important is understanding the degree of patience in new arrivals: how many prospective customers will simply balk at the apparent length of the line and walk away? What proportion of those waiting for service will give up (or "renege") after a certain amount of time and leave the line?

Segmentation research may suggest situations in which it is appropriate to establish priority lines for certain customers--those who are valued and frequent users, and those whose business is either more profitable (first class passengers) or faster to process (eight grocery items or less at a supermarket checkout).

Customers dislike being kept waiting for service and, as everyone knows, reservation systems are fallible. There's a risk that "overflow" customers may decide to try a competitor and never return. Marketers should look for ways to make waiting more palatable. There may be opportunities to take information, cross sell other services, and entertain the customers while they wait.

Facilities Design and Location

Operations and marketing personnel are often at odds on where service facilities should be located and how they should be laid out internally and externally. Operations concerns tend to revolve around issues such as least-cost-per-square-foot, good access for delivery trucks, simplified maintenance, good security, and easy supervision of employees. Pushed to an extreme, such concerns may lead to a mindset that views the customer as a nuisance who gets in the way of running an efficient operation.

Marketers, by contrast, tend to want a site that customers will find easy to reach by car, public transportation, or on foot. They seek a pleasant and safe location, perhaps convenient to other services that the customer may need. They may argue for an attractive exterior with ample parking, and an interior design geared to customer comfort and convenience. They want their customers to feel that they are being served , rather than being processed like some inanimate object in a factory.

Learning Curve

The learning curve concept is applicable to both individual and organizational learning. It is represented graphically by a line (or curve) displaying the relationship between unit production time (and/or cost) and the number of consecutive units of production. Normally, one would expect unit production time/cost figures to decline with experience. While practice does not always make perfect, it usually results in improved speed and quality at lower unit cost--giving rise to the operational goal of "moving down the learning curve."

Although marketers may support the lower costs and reduced error rates associated with such learning, they sometimes worry that not all customers necessarily want faster service interactions. Indeed, pressuring employees to work faster may reduce customer satisfaction with the quality of service.

Marketers can contribute to operational efficiency by pointing out that when new services are being introduced (or new customers are being attracted to existing services), then there is a learning curve for consumers, too. Providing extra assistance and advice to these customers when they first make use of the service in question may lead to faster and smoother interactions later, to the benefit of all parties.

Quality Control

Quality control is basically concerned with ensuring that service execution conforms to predefined standards. The marketer's task is to ensure that these standards reflect the needs and preferences of target market segments.

Quality problems are often perceptual: what an operator may consider to be quality work may not be so perceived by the customer. Sometimes this results from unrealistic expectations on the customer's part (perhaps stimulated by advertising messages that imply unrealistically high standards of performance). On other occasions, customers may not realize just how good service execution actually was, since the operations personnel failed to point out the quality of work performed.

Conclusion

Coming to terms with the differing and sometimes conflicting perspectives of marketing and operations personnel poses a challenge for both types of managers.

Marketers need to understand operational concepts and strategies, both in general terms and as these apply to a specific situation. They must recognize how pursuit of a particular operational strategy will contribute to the efficiency of the organization and result in cost savings (or other benefits). In addition to determining how a given operational strategy may affect customers and thereby impact marketing strategy, marketing managers should also ask themselves how a proposed marketing activity may impact operations.

Operations managers should recognize that an operational strategy designed to reduce costs may be equally--or even more--effective in turning off customers and thereby eroding revenues. Above all, when working in high-contact service environments, "ops" personnel should recognize that processing human beings is much more complex than processing inanimate objects.

Finally, both groups of managers should be looking for ways to work together: marketers may be able to develop customer-oriented strategies designed to make the operation run more efficiently, while operations concepts can be employed to provide better service to customers.

References

Chase, Richard B. (1978), "Where Does the Customer Fit in a Service Operation?" Harvard Business Review (November-December), 137.

Langeard, Eric, John E. G. Bateson, Christopher H. Lovelock, and Pierre Eiglier (1981), Services Marketing: New Insights from Consumers and Managers.

Cambridge MA: Marketing Science Institute.

Levitt, Theodore (1972), "Production Line Approach to Service", Harvard Business Review (September-October).

THE NEW SERVICE DEVELOPMENT PROCESS: SUGGESTIONS FOR IMPROVEMENT

Michael R. Bowers, University of Alabama at Birmingham

ABSTRACT

Service organizations tend to use an incomplete means of developing new services. The result is a lack of attention to the needs of the marketplace. A model for developing new services is suggested that allows greater input on the part of the service recipients.

INTRODUCTION

For many service organizations the marketplace today is rapidly changing. Old ways of doing business are no longer adequate, services once popular are no longer in demand. There has been massive changes in the areas of regulation and consumer demand for services. These changes have to a large extent antiquated existing services and created a tremendous demand for new and innovative services. Service companies attempting to serve yesterday's product to today's consumer will not remain competitive.

Despite the importance of developing new services for today's market, little is understood about how new services are or should be developed. The purpose of this article is to report the results of preliminary research on the process of new service development; how it differs among service industries and how it might be improved.

LITERATURE REVIEW

The services marketing literature was reviewed for insight into how developing new services had been addressed by other authors. Table 1 presents a listing of publications written since 1980 that deal with aspects of the new service development process. The articles tend to focus on a particular component of new service development such as concept testing (Murphy and Robinson 1981), or service design (Shostack 1981, 1984a and Chase 1983). Distinction is made as to the role of service employees in developing new services (Schneider and Bowen 1984; Zimney 1984). Two articles address the process of new service development in a systematic and holistic fashion (Lovelock 1984; Shostack 1984b).

Lovelock argues that there is no need to discard useful concepts developed from research into manufactured goods. Therefore he suggests that with modification, the principles of new product development derived from manufacturing fit new service development as well. With regard to the process of developing new products Lovelock (1984 p. 50) states, "There is general agreement that the new-product-development process should proceed systematically through a series of steps, beginning with a review of corporate (institutional) objectives and constraints and continuing through product introduction."

Shostack (1984b) has developed a model of new service development based on her own work experience. To a certain extent, the steps in the Shostack model mirror the elements of product development models formulated by other researchers (Booz-Allen & Hamilton 1982, Urban and Hauser 1980, and Wind 1982). For example, First Phase Definition is essentially the same as concept testing, First Phase Analysis is equivalent to concept screening, and First Phase Implementation is equal to product testing.

To summarize, new service development has been treated as an extension of the product development process. Writers have accepted generally recognized stages of goods development and provided a service oriented corollary. Except for Lovelock's (1984) and Shostack's (1984b) articles, new service development has not been addressed as a total system.

METHODOLOGY OF THE STUDY

Three service industries were chosen as the sampling frame for the study; banks, hospitals and insurance companies. These service industries were chosen because they are active innovators in new service development. Johne's findings indicate that experienced product innovators develop new products differently from inexperienced ones. On average, companies in this sample have introduced twelve new services over the past five years, or one every six months.

A total sample size of nine hundred was drawn for this study; three hundred randomly selected from each of the three service industries. The questionnaire was mailed to individually identified marketing managers or hospital administrators within each firm. If the addressee felt there were others more qualified to answer questions about new service development in their organization they were asked to forward the questionnaire to those individuals. Beyond operating in the specified industry, no other organizational characteristics were stipulated.

TABLE 1

NEW SERVICE DEVELOPMENT LITERATURE
SINCE 1980

AUTHOR	THEORY DEVELOPMENT	NEW PRODUCT DEVELOPMENT PROCESS - STRATEGY	IDEA GENERATION	SCREENING AND EVALUATION	BUSINESS ANALYSIS	PRODUCT DEVELOPMENT	TESTING: PRODUCT, MARKET	COMMERCIAL-IZATION
Beckwith & Fitzgerald, 1981	Design flexibility into delivery system							
Murphy & Robinson, 1981				Concept Testing				
Sandeman, 1981						Molecular model for new services		
Shostack, 1981						Blueprinting new services		
Chase, 1983						Modeling service process		
Dixon & Smith, 1983	Customer perspective							
Langeard & Eiglier, 1983		Multi-site multi-service typology						
Robinson, 1983					Business analysis of services			
Lovelock, 1984		New service development process						
Meyers, 1984	Managerial influences of innovation							
Schneider & Bowen 1984		Employee's role						
Schwartz, 1984	Role of culture in service innovation							
Shostack, 1984		New Service development process (b)				Designing new services (a)		
Zimney, 1984							Employee's role	

TABLE 2

Mean Scores for Banks on the Activities of New Product Development[a]

	Banks
Develop a Business Strategy (Long-term strategic direction)	3.70
Develop a New Product Strategy (Plan that outlines the type of new products to be developed)	3.13
Idea Generation (Formal process for soliciting ideas for new products)	2.70
Concept Development and Evaluation (Refining and developing the concept of the new product)	3.26
Business Analysis (Determining the profitability and feasibility of the new product)	3.83
Product Development and Testing (Developing and testing prototypes)	2.38
Market Testing (Limited testing of both the product and the marketing mix variables)	2.22
Commercialization (Full-scale introduction to the public)	3.86

[a] A score of three is midpoint on a five point scale. Therefore, a mean less than three indicates the sample participants are more likely to not engage in a given activity than they are to perform the activity.

TABLE 3

Mean Scores for Insurance Companies on the Activities of New Product Development

	Insurance Companies
Develop a Business Strategy (Long-term strategic direction)	3.80
Develop a New Product Strategy (Plan that outlines the type of new products to be developed)	3.51
Idea Generation (Formal process for soliciting ideas for new products)	3.10
Concept Development and Evaluation (Refining and developing the concept of the new product)	3.29
Business Analysis (Determining the profitability and feasibility of the new product)	3.77
Product Development and Testing (Developing and testing prototypes)	2.97
Market Testing (Limited testing of both the product and the marketing mix variables)	2.58
Commercialization (Full-scale introduction to the public)	3.38

TABLE 4

Mean Scores for Hospitals on the Activities of New Product Development

	Hospitals
Develop a Business Strategy (Long-term strategic direction)	3.93
Develop a New Product Strategy (Plan that outlines the type of new products to be developed)	3.24
Idea Generation (Formal process for soliciting ideas for new products)	3.05
Concept Development and Evaluation (Refining and developing the concept of the new product)	3.50
Business Analysis (Determining the profitability and feasibility of the new product)	4.10
Product Development and Testing (Developing and testing prototypes)	2.02
Market Testing (Limited testing of both the product and the marketing mix variables)	2.20
Commercialization (Full-scale introduction to the public)	3.50

TABLE 5

Mean of the Means for the Three Service Industries on the Activities of New Product Development

	Unweighted Means
Develop a Business Strategy (Long-term strategic direction)	3.81
Develop a New Product Strategy (Plan that outlines the type of new products to be developed)	3.29
Idea Generation (Formal process for soliciting ideas for new products)	2.95
Concept Development and Evaluation (Refining and developing the concept of the new product)	3.35
Business Analysis (Determining the profitability and feasibility of the new product)	3.90
Product Development and Testing (Developing and testing prototypes)	2.46
Market Testing (Limited testing of both the product and the marketing mix variables)	2.33
Commercialization (Full-scale introduction to the public)	3.58

Respondents were asked how often they engaged in a series of well established new product development activities. The activities mirror those steps identified in the Booz-Allen & Hamilton (1982) model of new product development. The Booz-Allen & Hamilton model incorporates the essential activities of other new product development models and is empirically derived from a large sample of both consumer goods and industrial manufacturers.

Participants in the study indicated the frequency in which their organization engaged in a given activity on a five point scale. Possible responses ranged from Never (1) to All the Time (5). Table 2 through Table 4 provide brief descriptions of the activities as well as the means of the responses for the three individual service industries. These statistics were used to identify differences in the process among the sample's service industries.

Table 5 presents the unweighted mean of the means for the activities of new product development, derived from the sample. These were calculated in order to understand the general pattern of new service development across industries without the bias of unequal sample size.

CHARACTERISTICS OF THE RESPONDENTS

An initial and follow up mailing yielded 253 useable questionnaires, for a response rate of 28%. Individual industry response rates were: a) banks - 109 questionnaires returned (36.3%); b) insurance companies - 83 questionnaires returned (27.7%); hospitals - 61 questionnaires returned (20.3%).

The sample organizations varied tremendously in the number of employees. The smallest company had 20 employees, the largest had over 14,000. The mean number of employees for the sample was 1097 with a standard deviation of 2018. When asked about the geographic range of their operations 48.36% of the respondents stated they were local. Over 28% of the sample participants claimed they operated on a statewide or regional level. Almost 23% of the respondents said they operated at a national or international level.

The sample firms were asked to rate themselves in terms of competitive strength. About 58% of the respondents felt they were above average in comparison to their competition. Approximately 42% felt they were average or below average relative to their competitors.

RESULT FROM THE STUDY

From studying Table 2 through Table 5, it is apparent that the service industries of hospitals, banks and insurance companies differ from the Booz-Allen & Hamilton (1982) model in developing new services. Responding service organizations tend to not engage in formalized idea generation, product development and testing or marketing testing. Development of a business strategy and business analysis are the two most likely activities to be undertaken. Development of a new product strategy, concept development and evaluation, and commercialization occur in moderate amounts.

An analysis of variance combined with Fisher's test of Least Significant Difference (LSD) on the means from the three service industries reveals that banks are significantly less likely to engage in idea generation than insurance companies or hospitals (alpha=.05). This is not surprising given the tendency for the

banking industry to rely upon regulatory agencies for new product initiatives. The same type of analysis indicates that insurance companies are significantly more likely to perform product development and testing than hospitals or banks (alpha=.05). Even though this is statistically significant, the performance of product testing and evaluation among insurance firms is an occasional event.

Results from an earlier study (Bowers 1985) indicates that the more service firms seek to understand their environment, the greater the success rate of their new services. It is therefore distressing to note the lack of customer exposure a new service receives before being released on the market. The activities which the sample respondents tend to not engage in are those activities which manufacturers use to insure they stay in touch with the market.

Manufacturers often solicit new product ideas from their salesforce (those who deal with the marketplace) or directly from consumers. Product testing is frequently performed by selected consumers to identify unforeseen strengths and weaknesses of the product. Market testing is done to see how the product, in conjunction with the other marketing mix variables, will fare in a controlled exposure to market forces. From the results of this study, it appears likely that the first time a new service is seen by consumers is during commercialization.

RECOMMENDATIONS

It is widely assumed that new product development is a critical function of any firm. Yet a general conclusion of this study is that service firms are doing an incomplete job of managing the process. It does not seem wise to develop new services in a vacuum, without input from the marketplace. The Normative Model presented in Figure 1 suggests the answer to this problem in three ways.

First, a formal process of searching for ideas outside as well as inside the organization should be established (Idea Generation). Active searching for new service ideas will allow the innovative firm to stay in touch with changes in the environment. The firm might be able to anticipate the moves of regulatory agencies and gain time on their competitors. More importantly, they may be able to creatively repackage existing services into more meaningful products or develop innovative new services within existing regulatory constraints.

There are many avenues for new product ideas. Competitive shopping and focus groups with consumers are popular means of discovering new ideas outside of the company. Using focus groups, a homogenous collection of consumers are asked how existing products could be made better and how their needs could be better satisfied with new products. The important point here is that the search for new service ideas should be made a routine part of the product development process.

Second, the Normative Model suggests that prior to substantial investments in creating the product itself, a rigorous definition of the policies, procedures and standards of performance should be created (Service Development and Evaluation). This document should then be evaluated not only by those associated with the new service project, but also by line personnel and consumers. Input from those charged with creating the service as well as those consuming it will validate the viability of the new product. It is much easier to make changes in this document than to correct errors once the service is operational. As a consequence, a critical look should be given for potential operating problems.

FIGURE 1

A NORMATIVE MODEL OF NEW SERVICE DEVELOPMENT[a]

1. Develop a Business Strategy
   (a long-term strategic direction for the firm)

2. Develop a New Service Strategy
   (a plan that outlines the type of new products to be developed)

3. Idea Generation
   (a formal process for soliciting ideas for new services)

4. Concept Development and Evaluation
   (refining and expanding the concept of the new service)

5. Business Analysis
   (determining the feasibility and profitability of the new service)

6. Service Development and Evaluation
   (establishing standards for performance of the new service)

7. Market Testing
   (testing of the marketing mix variables and of the service itself)

8. Commercialization
   (introduction to the public)

[a]Based on the Booz-Allen (1982) Model of New Product Development

Third, a major source or risk for new products is the failure of marketing mix variables. It is possible to gauge consumer reaction to advertising, sales promotions and personal selling campaigns as well as sensitivity to price. The results of this research suggest that determining consumer reaction to marketing mix variables is one of the most underutilized means of improving the chances for success of new services (Market Testing).

When possible, the Normative Model suggests that testing the service is appropriate in the context of a market test. This allows the service to be evaluated in comparison with the other marketing mix variables. Market testing the service permits the organization to judge the impact and interaction of the marketing mix. Market testing occurs after the service has passed all the other less expensive screening mechanisms. Marketing testing should take place only for the most promising new services.

SUMMARY

This research suggests that service organizations employ a process of new service development that is not open to marketplace influences. The path to developing better new products appears to lie in a systematic process of new service development that is sensitive to external change and incorporates consumer reactions and criticisms.

Three ways are suggested to carry out this improvement. First, routinely search for new product ideas outside of the organization. Second, completely define, develop and evaluate the service with the assistance of contact personnel and consumers. Third, put the new service in a market test to determine how well the marketing mix will work in the marketplace. By allowing new services to face the crucible of the market before commercialization, better new products will be introduced.

REFERENCES

Beckwith, Neil E. and Thomas J. Fitzgerald (1981), "Marketing of Services: Meeting of Different Needs," Marketing of Services, James H. Donnelly and William R. George, eds., Chicago: American Marketing Association, 239-241.

Booz-Allen & Hamilton (1982), New Product Management for the 1980s, New York: Booz-Allen & Hamilton.

Bowers, Michael R. (1985), An Exploration into New Service Development: Process, Organization and Structure. a dissertation, College Station Texas: Texas A&M University.

Chase, Richard B. (1983), "Modeling Service Processes," Emerging Perspectives on Services Marketing, Leonard L. Berry, G. Lynn Shostack and Gregory D. Upah, eds., Chicago: American Marketing Association, 137-138.

Dixon, Donald F. and Michael F. Smith (1983), "Theoretical Foundations for Services Marketing Strategy," Emerging Perspectives on Services Marketing, Leonard L. Berry, G. Lynn Shostack and Gregory D. Upah, eds., Chicago: American Marketing Association, 77-81.

Johne, Frederic A. (1984), "How Experienced Product Innovators Organize," Journal of Product Innovation Management, Volume 1, Number 4 (December), 210-223.

Langard, Eric and Pierre Eigler (1983), "Strategic Management of Service Development," Emerging Perspectives on Services Marketing, Leonard L. Berry, G. Lynn Shostack and Gregory D. Upah, eds., Chicago: American Marketing Association, 68-72.

Lovelock, Christopher (1984), "Developing and Implementing New Services," Developing New Services, William R. George and Claudia E. Marshall eds., Chicago: American Marketing Association, 44-64.

Meyers, Patricia (1984), "Innovative Shift: Lessons for Service Firms from a Technology Leader," Developing New Services, William R. George and Claudia E. Marshall, eds., Chicago: American Marketing Association, 217-220.

Murphy, Patrick E. and Richard K. Robinson (1981), "Concept Testing Services," Marketing of Services, James H. Donnelly and William R. George, Eds., Chicago: American Marketing Association, 217-220.

Robinson, Richard K. (1983), "New Service Development: The Cable TV Connection," Emerging Perspectives on Services Marketing, Leonard L. Berry, G. Lynn Shostack and Gregory D. Upah eds., Chicago: American Marketing Association, 73-76.

Sandeman, Graham (1981), "Implications of the Molecular Marketing Model in the Design of Retail Concepts," Marketing of Services, James H. Donnelly and William R. George, eds., Chicago: American Marketing Association, 230-235.

Schneider, Benjamin and David Bowen (1984), "New Services Design, Development and Implementation and the Employee," Developing New Services, William R. George and Claudia E. Marshall, eds., Chicago: American Marketing Association, 82-101.

Schwartz, Howard (1984), "Developing a Climate for Innovation of New Services," Developing New Services, William R. George and Claudia E. Marshall, eds., Chicago: American Marketing Association, 1-8.

Shostack, G. Lynn (1981), "How to Design a Service," Marketing of Services, James H. Donnelly and William R. George, eds., Chicago: American Marketing Association, 221-229.

_____ (1984a), "Designing Services that Deliver," Harvard Business Review, January-February, 133-139.

_____ (1984b), "Service Design in the Operating Environment," Developing New Services, William R. George and Claudia E. Marshall, eds., Chicago: American Marketing Association, 27-43.

Urban, Glen L. and John R. Hauser (1980), Design and Marketing of New Products, Englewood Cliffs, New Jersey: Prentice Hall.

Wind, Yoran J. (1982), Product Policy: Concepts, Methods, and Strategy, Reading, Maine: Wesley.

Zimney, Stephen A. (1984), "New Services Development and the Employee," Developing New Services, William R. George and Claudia E. Marshall, eds., Chicago: American Marketing Association, 68-81.

MARKETING FOR TELECOMMUNICATIONS: EMPHASIZING LONG-TERM STRATEGY

Thomas L. Powers, University of Alabama at Birmingham

ABSTRACT

The Marketing of telecommunication systems and other services has increased at a rapid rate in recent years. This has included an increase in expenditures on both advertising and sales promotion. This paper examines the use of these activities focusing on the relative benefit of each type. Recent telecommunication industry experience is reviewed that illustrates the comparative benefit of these efforts.

INTRODUCTION

Recent changes in the structure of the telecommunications industry have caused the degree of competitiveness between firms to increase at a rapid rate. The breakup of the Bell system, rapidly changing technologies, and increased participation of the consumer in the selection process have all caused this phenomona to occur. Because of this increased state of competition, telecommunication firms have embraced marketing and are actively attempting to integrate the marketing concept into their operations. By doing so, they are following the overall philosophy of this concept which has historically been seen to include listening to customers, coordinating the organization's activities, and measuring success by increases in profits or market share (McKitterick 1957).

This paper examines the benefits and limitations of obtaining and holding market share by using short-term promotional activities. A review of the traditional marketing literature on the subject is made and recent events within the long distance market are cited. Research in the area of consumer acceptance of promotional appeals provides an opportunity to examine the reaction that consumers have traditionally had to these activities for various products. This overview and the conclusions drawn from it can provide insight into possible consumer reaction to these activities in the telecommunications industry. In addition, the causes for the rapid development of these activities within organizations can be observed for traditional consumer product firms and related to developments in the telecommunications industry. The overall conclusion drawn is that the telecommunications and other service industries should carefully allocate their efforts on advertising and promotion that emphasizes image and long-term benefit as opposed to those activities that might cause the consumer to notice or be attracted to the firm's offering based on shorter term factors, such as price. Research that has taken place for product areas indicates that short-term promotion may not be beneficial over the long-term. Future research is warranted in the service sector to determine the exact impact of these activities.

BACKGROUND

The telecommunications industry is currently actively engaged in competition to attract and retain customers for its products and services. This is particularly true of long distance carriers who are competing for business once held exclusively by American Telephone and Telegraph Company. Efforts to maximize market share include many of the techniques used by traditional product and service firms to develop loyal market segments for their products. These methods include the use of brand or image advertising where ultimately a consumer insistence on that product or service is developed. Efforts to build brand loyalty include advertising that is designed to reinforce the brand image to the consumer, and position the brand according to the needs of the consumer and the position of the firm's competitors. In addition to this type of promotion, many times firms engage in shorter term activities that encourage brand switching and trial in an effort to gain new consumers at the expense of competition.

Firms may make marketing expenditures for essentially two purposes. The first is to increase loyalty to the brand, product, or institution. This involves a process whereby the consumer is conditioned over a period of time to recognize the firm's offerings as being better than competition, or in some way offering superior benefits for that consumer. Marketers typically achieve this objective by focusing on the variables of the marketing mix as they relate to the needs of the target market. Within these variables of place, promotion, price, and promotion an attempt is made to create some form of competitive advantage that can be maintained for a long period of time. Price advantages, and to a lesser extent promotional activities, can be matched by competitors in a relatively short period of time. The use of price promotion consequently may be limited in many long-term strategies, and is not utilized unless the primary focus on the consumer benefit is a low price position. Otherwise, this type of strategy may prove costly as it can provoke additional price competition where all competing firms lower price to their mutual detriment. This effect has been observed in he telecommunications industry (Business Week 1984).

A second category of advertising and promotion is sales promotion where the objective is to shift the demand curve in the short-term (McCarthy and Perrault 1985). This type of activity is typically seen for traditional consumer goods in the form of displays, price discounts, and additional merchandise offered. This type of promotional activity is similar to outright price competition as it may result in increased costs for the firms involved without any long-term benefit for them.

Recently there has been a substantial shift in the type of expenditures made by many firms. It has been shown that for some consumer goods the expenditures on promotion have increased at a rate twice that of advertising (Strang 1976). It has also been reported that these activities may take up over one-half of marketing budgets, where the amount spent on promotion exceeds the amount spent on consumer advertising. Competition that has historically been seen in these industries is relatively new to the communications industry, however, it is increasing at a rate that has caused these shorter term programs to be utilized more heavily.

Short-term promotional activities that have been used by product firms include trade discounts, retail price reductions, free merchandise, coupons, stamps, extended credit terms, cash rebates, and contests. These activities are quickly finding their way into the telecommunication industry and other service areas where increased competition is taking place.

Other service industries are increasing the utilization of shorter term promotional activities. The health care industry, for example, has moved in the direction of requiring more accountability in measurement of results of its marketing expenditures. This in some cases has resulted in a shirt to programs that have a quicker and more measurable response such as mail-in response cards and coupons (Powills 1986).

THE INTEGRATION OF MARKETING IN THE FIRM

As telecommunications and other service firms integrate and expand marketing into their operations they may follow the pattern of traditional product firms of increasing the emphasis on shorter term marketing programs at the expense of activities that may prove beneficial in the long-term. Reasons for this shift in emphasis has been cited for traditional products (Strang 1976) and may be applied to the telecommunications industry.

The emphasis on short-term marketing tactics for traditional goods can be linked to the willingness of management to accept and engage in this type of activity. In traditional product and service areas, management training in marketing and experience in promotional activity has been a common occurrence for many years. It is not surprising that they have a high degree of willingness to engage in this activity. The situation is somewhat dissimilar in the telecommunications field. Here, administrators trained in marketing and experienced with this type of activity have been in the minority. This situation is changing rapidly as more and more marketing positions are being created and filled with persons trained in these areas. Consequently, the presence of these people may serve as a facilitator to encourage this activity in this and other service industries that have not been previously subject to intense competition.

Management reward systems within traditional product firms have also encouraged this type of activity, as they have rewarded short-term increases in sales and market share. The product manager system, which places an individual manager in charge of a given product or service area, typically rewards the manager for gains within that product area. A manager placed in this situation who has the option of devoting marketing expenditures for sales promotion or for long-term brand image building is strongly motivated to spend that money on shorter term sales promotion. The same argument can be made for the operation of the firm in total, as the overall reward structure for top management has also historically stressed a short-term framework.

These reward systems that stress short-term results have not been as prevalent in the telecommunications industry. Emphasis has historically been placed on providing adequate return on investment, network development and maintenance, and other factors that are longer term in nature. The increased competitiveness of the telecommunications industry, including pressures originating from government deregulation, has caused a shift in emphasis, where managers are seeking results that are more immediate. At the same time the reward systems in the telecommunications industry are shifting in recognition of these goals. Although the current reward system is still a long way from that of traditional product and service firms, it clearly has the potential to move in that direction at a rapid rate.

Another reason for the increased use of promotional activity by traditional firms has been cited as the increased number of brands available to the consumer.

The increased number of brands in the marketplace has had a profound impact on the increased emphasis on short-term marketing efforts. As products typically rely on promotional activities at the time of introduction, the number of brands being introduced has a direct bearing on the use of this technique. As new brands are introduced, pressure is placed on the demand for shelf space. Promotion is then used as an intermediary level to maintain or increase shelf space for that product. This proliferation of brands may also greatly decrease the expected life cycle for products. Consequently, promotional activities may be engaged in to prolong the product life cycle.

These reasons for the increased use of short-term promotions has a parallel in the telecommunications field. First, the increased number of brands may be seen similar to the increased number and types of communication systems. Not only are there more competitors in the telecommunications market, but there are also different types of systems being offered. The issue of shelf space for traditional consumer products may be related to the need for competing telecommunication firms to gain and hold share within a infrastructure that is limited in its capacity. Here again, because of the pressure of the moment, inducements that are short-term in nature may be implemented. The issue of life cycle can be viewed in terms of service offerings that are on the decline being promoting heavily in order to prevent their ultimate demise. In the historically less competitive environment of telecommunications, this would not have been necessary.

A third area that has been seen to influence the use of shorter term promotional activities has been the decline in the overall economic environment. This has included the slow growth in population seen in recent years, the leveling off of discretionary income, high interest rates, and decreasing levels of consumer confidence. This situation has created an environment in many cases for traditional producers where, in addition to the increased competition noted earlier, there is simply less demand. This situation has caused many producers to resort to promotional activities that would have been unheard of a few years earlier. For example, the use of rebates on very small dollar amount purchases such as motor oil, hair dryers, and other small appliances were non-existent a few years ago. These factors may also cause telecommunciations firms to concentrate on increasing, or shifting in a favorable direction on a short-term basis.

ARE SHORT-TERM STRATEGIES EFFECTIVE?

Despite the widespread use of this type of short-term promotional activities, there have been questions as to their overall effectiveness. One such question focused on a parallel between promotional activities today and advertising years ago (Lemont 1981). In this comparison it was observed that, as with advertising twenty years ago, promotional activities represent "large, rapidly growing budgets with no real measurement, planning or management tools to apply these budgets." Other writers have noted that these activities will continue to increase unless it is demonstrated that they are unprofitable (Haugh 1979).

Although additional research is warranted in the area of the effectiveness of promotional activities, there are many reasons to believe that these activities are marginal in their benefit. Empirical research has shown that they may adversely impact a traditional distribution channel's performance (Powers 1985). Research also has documented the reaction that consumers have had to these types of activities.

This research provides a background that can provide insight into the application of these activities in the telecommunications area.

Previous research has shown the rationale of consumers in taking advantage of short-term offers, which includes a process of buying ahead, and then delaying future purchases (Blattberg, Eppen, and Lieberman 1981). This study indicated that the reason that consumers take advantage of a short-term offer relates to a stockpiling activity. It was observed that the consumer had a lower storage cost than did a retailer, therefore a price discount would encourage the consumer to assume the holding of that inventory. The conclusion drawn in this research was that the consumer simply buys ahead when these deals are offered. The alternative theory that was not supported in the research is that the dealing activity lowered the consumer's cost of experimentation with a new brand, and thus would encourage brand switching.

A consumer cannot 'store' telecommunication services as they do product purchases, however they may buy ahead or increase their usage in a given time period. The conclusion that may be inferred to the telecommunication are is that this type of activity may not encourage new users to try a service as much as it might encourage present users to take advantage of that offer.

The non-price aspect of promotional appeals has been examined (Cotton and Babb 1978). Here it was observed that response to dealing activities was much greater than to simply a reduction in price alone. This effect was also seen by Woodside and Waddle (1975). In addition, response to these activities was greater for products that were less familiar to a consumer. For example, the response to promotions on yogurt was greater than for products such as milk, that were more familiar to the consumer. It was also observed that after the promotion ended, sales volumes decreased.

These findings again may be applied. First, non-price aspects of a short-term promotion are valuable in obtaining a response. Secondly, it would appear that short-term approaches on services that are familiar to the consumer might not be as effective as other categories. For example, a promotion on a product new to the consumer, such as a cellular telephone might prove effective in comparison with one that is more familiar. Lastly, the observation on reduction in volume after the promotion is concluded reinforces the notion that these activities are in fact borrowing from future business.

Loyalty to brands has been observed in the context of short-term promotion (Massey and Frank, 1965). Here it was observed that non-brand loyal consumers had a higher reaction to promotional deals than did brand loyal consumers. Also, it was seen that price elasticity was higher for larger sized containers, reinforcing the stockpiling notion. This loyalty effect was also observed by Webster (1965) who found a similar relationship between brand loyalty and response to a promotional deal.

These observations, if applied to the telecommunication field, would indicate that where loyalty to a firm or service firm existed, it might prove to be very difficult to influence that person in the short-term. Also, those persons who had the flexibility, financial or otherwise, to respond to a deal would be the market attracted. This might imply that a more affluent, or innovative market segment could be attracted by a short- term approach, if the loyalty factor was not an issue.

McCann (1974) observed that households that pay higher prices normally responded at a higher rate than did households that normally buy lower priced goods. This was thought to be due to the fact that households that pay higher prices may think of themselves as splurging, therefore they become price sensitive to changes within their evoked set. Another possible explanation was that consumers who normally buy lower priced merchandise are satisfying their price consciousness by paying lower prices initially. This may also be due to the financial ability of the former household type to stockpile. It was also observed that innovators were more responsive than non-innovators to these dealing activities.

Again, implications exist for the telecommunications field. Short-term appeals may work best with more affluent market segments and for innovative consumers that have a relatively high propensity to assume risk. This profile of a more affluent, adventuresome individual does not necessarily match the profile that would intuitively appear as being the most conducive to a promotional appeal. This individual, in addition to having the ability to pay for services, might also be more of an opinion leader than the segment that have been seen in the research to be less inclined to react to a price deal or promotion.

Response to these activities has been observed in the context of competitive market structures (Chevalier 1975). Here it was seen that responses were larger where no one product had a clear market share advantage. This might indicate for long distance service, where the market has historically dominated by one firm, that short-term promotional appeals would have minimal effect. As will be discussed later in the paper, this does appear to be the case with long distance carriers competing against AT&T. For service areas where there is not a dominant firm, such as cellular telephone service, promotions may prove more effective.

Market reaction has been observed (Sexton 1970; Brown 1974) whereby short-term activities resulted in immediate increases in sales and market share, however they did not produce long-term buyers. This perhaps is the most profound of the research findings for the present stage of telecommunication service promotion. The concept of using this type of activity to encourage trial, with the assumption that these individuals will become permanent users of that service, is very appealing. The research that has been done for traditional products indicates that this is not the case. The overall pattern seems to be one where demand is increased in the short-term, perhaps by trial, more so by pulling demand ahead. The long-term effects that are desired do not appear to materialize, however.

This literature in this area gives an overall pattern of behavior by the consumer. They appear to be engaging in a stockpiling or pulling ahead activity as opposed to permanently switching brands. Brand loyalty appears to be inversely related to acceptance of promotions whereas consumers that are more adventuresome respond at a higher rate. More affluent consumers respond at a higher rate, and finally, price reduction appears to have only a partial impact compared to other elements of these activities.

The research described briefly in this paper has numerous implications for telecommunications and other service areas. The primary implication is that these activities may not necessarily result in the increase of long-term users. As part of this issue it has been seen that promotional activity appeals to certain market segments, on a short-term basis, and that a reduction in future market share may occur as the gains made in the promotion are paid back.

Differences clearly exist between products and services such as telecommunications that must be taken into account. First, services cannot be stockpiled as products are, however their use might be increased for a certain period and then reduced in future periods as the consumer compensates for higher usage in previous periods. For example, a promotion aimed at increasing long distance usage might result not in a permanent change in behavior, but in a temporary increase followed by a level below the original rate. Secondly, services are not as easily switched as product purchases are. This might result in a short-term promotion being ineffective to begin with, as consumers might not be able or willing to switch on a short-term basis. It might also result in a switch becoming permanent as it might be difficult to change back after the impact of the short-term program has passed.

The void between the knowledge of traditional goods and telecommunication promotion is immense, however the research done in product areas may provide guidelines until further research is conducted for the management of service promotion activities. Based on the research discussed, these activities should be approached with caution relative to their long-term benefit, especially considering that they will typically be funded by funds taken away from other marketing areas.

THE AT&T EXPERIENCE

The recent competitive battle for long distance customers also reflects the relative benefit of stressing long-term image above a short- term advantage to the consumer, such as a lower price. In the current marketplace, AT&T has stressed an image to the consumer via media advertising stressing quality and service. It has also provided services to the consumer that were not offered or were charged for by competitors such as MCI, Sprint and others (Business Week 1986). These efforts were designed to create a long-term competitive advantage that could not be quickly overcome. Their competitors on the other hand, oftentimes concentrated on price appeals as their primary advantage. This form of competitive advantage can be overcome and was in the long distance market through price reductions by AT&T and the phasing out of connection fee discounts to new long distance carriers by the FCC. The result has been that AT&T has held on to a very large portion of the market ant that the majority of consumers do believe that AT&T offers more reliable and better quality service than its competition (Business Week 1986). These results, of course, must be considered in light of the fact that AT&T had the benefit of just trying to hold on to present customers, as opposed to taking them away as did their competitors. In addition, they do have an obviously large time in market and size advantage.

While these results do not empirically support the notion advanced in this paper that long-term image building may prove to be the best marketing strategy in the increasingly competitive telecommunications industry, they do point out that this may in fact be the case. Empirical research is warranted to determine the reaction of consumers to various combinations of marketing mixes for telecommunication and other service offerings.

SUMMARY AND CONCLUSIONS

The increase in advertising and promotion in the telecommunications industry has created a real need to understand some of the factors surrounding its potential to increase the size and loyalty of target markets. If the pattern of events that has transpired for traditional goods can be applied to telecommunications and other service areas, the emphasis on short-term results will probably increase in future years. Furthermore, if the experience gained in the traditional segment hold true for the telecommunication field, these activities may be questionable in their benefit, with the only positive one being a momentary increase in demand. In order for telecommunications and other service industries to properly allocate marketing expenditures between short and long-term activities, substantial research is required to understand their exact effects.

REFERENCES

Blattberg, Robert B., Gary D. Eppen, and Joshua Lieberman (1981), "A Theoretical and Empirical Evaluation of Price Deals for Consumer Nondurables," Journal of Marketing, 45 (Winter), pp. 116-120.

Brown, Robert G. (1974), "Sales Response to Promotions and Advertising," Journal of Advertising Research, (August), pp. 33-39.

Business Week (1984, "A Marketing Blitz to Sell Long Distance Service," (July 2), pp. 86-88.

Business Week (1986), "The Long Distance Warrior," (February 17), pp. 86-94.

Chevalier, Michel and Ronald C. Curhan (1975), "Temporary Promotions as a Fuction of Trade Deals: Descriptive Analysis," Working Paper, Marketing Science Institute, Cambridge, Mass.

Cotton, B.C. and E. M. Babb (1978), "Consumer Response to Promotional Deals," Journal of Marketing, 42 (July), pp. 109-113.

Donnelly Marketing (1981), Thrid Annual Survey of Promotion Practices, (July).

Lemont, F. L. (1981), "Room at the Top in Promotions," Advertising Age, (March 23).

Massey, William F. and Ronald E. Frank (1965), "Short-Term Pricing and Dealing Effects in Selected Market Segments," Journal of Marketing Research, 2 (May), pp. 171-185.

McCann, J. M. (1974), "Market SEgment Response to Marketing Decision Variables," Journal of Marketing Research, 11 (November), pp. 399-412.

McCarthy, E. Jerome and William D. Perreault, Jr. (1984), Basic Marketing, Richard D. Irwin, Inc., pp. 471.

McKittereck, J. B. (1957), "What is the Marketing Management Concept?," The Frontiers of Marketing Thought and Science, The American Marketing Association, (December), pp. 71-82.

Powers, Thomas L. (1985), "An Examination of the Effects of Trade Incentives on Logistical Performance in the Grocery Products Industry." Ph.D. Dissertation, Michigan State University, East Lansing, Michigan.

Powills, Suzanne (1986), "Hospitals Call a Marketing Time Out," Hospitals, (June 5), pp. 50-55.

Sexton, E. E., Jr., (1970), "Estimating Marketing Policy Effects on Sales of a Frequently Purchased Product," Journal of Marketing Research, 7 (August), pp. 338-347.

Strang, Roger A. (1976), "Sales Promotion-Fast Growth, Faulty Management," Harvard Business Review, (July-August), pp. 115-124.

Webster, Frederick, E., Jr. (1965), "The Deal-Prone Consumer," Journal of Marketing Research, 2 (May), pp. 186-189.

Woodside, Arch D. and Gerald L. Waddle (1975), "Sales Effects of In-Store Advertising," Journal of Advertising Research, 15:3 (June).

77

THE ROLE OF THE ENVIRONMENT IN MARKETING SERVICES:
THE CONSUMER PERSPECTIVE

Julie Baker, Texas A&M Univ., College Station

ABSTRACT

There is agreement among service marketers that the physical
environment is critical in the services marketing mix. This
paper explores how the service environment is perceived from
the consumers' viewpoint. A framework that classifies
environmental variables is developed, key questions for
managers are posed and research priorities are discussed.

INTRODUCTION

The services marketing literature has established the
importance of the physical environment as a means to accomplish what Berry (1980) calls "managing the evidence" in a
service firm. Shostack (1981) notes that physical evidence
provides the clues that consumers need in order to formulate
a mental "reality" for a service. Research confirms that
people use appearances to form opinions about realities, and
the more intangible the product, the more the packaging--how
it is presented, who presents it--influences a consumer's
judgement (Levitt 1981). Consumer's perceptions are influenced by tangible clues, because they must form their
expectations about services through means other than actual
physical contact with the product they are buying (Booms and
Bitner 1982).

While agreement exists that the physical environment is a
significant aspect of the service offering, it has not been
clearly established exactly what role the environment plays,
and under what circumstances the environment becomes important from the consumer's point of view. The purposes of this
paper are as follows: 1) to classify environmental
elements; 2) to develop propositions about the consumer's
relationship with the service environment; 3) to discuss
managerial implications of the propositions and 4) to
develop a program of research based on the propositions.

COMPONENTS OF THE PHYSICAL ENVIRONMENT

Authors in the marketing literature have discussed various
elements relating to the physical services environment.
Kotler (1973) suggests the term "atmospherics" to describe
four relevant environmental dimensions, which include: (1)
visual perceptions (color, brightness, size, shapes); (2)
aural perceptions (volume, pitch); (3) olfactory perceptions
(scent, freshness); and (4) tactile perceptions (softness,
smoothness, temperature). Characteristics such as the use
of space and style of furnishings have been noted by Grove
and Fisk (1982). Booms and Bitner (1982) defined tangible
clues as architecture, lighting, temperature, furnishings,
layout and color. The elements of a retail store's
environment in a study by Westbrook (1981) included layout,
spaciousness, organization, cleanliness and attractiveness.

While dimensions of the environment have been described, a
definition and comprehensive framework that classifies these
dimensions for an applied use has not been developed.
Classification schema are important in the development of a
field, because phenomena that are organized into classes or
groups become more amenable to systematic study and theory
development (Hunt 1984). For purposes of this paper, the
term "environment" will encompass the physical facilities
where the service is delivered. Elements included are
exterior architecture, interior architecture and decoration,
and atmospheric conditions (temperature, lighting). The
service audience will be included because audience size,

type and behavior will impact upon the way the environment
is perceived by consumers. Service personnel are also
included because they too form an important part of the
environment.

It is proposed that the concept of environment can be broken
down into three basic components: (1) ambient factors; (2)
design factors; and (3) social factors (itemized in Table
1). There has been support for these categories in the
environmental psychology literature.

"Ambient" implies background conditions that tend to impact
upon the subconscious (Steele 1981, Campbell 1983). Wineman
(1982) identifies heating, ventilation and air conditioning
as three aspects of the ambient environment. Lighting and
acoustics were noted by Deasy (1985) as ambient conditions
that affect personal communications. Ward and Russell
(1981) refer to temperature as a sensory dimension of the
environment. Scent and cleanliness are proposed by the
author to be included in this category. Ambient factors
generally exist below the level of customers' immediate
awareness, so they may be less than totally conscious of
these conditions in the environment. Consumers expect a
certain level of ambient environmental conditions to exist
and may be unaware of these background factors unless they
are absent or exist at an unpleasant level.

"Design," on the other hand, suggests stimuli that exist at
the forefront of our awareness; visual cues that "make us
think verbally of what we see" (Steele 1981, p.28). Deasy
(1985) and Holahan (1982) distinguish between ambient and
design characteristics. Spatial (scale) dimensions and
relationships among dimensions are suggested as ways to
classify the environment by Ward and Russell (1981)--these
also relate to design components. The design component has
two dimensions: a functional dimension that includes layout
(space arrangement) and comfort, and an aesthetic dimension
that includes architecture, color materials and others (see
Table 1). Because these factors are generally more perceiv-
able, they may have more of a role in motivating purchase
behavior than ambient factors. This idea will be expanded
later in the paper.

Social factors are the people component of the environment.
This factor can be broken down into two dimensions: (1)
audience, which refers to other customers in the service
environment, and (2) service personnel. The appearance,
behavior, and number of other customers and contact personnel can clearly affect the way consumers perceive the
service firm.

Grove and Fisk (1982), in their dramaturgical framework,
used the term "audience" to describe a number of people
being served simultaneously by the service provider.
Audience factors become important in the environment when
consumers are required to share the same service facility.
The size of the audience can have an impact (positive or
negative) on the service experience. In the case of a
college football game, a large audience adds to the excitement of the experience, whereas a crowd in the grocery store
may have a negative impact. The nature of the audience, as
suggested by Lovelock (1984b), is also a significant factor
because the customer base contributes to the atmosphere of
many high-contact services. Audience characteristics such
as age, income or social class will affect the consumer's
perception of the environment. Audience behavior is a third
dimension of this component. Given the football game
mentioned above, a participative crowd would have a differ-

ent effect on the experience than would an uninterested crowd.

Service personnel can also affect the way consumers perceive the service environment. An example noted by Markin, Lillis and Narayana (1976) is the case where designers have created a store atmosphere that induces a buying mood, yet customers can be put off by haughty behavior in a salesperson. The appearance of service personnel can function in a similar manner: a salesperson that appears dirty or unkempt in an otherwise attractive environment may cause consumers to avoid that firm.

Using this framework to view the environment can help marketers to focus on the relative importance of ambient, design and social factors in facilities planning. The framework will appear in subsequent sections of this paper to suggest under what conditions consumers might respond to these factors.

Table 1

COMPONENTS OF THE PHYSICAL ENVIRONMENT

Ambient Factors	Background conditions that exist below the level of our immediate awareness	. Air Quality
		    . Temperature
		    . Humidity
		    . Circulation/
		       Ventilation
		. Noise (level, pitch)
		. Scent
		. Cleanliness

Design Factors*	Stimuli that exist at the forefront of our awareness	1) Aesthetic . Architecture . Color . Scale . Materials . Texture, pattern . Shape . Style . Accessories 2) Functional . Layout . Comfort . Signage
Social Factors	People in the Environment	1) Audience (Other Customers) . Number . Appearance . Behavior 2) Service Personnel . Number . Appearance . Behavior

* Interior and Exterior

PROPOSITIONS ABOUT THE SERVICE ENVIRONMENT: THE CONSUMER PERSPECTIVE

Much of the literature regarding the service environment has focused on the marketer's point of view, on ways the physical facilities can be designed to fulfill the firm's objectives. Insights are also needed into how the service environment is perceived from the consumer's point of view.

Emotional Response to the Service Environment

According to Ittleson (1973), "The first level of response to the environment is affective. The direct emotional impact of the situation... very generally governs the directions taken by subsequent relations with the environment" (p.16). Donovan and Rossiter (1982) propose that pleasurable emotions brought about by a store's environment is a powerful determinant of the extent to which consumers spend beyond their original expectation, and that positive affective states may prolong the time consumers spend in a

store. Similarly, Kotler (1973) noted that store atmosphere can influence consumers by arousing visceral reactions that may increase purchase probability.

A framework proposed by Mehrabian and Russell (1974) dichotomizes affective responses to an environment as being either approach or avoidance behaviors. Four aspects of approach-avoidance behavior can be examined:

1. A desire to physically stay in (approach) or to get out of (avoidance) the environment.

2. A desire to explore the environment (approach) or to avoid moving through or interacting with the environment (avoidance).

3. A willingness to communicate with others in the environment (approach) versus a tendency to shun interaction and communication (avoidance).

4. The degree of enhancement (approach) or hindrance (avoidance) of task performances and satisfaction (Donovan and Rossiter, 1982).

These components of approach-avoidance behaviors are appropriate for describing behaviors in a service or retail environment. Physical approach and avoidance relates to store patronage intentions, while the exploratory component can determine the length of in-store search, resulting in a broad or narrow exposure to product or service offerings. Communication approach and avoidance is related to interaction with service personnel. The last component, task performance and satisfaction, can be related to repeat-shopping frequency and to time and money expenditures in the firm (Donovan and Rossiter 1982). Stated another way, approach behaviors will tend to increase the probability of purchase, whereas avoidance behaviors will decrease that probability.

In order to investigate what factors in the environment motivate approach and avoidance behaviors, it is useful to refer to the classification scheme proposed earlier in the paper. How do ambient, design and social factors affect a consumers' desire to approach or to avoid a service firm?

As defined, ambient factors (temperature, lighting, etc.) generally impact on the subconscious of consumers. Awareness of these factors therefore tends to be low, unless the factors exist at an unpleasant level, or are absent in the environment. Consumers generally take for granted that the temperature will be comfortable (i.e. not noticeable), or that a certain level of lighting will be present. Consumers would probably expect most places of business to be clean. Since ambient conditions generally exist below awareness levels, they have little potential for encouraging approach behaviors. However, these conditions can provide disincentives if they demand heightened attention from the consumer. Lighting that is too bright, or music that is too loud can distract consumers from their task, and ultimately cause avoidance behaviors. If the temperature in a grocery store is acceptable to consumers, it does not directly motivate purchase behavior. However, when temperatures are colder or warmer than normal, the consumer's awareness is heightened, and dissatisfaction may result. Instead of taking more time to shop, consumers who are uncomfortable may hurry to make their intended purchases and leave the store.

While the above relationships may normally hold, there are circumstances in which ambient factors may motivate approach behaviors. These circumstances would occur when the factor is directly related to the product or service being marketed. An example would be a bakery, where the delicious smells that greet consumers as they walk in the door would likely increase approach behaviors and purchase probability.

Proposition #1: From the consumer's standpoint, awareness

of ambient factors will increase the probability of avoidance behaviors.

Exception: When heightened awareness of an ambient factor directly enhances the product or service offered.

Design factors are more perceptible than ambient factors, and consumers can more easily evaluate what they perceive. Therefore, the design component has greater potential for producing a positive emotional state which should encourage approach behavior and increase purchase probability. Aesthetic elements such as color, style, pattern, or merchandise presentation are the extras that contribute to a consumer's sense of pleasure in experiencing a service. Layout, a functional element, can also increase the probability of approach, as in the case of complementary merchandise located in adjacent departments (i.e. shoes and purses). Consider two women's apparel shops. Shop A is elegantly decorated with soft, feminine colors, and the clothing is appealingly displayed with coordinating accessories. Shop B is clean and neat, but little attempt has been made to decorate attractively. Intuitively, Shop A's environment would provide more pleasure to consumers than would the environment in Shop B. Therefore, given that factors such as service level or merchandise quality are held constant, consumers may stay longer and buy more in Shop A, and they may also be motivated to choose Shop A over Shop B.

Proposition #2: From the consumers standpoint, appropriate design factors in the service environment will increase the probability of approach behavior.

Social factors--the people component--can function to motivate either approach or avoidance behaviors, depending on their relationship to the service experience. This is true of both the audience and the service personnel components.

For some services, audience size and participation could encourage approach. Imagine a rock concert attended by only a handful of people: much of the excitement generated by a large crowd would be lost. The consumer's experience will also be affected by whether or not the audience participates, as well as by how they participate. Other experiences such as attending a dance or a football game are also enhanced by this sense of participative excitement.

Service personnel can also serve to motivate approach behavior. Attractive appearance and pleasant behavior of those individuals that deal directly with the customer can greatly enhance the service experience. Also, the number of personnel available to manage demand can be important for the physical and task performance components of consumers' approach behavior.

Social factors can motivate avoidance as well as approach behaviors. Sandeman (1981) suggests that queues at checkouts and crowded sales floors can lead to dissatisfaction because they increase the amount of effort consumers feel they have to expend to shop. Similarly, consumers may avoid patronizing service firms where personnel or other customers exhibit unpleasant appearance or behaviors.

Proposition #3: From the consumer standpoint, social factors that enhance the service experience will increase the probability of approach behavior.

Proposition #4: From the consumer's standpoint, social factors that inhibit the service experience will increase the probability of avoidance behaviors.

Environmental Needs of Consumers and Contact Personnel

Robert Sommer (1969, p. 171), a noted environmental psychologist, states, "A design problem is a value problem:

Whose interests are to be served?" The environment of a service firm must meet the needs of two groups of individuals--consumers and contact personnel--whose interests may conflict. Should the service environment be designed to satisfy the needs of employees, who spend more time at the facility than the customer, and who may need certain conditions in which to effectively perform their jobs? Alternatively, should the environment be designed to please the consumer, upon whose repeat business the firm depends? Ideally, the environmental experience should be positive for both groups, but pleasing both may be difficult. A few examples will illustrate the dilemma.

For many hospitals, the most important design criterion is the facilitation of medical-staff activities, which, in turn, is assumed to promote patient well-being. However, the needs of the staff may conflict with the needs of the patients, so that one must be favored over the other (Heimstra and McFarling 1978). For instance, the optimum ambient conditions for a surgeon and his staff under great stress in the operating room would include cool, dry air. The patient's physical well-being, on the other hand, calls for warm, moist air (Fitch 1965). Similarly, design factors that are chosen to increase the hospital staff's efficiency may have a negative effect on the patients' psychological well-being. Results of a study by Jaco (1967) investigating patient reactions to a radial nursing station showed that patients reported a lack of privacy, apparently because the nurses could look directly into their rooms.

Researchers investigating design preferences of nursing home residents and administrators found significant differences existed between these two groups on many design choices. Participants were presented with two or more alternatives on design issues such as: lounge design, dining room seating arrangements, overall nursing home design and residents' room furnishings. Findings suggested that while administrators favored designs that promote social interaction, nursing home residents preferred designs that enhanced privacy (Duffy et al. 1986).

Airport terminals are another example of potential conflict between service personnel and the consumer with respect to design factors. Many waiting areas are furnished with uncomfortable chairs that are bolted together, so passengers who wish to arrange their seating to facilitate conversation may not do so. One reason for bolting down the chairs is to make it easier for janitors to sweep the floor (Sommer 1974).

Consumers may have different perspectives on the environment than service personnel, thus:

Proposition #5: Consumers may expect or want different attributes (or levels of attributes) in the service environment than service personnel.

Environmental Needs of Consumers and Goals of the Firm

Just as differences may exist between consumers and service personnel, a similar situation could exist between consumers and the service firm itself. Often, physical facilities are designed to achieve the firm's goals without consideration of how the environment will affect consumers. For example, the open-planning used in some banks may serve a bank's objectives for efficiency and reduced utility bills, but does not address the consumer's needs for privacy and confidentiality.

Airport terminals, as previously suggested, are often not designed with the passenger in mind. One reason is that a large portion of the income generated by airports comes from the shops, restaurants, bars and insurance counters that proliferate in most terminals. If design factors are chosen to make waiting between flights more comfortable, or loading passengers more convenient, fewer passengers may patronize these concessions (Sommer 1974). For example, a proposal for the Houston Intercontinental Airport that outlined a system of loading or unloading automobiles within 100 feet of the aircraft was rejected because it did not draw passengers through the commercial enterprises in the terminal (Cannady 1970).

Because the objectives of the firm may preclude the environment needs of consumers, the following proposition is offered:

Proposition #6: Consumers may expect or want environmental attributes (or levels of attributes) in the service firm that run counter to environmental attributes that may be dictated by the objectives of the firm.

Service Experience

First impressions of a service firm, formed in part by evaluation of the environmental "package", influence customers' ultimate purchase decisions (Booms and Bitner 1982). Wyckham, Fitzroy and Mandry (1975, p. 61) noted that consumers "desire the security of evaluating something tangible, and do so by analyzing what they can: the appearance of the physician's waiting room, the venue of the travel agent's office, the colour of the aircraft." Tangible clues become an indicator of the quality and nature of the service to be performed, especially where consumers have little or no previous experience with a service offering (Upah and Uhl 1980).

What can the environment tell an inexperienced consumer about a service firm? Fisk's model of consumer evaluation of services proposes two concepts that are relevant to this question: (1) it assumes that consumer evaluation is the result of comparing expectations with perceived performance, and (2) the consumer evaluates a service at three stages--before, during and after consumption (Fisk 1981). If the first assumption is true, it follows that consumers who have little or no experience with a type of service offering have fewer expectations. The environment can provide tangible clues that will assist the new and unfamiliar customer in forming expectations and in evaluation of the service before consumption. Environmental clues may also help to reduce cognitive dissonance for the first-time user during and after service consumption. Consumers who have experience with a service, on the other hand, form their evaluations based on previous use, so will rely less on tangibles and more on performance for evaluation at all three stages of consumption.

Consumers' expectations about service quality could be affected by their evaluation of the physical facilities. Parasuraman, Zeithaml and Berry (1985) found that tangibles (physical evidence of the service) comprise one of ten dimensions consumers use to evaluate service quality. This characteristic was one of only two that were classified as search properties-those properties that can be known in advance of purchase. Consumers who are unfamiliar with a firm would rely more heavily on search properties in making a purchase decision and the tangibles provided by the environment in evaluating quality.

The physical environment can influence new consumers' expectations of prices charged. For example, consumers may expect that a lawyer whose offices are expensively furnished will charge more than a lawyer whose offices are nondescript. While this may not actually be the case, consumers who lack price information may use available environmental clues to make a purchase decision.

Environmental clues can also help to reduce consumers' perceived risk in using a new service. Services are more risky to purchase than goods because the consumer has few tangible factors to evaluate (Guseman 1981). This is especially true for certain "knowledge" services such as law, medicine, or architecture. These are services about which consumers generally have limited understanding, so the locus of control shifts to the service supplier (Lovelock 1984a), causing a higher perceived risk. Since the physical facilities are a visible symbol of the service, inexperienced consumers may judge the provider's competence by evaluating the firm's environment.

Because a consumer who is inexperienced with a service firm brings few expectations to the exchange process, it is proposed that:

Proposition #7: Consumers who have no experience with a service category are more likely to use the environment as an evaluation tool than consumers with experience.

Time Spent in the Service Facility

The nature of a service will determine the amount of time consumers spend in the service facility. Lovelock (1984c) distinguishes between services for the customer and services for the customer's possessions. Most services in the latter category require a customer to drop off the item on which service is to be performed and pick it up later. Customers normally spend little time in these facilities, so the role of the environment would be relatively less important than it would for a service in which a consumer spends more time. There are also some services that are performed on the customer's person that require less time than others, where environmental impact will change.

Consider consumer A, who patronizes a dry-cleaner, versus consumer B, who is staying in a hotel. Consumer A enters the cleaners, possibly waits in line for a few minutes, drops off the clothing and leaves. On the other hand, consumer B may spend a week at a hotel during the course of a business trip. It seems logical that consumer B would place more importance on ambient, design and social factors than would consumer A, since time spent in the service facility is greater for B. Similarly, the importance of the factors for consumer B will probably decrease as the time of stay decreases. A consumer staying overnight in a hotel will probably not place as much importance on certain environmental factors (or may be willing to endure unfavorable conditions) than if that person were to spend a week in the facility. If the air conditioning malfunctioned during July, an overnight consumer might tolerate the discomfort, while one who needs or wants to stay longer is less likely to put up with the situation.

The amount of time a consumer spends using a service will impact upon the role of the environment such that:

Proposition #8: The more time a consumer spends in a service facility, the more important the role of the environment becomes.

Facility-Based Attributes

Services, by nature, are experiential (Lovelock 1981). In many cases, when consumers patronize a service firm, they are buying not only the performance of the service, but also the experience associated with the process of service delivery (Lovelock 1984a). A significant part of this experience is the atmosphere of the physical environment in which the service is delivered. Kotler (1973) suggests that in some cases the atmosphere of the firm is the primary product, having more influence on the purchase decision than the product offering. In other words, the environmental experience itself becomes an inherent benefit. For example, the unique atmosphere or character of a retail store can influence consumer choice behavior. The president of Federated Department Stores remarked that "this distinct character...is, in our opinion, the single most important reason why customers select one store over another..." (Federated Department Stores 1984). Retail stores, resort hotels, restaurants and amusement parks are all examples of businesses that use the physical environment to shape the service offering. Alternatively, there are other services in which the environment, while it may be important, does

not offer unique intrinsic benefits: examples are professional services, dry cleaning or repair services. The
difference between the former and the latter service categories lies in what Lovelock (1984a) has described as the
extent to which facility-based attributes form part of the
service product. Within this framework, services are
classified as: (1) high facility-based (hotel); (2) medium
facility-based (dentist); and (3) low facility-based
(corporate banking). Consumers who want to patronize a
resort hotel would give greater weight to environmental
attributes than consumers who are choosing a dentist or a
bank, because atmosphere forms a larger part of the total
product that the hotel has for sale.

Because service firms offer different relative amounts of
environmental experience as an intrinsic benefit, it is
proposed that:

Proposition #9: Consumers are more likely to use the
physical environment as a basis for service selection when
facility-based attributes form a large part of the total
service offering.

Service Classifications

Consumer goods have been classified as convenience goods,
shopping goods and specialty goods. This system of
classification may be a useful way to look at the importance
of the environment to services.

Convenience goods have two characteristics: (1) the consumer has complete knowledge of the product before going to buy
it, and (2) the product is purchased with a minimum of
effort (Stanton 1984). These characteristics parallel those
that could exist with a convenience service: (1) the
consumer is knowledgeable about the service offering, and
(2) the consumer's need from the service convenience--he/she
does not want to spend time and effort in using the service.
These services tend to involve low prices and relatively low
risk. Dry cleaners, convenience stores, photo-processing
outlets and the post office are examples of service firms
that would fit in this category. For convenience services,
ambient factors probably have more relative importance than
design factors. In other words, the design factors in the
environment do not influence choice behavior, nor are they
likely to motivate purchase behavior once the consumer is in
the facility. However, if the ambient environment does not
meet expectations of cleanliness or temperature, the consumer may become dissatisfied, and exhibit avoidance behaviors.

Shopping goods are those goods for which consumers lack full
knowledge and so want to compare quality, price and style
before purchasing (Stanton 1984). For a shopping service,
consumers may not lack knowledge of a general service
category, but may lack knowledge of a specific offering,
such as a newly opened retail store. Consumers may shop
certain services, not necessarily to compare price or
quality (although this may be the case, as with a bank
loan), but to enjoy the experience of shopping. For instance, while a consumer may always shop at a particular
department store, she probably also likes to shop other
places as well. A key factor that distinguishes shopping
services is consumer loyalty: consumers are not as likely
to be loyal to a single firm at the exclusion of other
firms. More money and higher risk are generally involved
with shopping services than with convenience services.

The physical environment is critical to shopping services
for two reasons. First, consumers are likely to spend more
time patronizing a shopping service. Managers could encourage them to spend more time (and possibly more money) by
designing a pleasant environment. Second, the environment
can provide shopping services with a competitive edge,
especially when facility-based attributes form a large part
of the total service offering. This becomes even more
important as the number of offerings in a service category
increases. Ambient, design and social factors should all be
carefully coordinated and managed for shopping services.
For the sometimes difficult task of managing the service
audience, see Lovelock (1984b).

Specialty goods are those products for which the consumer
shows strong brand preference, and a willingness to spend
time and effort in the purchasing process (Stanton 1984).
Similarly, services could be classified by strength of
consumer preference for, or relationship to, a specific
service provider. The concept of particularism--strong
preference for a specific service provider--has been
discussed by Miller (1985), who proposed that consumers are
likely to develop strong preferences for specific providers
in services of a personal nature. Thus, consumers tend to
exhibit more loyalty to a specialty service than to a
shopping service. Consumers are likely to develop a strong
loyalty to their doctor or lawyer, because a continuing
relationship with these professionals leads to better, more
personal service. Consumers would also view a service
provider with a strong reputation in the specialty category:
time and effort become less important if consumers can
purchase "the best." Specialty services tend to involve
relatively high risk, and high involvement.

The physical environment will have a greater impact upon the
inexperienced consumer of specialty services, for reasons
discussed previously: price and quality cues, and risk
reduction. While attributes not related to the environment
(i.e. expertise, price, etc.) may be more important to the
consumer of specialty services, first impressions created by
design and social factors may determine initial approach or
avoidance behaviors. For example, the environment can help
reduce risk in an uncertain prospect. A New York pedia-
trician designed her waiting room using bright colors,
interesting posters on the walls and lots of toys in order
to help reassure anxious patients and parents, thereby
reducing psychological risk (Greenberg 1985). As the
relationship develops between the consumer and the service
provider, the environment becomes less important and service
performance can be evaluated on its own merits.

It is important to note that one service provider could
encompass two or more of these classifications. For instance, a bank could simultaneously provide convenience
(teller services), shopping (loans) and specialty (advisory)
services.

When services are classified as convenience, shopping or
specialty services, it is proposed that:

Proposition #10: Consumers place relatively little importance on the physical environment for convenience services.

Proposition #11: Consumers place a high degree of importance on the physical environment for shopping services.

Proposition #12: New consumers place more importance on the
physical environment than experienced consumers for specialty services.

Facilitation of Behavior

The physical environment can be designed to facilitate
consumer participation in and use of a service. When
customers arrive at a service facility, they may be expected
to find their own way, or their progress can be carefully
"stage-managed" (Lovelock 1981). One of the ways this
direction can be accomplished is through attentive planning
of various design factors. For example, color can be used
to identify a pathway system in a complex environment (such
as a hospital), or as an orienting device on different floor
levels of a multistory building (Wineman 1979). Strategic-
ally-placed signs can direct consumers and give them information about aspects of the service. A salad bar in a
restaurant, if easily visible, cues consumers that they are
expected to participate in delivery of the service. The
physical environment can also be designed to influence

customer behavior by inhibiting or encouraging customers to interact with each other. A chain of Japanese restaurants uses round-table seating arrangements that permit large groups whose members may be strangers to one another to be seated together, thus encouraging customer interaction. Alternatively, a restaurant may use dim lighting and physical barriers to limit consumer interaction and enhance privacy (Booms and Bitner 1982).

Because the environment provides visible evidence of the nature and process of service delivery:

Proposition #13: From the consumer's standpoint, the physical environment in a service influences behavior.

Interactions Between Propositions

The assumption behind each proposition offered has been that all other factors in the service situation are constant. In practice, however, this is seldom the case, and it is important to realize that interactions occur between several of the concepts proposed. Proposition #8, which deals with the amount of time spent in the service facility, has an impact upon several other propositions. For example, services in which facility-based attributes form a large part of the offering tend to be those in which consumers spend relatively more time, such as hotels, restaurants, amusement parks, or certain retail stores. In turn, time and facility-based attributes are related to the importance of the physical environment for shopping services: these services are likely to offer the environment as an intrinsic benefit, and consumers may spend more time in the facilities than they would in a convenience service.

The time factor would also impact upon Proposition #7, which contends that inexperienced consumers place more weight on the environment as an evaluation tool. This concept would not hold for customers who spend some time in a facility, and who may not return if the environment is unsatisfactory, regardless of whether they are experienced or inexperienced with a particular firm. Propositions #7 and #13 also interact because new/inexperi- enced consumers are more likely to look to the environment for behavioral clues.

Because services will differ along the dimensions in which the propositions are based, each individual proposition, as well as possible interactions between propositions, must be examined for their impact upon marketing strategy. The following section suggests key questions service firms should address in order to maximize environmental effective-ness.

MANAGING THE ENVIRONMENT: KEY QUESTIONS

The propositions offered lead to key questions a firm needs to answer before manipulating environmental variables. The answers to these questions, which will differ across service types, will have implications for the service firm's market-ing mix.

1. Does conflict exist between the environmental needs of the firm's employees and consumers? If so, how can these conflicts be resolved to satisfy both groups?

2. Is there a conflict between organizational goals and consumers' environmental needs or desires? If so, how can these conflicts be resolved to accommodate both the firm and the consumer?

3. Which environmental components (ambient, design, social) are most relevant to consumers using the firm's services? How can these components be manipulated to produce the desired effects?

4. What does the physical environment of the firm convey to the new/inexperienced consumer in terms of service quality, price and risk? How does the environment affect established customers?

5. How much time do consumers spend in the firm's facili-ties? Which components (ambient, design, social) are the most important to manipulate, and to what extent should they be manipulated?

6. To what extent is the service experience enhanced by the environment? Where would money budgeted for the physical facilities be most effectively spent?

RESEARCH PRIORITIES

The propositions discussed in this paper provide a framework with which to begin exploring the role of the physical environment in service firms. Key issues that need to be researched include the following:
1. Because so many elements make up the physical environment, a need exists to classify these elements. Such a classification would make the study and manipulation of the environment a more manageable task.

2. Relating components of the environment (once identified) to approach and avoidance behaviors could provide guidelines for determining which environmental elements are critical to consumers, and which ones may not be as critical, and under what circumstances (i.e., for which types of services).

3. Little has been done on the conflict that may occur between the environmental needs of consumers and those of service personnel. Research on this topic would have implications for both consumer and internal marketing.

4. Since conflict could also occur between consumers' environmental needs and the service firm's objectives, this area would be important to research.

5. Research should be undertaken to determine how new service consumers use the environment to evaluate firms in terms of image, quality and price. Research should also investigate how established customers evaluate the environ-ment in light of relationship marketing. It would be interesting to note the similarities and differences between these two groups of customers.

6. Time spent in the service facility interacts with several of the other propositions and should be incorporated into environmental studies. Another important topic is which environmental factors are perceived as salient as a function of time spent in the service facility. The issue of time was discussed from the perspective of a single use of the service facility. A related issue that needs to be addresssed is the perspective of time resulting from multiple facility uses.

7. It was proposed that consumers would be more likely to use the environment as a basis for service selection when facility-based attributes form a large part of the service offering. Criteria for classifying service firms based on these attributes is needed.

8. Research should determine if the categories convenience, shopping and specialty are appropriate for services. If this classification is found to be appropriate, then it would be important to study how the environment in each type of firm impacts upon consumers.

Another important aspect of these propositions that needs to be researched is whether the proposed environmental roles differ across service firms. Interaction between the propositions should also be investigated.

REFERENCES

Available upon request from the author.

A MODEL FOR CROWDING IN THE SERVICE EXPERIENCE: EMPIRICAL FINDINGS

John E.G. Bateson, The London Business School
Michael K.M. Hui, The London Business School

the physical environment. The basic model is illustrated in Figure 1.

ABSTRACT

This paper presents a new model for understanding the impact of crowding on the service experience. The model is an integration of the Mehrabian and Russell model of human-environment interactions and the perceived control model of crowding. Preliminary support for the model is provided from existing literature and from an exploratory empirical study using a convenience sample.

INTRODUCTION

The pervasiveness of the problem of crowding to most service organizations has recently been discussed (Bateson and Hui 1985). It has been argued that crowding is a far more complicated and significant managerial issue than it appears to be intuitively. The main objective of this paper is to develop a fundamental theoretical framework for future research on crowding in service organizations as well as the service encounter; emphasis is laid on the influence of high-density service environments on customer perceived control and subsequent affective and behavioral responses to the service organizations. Preliminary empirical support is provided.

One peculiar characteristic of the service buying and consumption process is that it involves a series of interactions between customers and both contact personnel and environments of service firms (Eiglier and Langeard 1977). It is from these interactions that customers acquire their service experiences and get their needs and wants satisfied. Based on this argument, the quality of the service encounter has been hypothesized to be a crucial determinant of customer satisfaction in the buying of services (Czepiel et al 1985, Solomon et al 1985). As a result of the development of the service encounter as a core research area in the marketing of services, more attention has been granted to the psychological constructs and processes that are related to interpersonal and human-environment interactions. The proposed model of the impact of crowding on the service experience is an integration of the research on perceived control and Mehrabian and Russell (1974) comprehensive model of human-environment relations. This paper briefly outlines the Mehrabian and Russell model and the relevant crowding literature. Based on these reviews, a model of crowding is developed primarily for the explanation and study of the perceptual and emotional impact of high-density service settings. Finally, the details and results of a pilot empirical study are presented. The findings of this study provide preliminary support for the proposed model.

THE MEHRABIAN AND RUSSELL MODEL

Mehrabian and Russell (1974) have proposed a comprehensive model of human-environment relations (labelled as M&R model hereafter). With the support of some empirical findings, they argue that there are three basic bipolar emotional dimensions: pleasure-displeasure; arousal-unarousal; dominant-submissive, which modulate all human behavioral responses towards

FIGURE 1

The Basic Framework of M&R Model

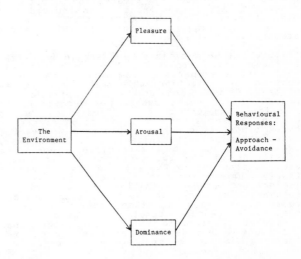

The model indicates that the three emotional dimensions are employed as intervening variables, linking the environment to a variety of human behaviors which can be generalized along an approach-avoidance continuum. However, hitherto, empirical evidence has provided only partial support to this formulation. In essence, a number of studies have failed to demonstrate "dominance" as a dimension of affective responses paralleled to pleasure and arousal. From the intercorrelations between similarly labelled emotional dimensions derived from four different methodologies: multi-dimensional scaling; successive-intervals scaling; semantic differential scaling; factor analysis of verbal self-report data, Russell (1978) has concluded that there is strong evidence to demonstrate the convergent validity of both pleasure and arousal as two dimensions of affect. Beyond these two dimensions, however, the psychometric property of a third dimension is equivocal. The findings also indicate that the third dimension accounts for only a small proportion of the variance in affective responses. Finally, dominance has been found to highly correlate with pleasure (r=.65) and modertaely correlate with arousal (r=.25). In other words, pleasure and arousal explain altogether 46% of the variance in dominance. These findings obviously contradict Mehrabian and Russell's proposition that dominance is a dimension of affect and is orthogonal to pleasure and arousal.

The findings of a study which applies the M&R model to retail environments also revealed that dominance has a negligible relationship with any in-store shopping behavior (Donovan and Rossiter 1982). In no case does dominance correlate significantly with the criterion variables such as approach-avoidance behaviors towards a particular retail environment.

The Revised M&R Model

Russell and his colleagues (Russell 1978, Russell and Pratt 1980, Russell, Ward and Pratt

1981) have attempted to clarify the confusing evidence related to dominance as an intervening variable between environment and human behavior. They contend that there are actually two categories of terms that people generally employ to describe their feelings on the physical environment. The first category refers to terms that consist of predominantly affective connatation; they describe primarily an individual's internal state. It is suggested that pleasure and arousal are two underlying dimensions that are sufficient to capture all the affective environmental meanings. By contrast, there are terms that can be interpreted as cognitive/perceptual rather than affective in nature. These terms are employed particularly to convey information about the antecedents and consequences of an individual's internal state. They suggested that dominance is an underlying dimension of this latter category of environmental terms.

Attitude has been defined by Fishbein and Ajzen (Fishbein and Ajzen 1975, Ajzen and Fishbein 1981) with a tripartite framework: conation is function of affection which in turn is an outcome of cognition. Whereas cognition is concerned with one's subjective judgements of an action, an object or an individual along certain salient attributes, affection refers to those "sympathetic nervous responses and verbal statements of affect" (Ajzen and Fishbein 1981, p.20). It can be recognized that the definitions of the two types of environmental terms as proposed by Russell and his colleagues closely correspond with Fishbein and Ajzen's distinction between cognition and affection. Employing the same cognition-affection-conation sequence, we suggest that dominance as a cognitive/perceptual construct should be an antecedent of pleasure and arousal rather than a variable independent and parallel to the two affective dimensions, as shown in Figure 2.

FIGURE 2

The Revised M&R Model

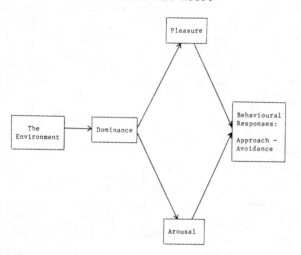

As a matter of fact, Russell and his colleagues (Russell and Pratt 1980, Russell, Ward and Pratt 1981) have ignored the dominant-submissive dimension in their recent model of environmental quality, which centers primarily on the affective properties of the environment. Survey findings reveal that adjectives commonly employed to describe the affective quality of the environment can be adequately defined within a two-dimensional space of pleasant-unpleasant and arousing-sleeply.

THE CONTROL THEORY OF CROWDING

Different theoretical frameworks have been proposed to explain the equivocal experiemntal results concerning the impact of crowding on human behavior. Findings from both laboratory settings (see, for example, Paulus et al 1976) and real-life settings (see, for example, Mackintosh, West and Saegart 1975) have indicated that crowding does have deleterious effects on human responsse such as interpersonal behavior and task performance. However, a number of other experimental studies have obtained the opposite results. They have shown that crowding can have no, or even positive, effects on human behavior (see, for example, Freedman et al 1971, Freedman 1975).

Stokols (1972) has asserted that there is a need to distinguish between the two theoretical constructs of "density" and "crowding". Density is defined as "the physical condition, in terms of spatial parameters" while crowding is a psychological experience characterized by stress, and at the same time is a motivational state. It is suggested that density is a necessary but not sufficient condition for crowding. Various social and psychological phenomena have since then been proposed by the theorists to explain the relationship between density and crowding.

There is considerable empirical and theoretical support for the paramount importance of actual or perceived control in modulating the impact of aversive stimuli such as noise and electric shock on human psychological and behavioral responses (see, for example, Glass and Singer 1972). Based on this line of thinking, some theorists have proposed that in any high density setting, an individual will experience crowding stress if, and only if he/she loses his/her personal control over the important situational outcomes (Schmidt and Keating 1979, Baron and Rodin 1978).

To date, an enormous amount of empirical evidence (see, fro example, Langer and Saegart 1977, Sherrod 1974, Rodin, Solomon and Metcalf 1978) has supported the argument that lack or loss of control is an essential antecedent of stressful crowding experience. As long as an individual can maintain his/her actual or perceived control over a high-density setting, he/she will not, or at at least to a lesser extent, suffer from any symptoms of crowding stress.

A MODEL OF CROWDING

In this section, a model of crowding (Figure 3) is developed through the integration of the control theory of crowding into the modified version of the M&R model (Figure 2). The proposed model provides a fundamental framework so that the impact of high-density service environments on service encounters and customer behavior can be further investigated.

FIGURE 3

A Model of Crowding in the Service Experience

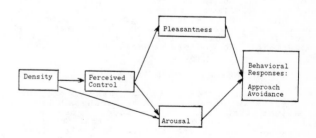

Semantic-differential scales have been developed to measure the three principal emotional dimensions of environmental responses (Mehrabian and Russell 1974, p.216). By examining the six individual items of the Scale of Dominance (Figure 4), one can easily recognize that dominance, as operationalized by Mehrabian and Russell, is virtually equivalent to perceived control.

FIGURE 4

The Scale of Dominance
(Mehrabian and Russell 1974, p.216)

Controlling/Controlled

Influential/Influenced

In Control/Cared For

Important/Awed

Dominant/Submissive

Autonomous/Guided

In addition to the two adjecyive pairs that consist of the word "control" explicitly (Controlling/Controlled; In Control/Cared for), the other four also carry a strong "control" connotation. Actually, in a latter article, the same two authors have proposed that perceived control is a crucial determinant of dominance:

"A person feels dominant when he is able to influence or control the situation he is in; he feels submissive when the environment influences him." (Russell and Mehrabian 1976, p.6)

In accordance with the revised M&R model, it is therefore hypothesized that in any physical setting, an individual's perceived level of control is a function of the physical characteristics of the setting (cf. Proshansky, Ittelson and Rivlin 1970). Perceived control in turn influences the individual's affective responses which can be expressed in terms of the Mehrabian and Russell's dimensions of pleasure and arousal. Finally, any human responses to the environment are hypothesized to be a function of the two affective dimensions only.

Crowding has been commonly operationalized or shown to be inversely correlated with pleasure (see, for example, McClelland and Auslander 1978). Furthermore, a number of authors have asserted that crowding is an arousing experience. The heightened arousal may be due to the higher information rate in high density environments. Information rate has been defined as the total amount of information embedded in the physical environment and hypothesized to be a direct correlate of human arousal (Mehrabian and Russell 1974). It is clear that people can be regarded as a source of environmental stimuli and information. As a result, it is expected that high density environments should inscribe a higher information rate and thus should elicit a higher level of arousal than low density environment. In addition, experimental findings have shown that lack or loss of personal control is usually associated with self-reported and physiological arousal (for a review, see Schmidt and Keating 1979). We can therefore conclude that crowding as a kind of psychological stress is actually an unpleasant and arousing experience. As a consequence, experience of crowding should be captured by the degree of pleasantness and arousal people attribute to a particular environment as a function of people density.

Rapoport (1975) has defined crowding as a tripartite sequence of physical density, perceived density and affective density. People per unit area (physical density) is suggested to affect an individual's perception of the number of people present in a given environmental setting (perceived density); this perceived density is then matched against norms and expectations, resulting in favorable or unfavorable appraisal of the setting (affective density). Owing to the fact that perceived control has been identified as a crucial component of perceived density, this conceptualization of crowding provides some support to our contention that perceived control is an antecedent of human affective responses to the physical environment rather than a dimension of affect per se.

In summary, the present model is primarily a modified version and an application of the M&R model. However, our model can be distinguished from the original M&R model by three characteristics. Firstly, our model is concerned with only one physical dimension of the environment - people density, instead of the molar physical environment. Secondly, perceived control has been employed and treated as an intervening variable linking density to the two affective dimensions of environmental responses - pleasure and arousal. In this way we can reconcile the equivocal evidenc related to the original M&R model and incorporate the control theory of crowding into our proposed model. Finally, since perceived control has been advocated as a crucial determinant of the customer perceived quality of the service encounter (Bateson 1985), we suggest that the present model can be extended to the study of human emotional and behavioral responses to the service encounter which composes of a bunch of human-environment and social interactions. The model is open to further modifi ation by the addition of relevant physical and social variables. For instance, the whole crowding process as suggested by our model can be modified by the kinds of social activities held in the setting.

A PILOT EMPIRICAL STUDY

A programme of research is being developed by the authors to test the proposed crowding model in the context of the service experience. It is an undeniable fact that high-density service environments can create deleterious effects on customers' evaluation of their service experience. Nevertheless, research designed to explore the major physical, social, personal and psychological determinants of crowding stress is necessary before any "crowding management" (Bateson and Hui 1985) strategies can be developed. A pilot study has been carried out to examine the basic assumptions and some of the hypotheses derived from by the model. Large-scale surveys are justified provided that such preliminary evidence as indicated by the findings of the pilot study turns out to be positive.

Thirty first-year MBA students of a business school in London, England, were selected as a convenience sample for the pilot study. Half of the respondents were requested to recall their most recent shopping experiences, and for the other half their most recent experiences in withdrawing cash through the human tellers of their banks. Their service experiences were then measured by a self-administered questionnaire. The respondents were asked to describe their feelings on their service experiences on the following scales:

(1) Mehrabian and Russell's (1974) Scales of Dominance, Arousal and Pleasure.
(2) Gurin, Gurin, Lao and Beattie's (1969) Scale of Personal Control.
(3) A Scale of Crowding.

The dominance scale was included so that it

could be compared to the results obtained from the Scale of Personal Control. This latter scale was developed by Gurin et al (1969) as part of their study of the motivational dynamics of Negro Youth. The Scale of Crowding consisted of five semantic differential items identified from the crowding literature. These items were:

* Stuffy/Not Stuffy
* Cramped/Uncramped
* Crowded/Uncrowded
* Free to Move/Restricted
* Spacious/Confined

A few modifications of the wordings of the original scales were performed so that the scales looked more appropriate to describe the service experience. All the scales were transformed into 5-point Likert-type (Personal Control, Crowding) or semantic differential (Pleasure, Dominance and Arousal).

RESULTS AND DISCUSSIONS

Pearson product moment correlation coefficients were computed among the major variables (Table 1). As the analysis is based on the retrospective evaluation of the service experience, there is no way to determine objectively the physical density of the service settings (the shops and banks). Consequently, a test of the whole model is not possible. Nonetheless, the correlation matrix of the variables reveals some exciting and encouraging results.

TABLE 1

Intercorrelation Matrix of Variables in Pilot Study

	DOMINANCE	PLEASURE	AROUSAL	PERSONAL CONTROL	CROWDING
DOMINANCE	1				
PLEASURE	.560**	1			
AROUSAL	.060	.163	1		
PERSONAL CONTROL	.515*	.541**	-.167	1	
CROWDING	-.705**	-.645**	-.193	-.563**	1
CRONBACH ALPHA	0.84	0.80	0.56	0.86	0.91

* P ≤ 0.05
** P ≤ 0.001

A highly significant correlation coefficient of .515 (p=.002) between Dominance and Personal Control confirms our assumption that dominance and perceived control are closely associated theoretical constructs. More importantly, both Dominance and Personal Control correlate strongly with Pleasure (r=.560, p=.001 and r=.541, p=.001 respectively). These findings provide preliminary evidence to support Bateson's (1985) argument that in the service encounter, perceived control is a crucial determinant of customer satisfaction.

An examination of the correlation between Crowding and Pleasure (r=.645, p=.000) reveals that crowding, as generally defined by the existing literature (see, for example, Stokols 1972) is an unpleasant psychological experience. Moreover, Crowding is inversely correlated with both Dominance (r=-.705, p=.000) and Personal Control (r=-.563 p=.000) confirming the prediction derived from the control theory of crowding that there exists an intense covariation between perceived control

and unpleasant crowding stress. Of course, a causal relationship between the two variables cannot be assumed.

The only unexpected finding is that Arousal is uncorrelated with any other variable. According to our model of crowding, significant correlations between Arousal and both Dominance and Personal Control are hypothesized. However, since an extreme low reliability has been found for the Scale of Arousal (Cronbach Alpha = .559), definite conclusions are obviously inappropriate. The low reliability of the scale may be caused by two factors. It has been suggested that emotional responses should be assessed during or as soon as possible after an event (Donovan and Rossiter 1982). In this pilot study, however, there was a time lapse of as long as over a month between the service experience and the measurement. Secondly, based on our observation in the pre-test of the questionnaire, a lot of the respondents seem to be rather confused with the concept of arousal.

Partial correlations were also obtained to gain preliminary insights into the possible links in the process. When controlling for Crowding, Pleasure has been found to be uncorrelated with Dominance (r=.195, p=.156) and only marginally correlated with Personal Control (r=.281 p=.070). The results reveal that consumer satisfaction varies with perceived control only because both variables are correlated with crowding. One possible interpretation of the findings could be that in such daily routine service encounters such as shopping or withdrawing cash in a bank, the physical density of the service environment can have a considerable impact on customer perceived control and customer satisfaction.

CONCLUSIONS

The proposed crowdng model is rooted heavily in existing theories from environmental psychology and the preliminary findings obtained in this study are supportive of the basic formulation of the model although they cannot be taken as proof in any way. Since the sample size and the range of services covered in this study are very limited and no objective measure of density exists, all the discussions related to the findings are therefore tentative rather than definite.

The results are, however, sufficiently encouraging to suggest that such a parsimonious model may provide a heuristic framework in the understanding and future research of crowding in service organizations as well as the service encounter. Extensions of the proposed model, particularly by the incorporation of additional situational and personal variables (see Rapoport 1975) may be particularly useful.

REFERENCES

Ajzen, I and M. Fishbein (1980), Understanding Attitude and Predicting Social Behavior, N.J.: Prentice-Hall, Inc.

Baron, R.M. and J. Rodin (1978), "Personal Control as a Mediator of Crowding," in Advances in Environmental Psychology (Vol 1), A. Baum, J.E. Singer & S. Valins, eds., Hillsdale, N.J.: LEA, 145-90.

Bateson, J.E.G. (1985), "Perceived Control and the Service Encounter," in The Service Encounter, J. Czepiel, M. Solomon, and C. Surprenant, eds., MA: Lexington Books.

---------- and M. Hui (1986), "Crowding in the Service Environment," in Creative Services Marketing - Proceedings, C. Marshall, D. Schmalensee, and V. Venkatesan, eds., Chicago: American Marketing Association.

Czepiel, J.A. et al (1985), "Service

Encounters: An Overview," in The Service Encounter, J. Czepiel, M. Solomon, and C. Surprenant, eds., MA: Lexington Books.

Donovan, R.J. and J.R. Rossiter (1982), "Store Atmosphere: An Environmental Psychology Approach," Journal of Retailing, 58(Spring), 34-57.

Eiglier, P. and E. Langeard (1977), "A New Approach to Service Marketing," in Marketing Consumer Services: New Insights, P. Eiglier et al, eds., Cambridge, MA: Marketing Science Institute.

Fishbein, M. and I. Ajzen (1975), Belief, Attitude, Intention and Behavior: An Introduction to Theory and Research, Reading, Mass.: Addison-Wesley.

Freedman, J.L. (1975), Crowding and Behavior, N.Y.: Viking.

_____ et al (1971), "The Effect of Crowding on Human Task Performance," Journal of Applied Social Psychology, 1, 7-25.

Glass, D.C. and J.E. Singer (1972), Urban Stress, N.Y.: Academic Press.

Gurin, P. et al (1969), "Internal-External Control in the Motivational Dynamics of Negro Youth," Journal of Social Issues, 15, 29-53.

Langer, E.J. and S. Saegart(1977), "Crowding and Cognitive Control," Journal of Personality and Social Psychology, 35, no.3, 175-82.

Mackintosh, E., S. West, and S. Saegart (1975), "Two Studies of Crowding in Urban Public Spaces," Environment and Behavior, 7, no.2, 159-84.

McClelland, L. and N. Auslander (1978), "Perception of Crowding and Pleasantness in Public Settings," Environment and Behavior, 10, no.4, 535-53.

Mehrabian, A. and J.A. Russell (1974), An Approach to Environmental Psychology, Cambridge, MA: MIT Press.

Paulus, P.B. et al (1976), "Density Does Affect Performance," Journal of Personality and Social Psychology, 34, 248-53.

Proshansky, H.M., W.H. Ittelson, and L.G. Rivlin (1970), "Freedom of Choice and Behavior in a Physical Setting," in Environmental Psychology: Man and His Physical Setting, H.M. Proshansky, W.H. Ittelson, and L.G. Rivlin, eds, N.Y.: Holt, Rinehart & Winston, Inc., 173-83.

Rapoport, A. (1975), "Toward a Redefinition of Density," Environment and Behavior, 7, 33-58.

Rodin, J., S.K. Solomon, and J. Metcalf (1978), "Role of Control in Mediating Perceptions of Density," Journal of Personality and Social Psychology, 36, no.9, 988-99.

Russell, J.A. (1978), "Evidence of Convergent Validity on the Dimensions of Affect," Journal of Personality and Social Psychology, 36, 1152-68.

_____ and A. Mehrabian (1976), "Some Behavioral Effects of the Physical Environment," in Experiencing the Environment, S. Wapner, S.B. Cohen, and B. Kaplan, eds., N.Y.: Plenum Press.

_____ and G. Pratt (1980), "A Description of the Affective Quality Attributed to the Environments," Journal of Personality and Social Psychology, 38, 311-22.

_____, L.M. Ward, and G. Pratt(1981), "Affective Quality Attributed to Environment: A Factor Analytic Study," Environment and Behavior, 13, no.3, 259-88.

Schmidt, D.E. and J.P. Keating (1979), "Human Crowding and Personal Control: An Integration of Research," Psychological Bulletin, 86, no.4, 680-700.

Sherrod, D.R. (1974), "Crowding, Perceived Control, and Behavioral After Effects," Journal of Applied Social Psychology, 4, 171-86.

Solomon, M.R. et al (1985), "A Role Theory Perspective on Dyadic Interactions: The Service Encounter," Journal of Marketing, 49, 1(Winter), 99-111.

Stokols, D. (1972), "On the Distinction between Density and Crowding," Psychological Review, 79, no.3, 275-77.

John Bateson is Senior Lecturer and Ernst and Whinney Research Fellow at the London Business School. Michael Hui is a doctoral student at the London Business School.

EXPLORING THE CONCEPT OF LOYALTY IN SERVICES

John A. Czepiel, New York University, New York
Robert Gilmore, New York University, New York

ABSTRACT

Loyalty is defined as a specific attitude to continue in an exchange relationship based solely on past experiences and is differentiated from repeat purchase and preference based definitions. A model describing the process of the development of loyalty is presented. Based on that model it is hypothesized that services have a greater capacity for creating loyalty than do goods.

INTRODUCTION

Customer loyalty is to marketers what love is to pubescent children. Even though they don't know what it is or how to get it, they want it because they think it will feel good. This paper's purpose is to explain what customer loyalty is, why services have a greater capacity for creating customer loyalty than do goods businesses, and finally, how one goes about getting it.

Part of the difficulty marketers have with customer loyalty is that there are shortcomings in both the clarity of the concept and the exact words used to capture the idea. The paper deals with this issue first. It next presents a model which defines loyalty and the process by which it is developed. Third it uses that model to demonstrate what savvy service marketers probably already know; the "purer" the service, the greater the capacity for loyalty.

THE MEANING OF LOYALTY

William Safire, Edwin Newman and English professors should not be the only ones who are concerned about the accuracy of language usage. Marketers depend on concepts which allow us to understand marketplace phenomena and to share that meaning with others. Customer loyalty, however, is a concept whose meaning has changed with each user and whose metaphorical basis is severely flawed (Arndt, 1985). The point is that the word loyalty means things that can seldom be expected in marketplace relationships to such an extent that its usage ought to be restricted.

As it is typically used in our culture, loyalty connotes sentiment and the feeling of devotion that one holds for one's country, creed, family, friends. Loyalty is heavy-duty stuff -- going to face the lions rather than betraying one's faith; sticking with a cantankerous friend in need because of half-remembered but important experiences years ago; enduring the not-always-short-term costs of a marriage because of a commitment to one's spouse and the relationship. No market-based loyalty can ever be worth true loyalty in these senses.

Moreover, using the word to describe any marketplace relationship not only devalues the word, it plants in our heads the above meanings and associations -- no matter how often we say "well, you know what I mean". When we use the word to describe marketplace behavior, a little but important part of our brain still tries to assign non-market, emotional, family- and nation-based criteria to the situation. This only confuses us and obscures what is truly behind the marketplace behavior we observe and want to deserve.

The problem is that we have no better word to use. The lexicon of words and terms that exist to describe market-place exchange activity contains none that communicate the concepts "attachment" and "commitment" on the part of the customer to the offering or supplier. Words such as buyer or purchaser for example, imply nothing about the past or the future. Other words such as shopper, user, or consumer describe what a person is before or after a purchase but say nothing about whether they would do it again. The word customer implies some regularity of purchase but nothing about exclusivity, or more importantly, how the buyer would act when an attractive competitor arrived on the scene. Yet the phenomenon exists: customers exhibit feelings, beliefs, and behaviors toward offerings and suppliers that act to maintain existing exchange relationships -- sometimes apparently in the face of self interest. We approximate that phenomenon with the word loyalty and, protest as we will, we are stuck with it until someone can come up with a better term to which we will all be willing to be loyal.

MARKETPLACE LOYALTY

More confusing than the use of the word loyalty, however, is the confusion that marketers have when they use the word to understand and describe marketplace behavior. Some marketers use the word to capture purely behavioral phenomena -- repeat purchase -- while others include an attitudinal component reflecting preference (Jacoby and Chestnut 1978). A source of continued conceptual ambiguity is that the preference based notions of loyalty fail to understand that loyalty, at its core, is a noninstrumental value. Marketers know how to create instrumental preference-based repeat purchases; simply devise an offer too good for customers to refuse. Loyalty, however, is distinct from this instrumental aspect of preference.

We define marketplace loyalty in terms of an attitude which develops under specific conditions and as a result of particular psychological processes. The results of this process can usually be observed in repeat purchase behavior. As an attitude it is a disposition to continue in a particular exchange relationship based solely on the experiences of the past relationship; that is, regardless of the consequences to the actor. The marketplace behavior that results is not only continued patronage but a willingness to voice dissatisfaction rather than to defect and to give the supplying firm time to remedy its absolute or relative shortcomings. Note here the similarities to Hirschman's (1970) conception of voice and exit.

This developmental process is shown in Figure 1. Over the history of the relationship the buyer has had experience with the behavior of the supplier and the actual performance of the product/service. Alternative suppliers and products/services have vied for his patronage. In continuing to purchase, to choose the particular supplier - product/service combination, the buyer must justify his actions to himself, interpret the seller's behaviors and find ways to resolve the inevitable differences between expectations and reality.

These resolutions occur through four psychological processes. In inconsistency resolution the buyer must reconcile the choice he made in the face of changes in costs and rewards and especially in comparison to other, competing offers. Attitudinal consistency theories (e.g., Festinger 1957, Heider 1958) tell us that the cognitive reconciliation/justification process leads to more posi-

FIGURE 1

THE PROCESS OF LOYALTY DEVELOPMENT

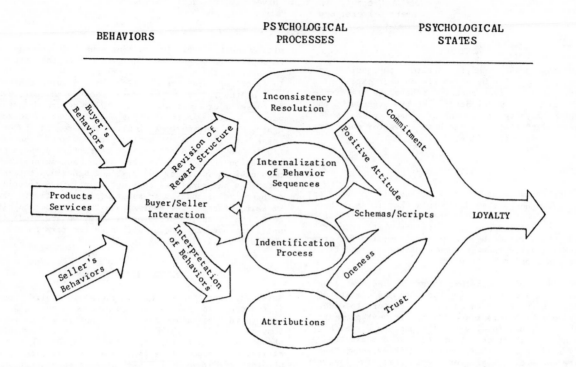

BEHAVIORS   PSYCHOLOGICAL PROCESSES   PSYCHOLOGICAL STATES

tive attitudes and commitment to the choice and object.

Similarly, the process of attribution leads to positive attitudes and trust. As the buyer observes and interprets the seller's (and his own) behaviors, he makes attributions as to causality (why did the seller act that way?). Attributions that the seller acted out of concern for they buyer's well-being lead the buyer to trust the seller. By way of contrast, an attribution that the seller "had no choice" or "feared a lawsuit" would not lead to trust or a positive attitude.

Finally, the buyer and seller have interacted in some way, negotiated the purchases perhaps. They may have had to deal with and resolve the inevitable changes in the substance, administration, and details of completing the transactions and servicing them over time. These interactions or behavior sequences between buyer and seller, over time, become internally encoded as schemas (e.g., Markus 1977). As they become more frequent, these choice and interaction behavior pairings increase the probability of continuing in the chosen relationship. Choosing a particular offering and working out the offer's wrinkles become well-worn paths, familiar to the buyer and easy to use. Closeness may develop to the point where the seller becomes identified with the buyer's way of doing business. Similarly, the buyer may simultaneously identify with the seller and think of the seller as my _____ (e.g., broker, accountant, hairdresser); that is, a sense of oneness develops.

While we can formulate that the resultant -- loyalty -- is a disposition supported by the components of commitment, trust, positive attitudes, oneness, and schemas/scripts; that is too static an approach. For as we have seen, loyalty develops in a dynamic process. Our understanding of loyalty must necessarily include not only its simple definition but the framework within which it develops (Figure 1).

Implications

Understanding loyalty in this manner offers several insights. The first and major among these is counterintuitive. It is that perfection in performance will not necessarily lead to loyalty. It may lead to "apparent loyalty" -- that is, continued purchase behavior over time -- but such a purchase sequence is based on self interest-based preference and habit, not trust and commitment. Faced with a superior alternative, the buyer has no reason not to defect. The relationship has been based on economic rationality -- choosing the "best" offer at each purchase decision point -- and it will die on that same basis.

Loyalty is necessary only in an imperfect world. Loyalty is desirable because loyalty is what binds customer to supplier in the face of increasingly attractive competitive offers or the supplier's own shortcomings. It is the identification with, trust in, and commitment to the supplier that underlies the customer's willingness to give the supplier time to redress those relative or absolute shortfalls in performance. The developmental process which led to the growth of loyalty also established the mechanisms by which the customer and supplier resolve differences. But it is loyalty which, when all else fails, provides a security net for the supplier.

The second implication is that fixed or invariant offers are less likely to engender loyalty than those in which there is room to maneuver. Where the product/service is "one-size-fits-all" and the terms and conditions "take-it-or-leave-it," there is little cause for a buyer to make positive attributions about the supplier's acts or even to have much reason to interact with the seller, let alone practice the give-and-take necessary to build and maintain a relationship. For loyalty can only be created and exist in a relationship. Loyalty has no relevance to the single, isolated transaction.

The third implication is that it is not appropriate to guage loyalty by behavior alone. There are too many explanations for regular purchase behavior which do not require trust, commitment, or even positive regard. Only by knowing why a behavior occurs can one begin to guage loyalty. A docile, never complaining customer is a more likely candidate for defection than is a client with whom one has successfully negotiated the inevitable shortcomings of the relationship.

LOYALTY IN SERVICES

Services have an inherently greater capacity to create loyalty than do goods because the service situation is one which is conducive to the loyalty process described above. The situation is best described in terms of three of the characteristics of services: intangibility, heterogeneity, and interaction intensity (Czepiel, 1980).

Services are intangible performances, acts, processes experiences, and abilities. They are ephemeral, flitting spirits that we find difficult to touch, hold, measure, weigh, evaluate, judge, communicate. Almost by definition, these acts are heterogeneous, never quite the same in performance or delivery. Even the most seemingly homogeneous, the complex physical sorting and computer act of clearing checks, isn't. Each transfer is unique in time, amount payee, routing, and purpose. Finally, services are interaction intensive. Generally we think of them as people intensive, but the interaction intensity need not be human to affect our purpose. This interaction is direct between client and supplier and may be in person, by phone, telex, facsimile, or mail, and be between humans, machines, or computers in any conceivable combination (Czepiel, et al., 1985). It is acknowledged, though, that the more personal the interaction the richer the relationship is and the more potential there is for loyalty to develop.

These characteristics of services form the kind of situation in which loyalty can best be formed. First, the nature of services, especially professional ones, is such that they are high on credence properties (Gummesson, 1981). Their ephemeral, intangible nature is such that the client must trust the supplier's competence and feel secure in the belief that the supplier will act in the client's best interest. In addition the interaction intensity of services gives the client the opportunity to observe the supplier's behavior and to form attributions which lead to the needed trust (Solomon, et al., 1985).

The heterogeneous nature of services is apparent to the client and at some conscious and unconscious level, creates an expectation that the service can be tailored to fit his exact needs. In fact, a study by Nyquist, Bitner, and Booms (1985) showed just that. Customer expectations which exceeded the system's ability to deliver accounted for 74% of "incidents" reported by hotel, restaurant, and airline service employees. At the production level heterogeneity has two effects. One is that the client's expectations as to the exactness of the service's fit to his or her needs will most frequently be disappointed. Seldom will the service type match perfectly with the service type needed. Second, even when they are a close match, the levels of expected and delivered performance may not coincide.

This heterogeneity engages two processes; inconsistency resolution as the client reconciles the expected with reality and internalization of behavior sequences as the client works with the supplier to correct discrepancies or simply to improve the match of the needed/desired with the possible potential. In this way the client builds commitment as he justifies his choice of the service and creates and elaborates on the script which details the choice, negotiation, tailoring, and problem resolution sequence of acts with the supplier. Fiebelkorn (1985) for example, found that bank

customers whose service problems were competently resolved were as satisfied as the average customer who had not had a problem.

To the extent that these actions between client and supplier are face-to-face, or human-to-human the impact is stronger. Human interactions are always more engaging and effective than impersonal ones. In addition to effectiveness, the presence of a human on the supplier side allows for the creation of a double bond: one between the client and the supplier's human representative, the other between the client and the supplier firm itself. When both are strong and positive one can assume a particularly strong loyalty is formed. On the other hand, some might point to this as simply doubling the potential for error. Since it is possible to have mixed attitudes towards the supplying firm and to its representative, such mixed loyalty situations are a matter of concern.

As one applies this model of loyalty across different service types, it becomes apparent that their capacities for loyalty are not all the same. Figure 2 suggests one framework by which this capacity may be analyzed. It classifies services by the ability and willingness to tailor the service to clients' needs (inherent and strategic heterogeneity) and the intensity of interaction. Services high on both can be said to have the capacity for Double Bond Loyalty, those high on only one to have the capacity for Service Loyalty or Provider Loyalty, and those low on both have a low relative capacity for loyalty.

FIGURE 2

Capacity for Loyalty by Service Type

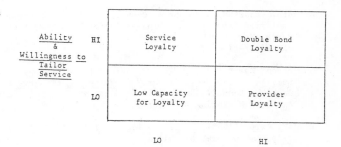

By this definition then, the "purer" the service the more loyalty comes into play. The CPA firm that specializes in financial planning and consulting rather than auditing will have the potential for a more loyal clientele. Consulting firms that work on problem identification and conceptualization can engender greater loyalty than those which sell and install computing system packages. Curiously, this route leads to the same conclusion which Porter (1980) arrived at from a competitive economic and strategic perspective: standard products and differentiated products products differ in the extent to which they can engender customer loyalty.

Summary

While no marketplace relationship can ever engender the same kind or degree of loyalty that the word suggests, the process and its result are important. While continued purchase is the result most marketers think of, it is the customer's willingness to give the supplier the time and feedback necessary to work through the deficiencies in the relationship that is important. It is the customer's willingness to endure temporary performance shortfalls in order to gain the long term benefits of the relationship that benefits both. Services, by their very nature, have a greater capacity to form loyal relationships and the "purer" the service, the greater this capacity. It is the heterogeneity, intangibility, and interaction intensity inherent in service offerings which actively engages the loyalty process.

REFERENCES

Arndt, Johan (1985), "On Making Marketing Science More Scientific: Role of Orientations, Paradigms, Metaphors, and Puzzle Solving," Journal of Marketing, 49 (Summer), 11-23.

Czepiel, John A. (1980), Managing Customer Satisfaction in Consumer Service Businesses. Cambridge, MA: Marketing Science Institute.

Czepiel, John A., Michael R. Solomon, Carol F. Surprenant, and Evelyn G. Gutman (1985), "Service Encounters: An Overview" in The Service Encounter: Managing Employee/Customer Interaction in Service Businesses, John A. Czepiel, Michael R. Solomon, and Carol F. Surprenant eds., Lexington, MA: Lexington Books, 3-15.

Fiebelkorn, Sandra L. (1985), "Retail Service Encounter Satisfaction: Model and Measurement," in The Service Encounter: Managing Employee/Customer Interaction in Service Businesses, John A. Czepiel, Michael R. Solomon, and Carol F. Surprenant eds., Lexington, MA: Lexington Books, 181-193.

Festinger, Leon (1957), A Theory of Cognitive Dissonance. Stanford, CA: Stanford University Press.

Gilmore, Robert F. and John A. Czepiel (1986), "Reconceptualizing Loyalty in Exchange Relationships," Working Paper, New York University Graduate School of Business Administration, July.

Gummesson, Evert (1981), "The Marketing of Professional Services -- 25 Propositions," in Marketing of Services, James H. Donnelly and William R. George eds., Chicago: American Marketing Association.

Heider, Fritz (1958), The Psychology of Interpersonal Relations. New York, NY: Wiley.

Hirschman, Albert O. (1970), Exit, Voice, and Loyalty. Cambridge, MA: Harvard University Press.

Jacoby, Jacob and Robert W. Chestnut (1978), Brand Loyalty Measurement and Management. New York, NY: Wiley

Markus, Hazel (1977), "Self-Schemata and Processing Information About the Self," Journal of Personality and Social Psychology, 35, 63-78.

Nyquist, Jody D., Mary J. Bitner, and Bernard H. Booms (1985), "Identifying Communications Difficulties in the Service Encounter: A Critical Incident Approach," in The Service Encounter: Managing Employee/Customer Interaction in Service Businesses, John A. Czepiel, Michael R. Solomon, and Carol F. Surprenant eds., 195-212.

Porter, Michael E. (1980), Competitive Strategy. New York, NY: The Free Press.

Solomon, Michael R., Carol F. Surprenant, John A. Czepiel, and Evelyn G. Gutman (1985), "A Role Theory Perspective on Dyadic Interactions: The Service Encounter," Journal of Marketing, 49 (Winter) 99-111.

MANAGING LONG-TERM RELATIONSHIPS

Carole A. Congram, Consultant

ABSTRACT

Many service industries are based on long-term relationships between a service organization's clients or customers and its service providers. Service providers can take an active role in managing the service experience to influence clients' expectations. Relationship management is the process of ensuring the effective delivery of services to meet clients' or customers' needs. The relationship is discussed in terms of two phases: pre-purchase and post-purchase. Four examples of critical post-purchase points which can be managed are presented.

WHAT IS RELATIONSHIP MANAGEMENT?

Many services are based on frequent, intense, continuing personal relationships. Consider the professions -- accounting, architecture, engineering, law, medicine -- as well as certain banking specialties, consulting, insurance, and personal financial planning. The clients or customers in these industries and their service providers have the potential for long-term, constructive, mutually rewarding relationships. The potential frequently is not realized -- in part, because service providers do not understand the nature of relationship management.

Relationship management is the process of ensuring the effective delivery of services to meet clients' or customers' needs. This definition implies that:

1. Relationship management is ongoing and systematic.

2. Relationship management is predicated on an organized approach to identifying client segments and the appropriate services for these segments.

3. Service providers can become sensitive to an individual client's or customer's needs.

4. A client's or customer's experiences and expectations can be directed in a positive way.

The definition also sets these priorities for service organizations:

1. Understand your organization's client or customer base;

2. Align services with needs of client or customer subgroups; and, then,

3. Develop relationship management systems.

Relationships exist over time. In a business setting, the purchase, i.e., the time when the client engages the service organization, is especially important because of the commitment made by both parties. In fact, the sale divides the relationship into two phases.

Pre-Purchase Relationship Phase

Pre-purchase relationship-building activities are concerned largely with shaping client expectations of the service experience. The service organization may use a broad range of marketing tools, techniques, and activities to influence expectations:

- Advertising

- Brochures

- Community involvement

- Direct mail

- Newsletters

- Personal selling

- Public relations

- Trade associations

- Word of mouth

In addition, in many relationship-based industries, the service providers make a formal proposal -- oral or written -- in which they may attempt to explain the service experience the prospective client can expect. It is difficult, if not impossible, to simulate the service experience in these industries.

Many service providers expend energy on pre-purchase relationship-building activities and assume that:

1. The purchase cements the relationship, and

2. The relationship will take care of itself during the service delivery process.

Post-Purchase Relationship Phase

Once the client purchases a service, he enters the organization's service delivery system. The client continually tests the expectations formed prior to the purchase against his experiences in the system. His experiences are of two types:

- Technical, i.e., the core work of the service organization, such as accounting or architecture; and

- Relationship, i.e., the functional aspects of service, such as timely delivery of reports, understanding of the client's business, or consistent coordination of service.

The client's observations of the firm's technical and relationship performance give him a measure of service quality. For those clients with limited understanding of the technical aspects of service, perceptions of quality derive from the relationship aspects, which tend to be subjective in nature.

Successful client-oriented service providers develop sensitivity to the relationship aspects of service, and management strives to provide educational programs and service experiences that help professionals develop this sensitivity. In relationship-based industries, marketing managers are most successful when they help service providers in their day-to-day dealings with clients.

CRITICAL POINTS IN THE POST-PURCHASE PHASE

Every service industry has critical times when service providers can use the opportunity to educate clients about the service delivery process and, in effect, manage clients' expectations. Although the critical times may differ across industries, there are several points that recur across relationship-based industries.

The Purchase

The purchase, or sale, is an especially important time for both the client and the service providers. On the one hand, the client is anticipating the service he will receive. He may be somewhat apprehensive, too, as he wonders whether he selected the right firm to meet his needs, and as he begins to evaluate the consistency between his expectations and the service received.

On the other hand, at the time of the purchase, service providers are happy because they have gained another client, but he is probably one of many. If they wooed the prospective client with some intensity, they probably neglected other activities, to which they must attend once the purchase is in hand. In doing so, they may disappoint the client by not giving him the attention he expects.

With planning, this disappointment can be avoided. For example, the managing partner of an accounting firm could hold a monthly luncheon for new clients. A personal invitation could state that the firm's partners value the opportunity to serve the client. Another example: Upon being retained, a member of the service management team could schedule a planning meeting with key client personnel.

Managing clients' post-purchase perceptions involves implementing a support system that meets the needs of your organization's service providers. The key is to identify the types of contact that are appropriate to the style of the service providers and to build the supporting systems to help them be successful.

Project Planning

The planning phase of any project offers the opportunity to manage perceptions by educating a client about the service process and the results anticipated at various stages in the process. Frequently, clients have no idea why a procedure is needed. If you can deal with questions or misperceptions in the planning stages, you remove them as sources of dissatisfaction later, during service delivery.

Project Completion

At the end of a project, it is critical for the service providers to ensure that the client's key personnel understand the benefits resulting from the project. The service provider should communicate the benefits in writing, as well as in any oral presentations, to top management and, if appropriate, other managers.

Periods of Inactivity

When your organization is not providing services to a client, it is imperative to continue communicating with him. Communications, both personal and non-personal, should be designed so that the client concludes: "This service organization is interested in me and my company.

The people have good ideas for me, and they do good work." Examples of facilitating communications include ideas that would help to improve the client company's performance, invitations to events he would consider worthwhile, and newsletters geared to issues in his industry.

Critical Points and Evaluation

Once you have identified the critical points in your organization's service delivery process, supporting systems and educational programs can be developed to help service providers improve performance. Developing this support requires a substantial investment. To be most effective, an ongoing service quality evaluation program could be used to monitor service providers' success in managing relationships.

AMA MASTERCLASS - INTRODUCTION

Tim Powell, Coopers & Lybrand, New York

The MasterClass was a chance for conference participants
to integrate services marketing theory with actual case
histories. In effect each session was an intensive
laboratory for the development of a case study suitable
for use in a business curriculum. Several of the case
authors, in fact, plan to extend them into full-length
classroom cases.

An informal MasterClass planning committee selected topics
to cover a range of issues: service branding and fran-
chising; service quality; new service development and
rollout; and service marketing in a turbulent environment.

We likewise tried for a cross-section of featured industries -- personnel services, banking, telecommunications, and cable TV were each represented -- and a
balance between services marketed to organizations and
those marketed to individuals. We felt this approach was
consistent with the "something for everyone" structure
of the conference as a whole.

Each session was structured like a business school case,
with an academic (or consultant) leading the audience
in the identification and discussion of the issues. Unlike a classroom case, a key executive in the case
actively participated in the presentation and discussion.
This kept the dialogue balanced between the theoretically
feasible and the practically possible.

Most of the sessions started with the executive's introducing the audience to the industry and the company being discussed. The particular marketing problem at hand
was then described, along with enough background to im-
part a flavor of the decision-making environment of the
situation. Options were proposed, and the audience was
invited to discuss them and make recommendations among the
alternatives.

Then we got the chance -- often missing from business
school cases -- to see what actually was done, and what
the results were. This provided four fascinating glimpses
into the world of marketing decision-making.

Participation from the audience was lively, in spite of
the relatively extended length and late hour of the
sessions. In several instances we observed presenters
jotting down ideas to take back and try out. The audience
was thus integrated not only into the case development
process, but also in some cases into the business process
itself.

The theme of functional integration pervaded the sessions,
although presenters had not been prompted to emphasize it.
In the case of Personnel Pool, we saw how corporate
organizational structure relates to delivery channel
structure. In Bankers Trust, we saw how integral the
quality of operations is to service marketing. In the GTE
case, we saw how market research was integrated into the
service design and development cycle. Rollins Cablevision
was a fascinating look at pricing options in an industry
being price-deregulated.

Robert J. Kopp, Babson College
Arvind Jadhav, GTE

ABSTRACT

This article is a case study of the introduction of a new service -- GTE TeleMessager.
The case records the progress of Telemessager
through the new product development stages of
idea generation; screening; business analysis;
product development and testing; test marketing;
and commercialization. The case also illustrates the key role played by the "product
champion" in shepherding a new business idea
along the long and difficult path toward
commercialization.

INTRODUCTION

In 1980, GTE Corporation (formerly General
Telephone & Electronics) had sales of $9.7
billion, ranking it as the 2nd on Fortune's
list of the top 50 U.S. utilities. GTE was
second only to AT&T in providing telephone
service to residences and businesses. The
Telephone Operating Group (Telops), which was
also involved in data processing and satellite
communications, accounted for roughly sixty
percent of company sales. The remaining forty
percent of sales was derived from the
Diversified Products Group, GTE's manufacturing
arm; key products included communications and
telephone equipment, and consumer products
marketed under the Sylvania name.

It was at this time that Telops management
decided that more new products were needed to
meet the Group's long-run growth objectives.
In 1981, a New Business Development (NBD) team
was formed and was charged with identifying and
developing new product ideas. William Bradford
was transferred from Corporate Marketing
Research to become a Manager of New Business
Development.

Bradford had joined GTE ten years earlier as a
Senior Economist and had worked in several
other functional areas including Engineering,
Forecasting and Planning. Also at this time, a
New Business Task Force (NBTF) was formed to
oversee NBD's new product development efforts.

THE BIRTH OF A NEW SERVICE

With the NBD and NBTF in place, Bill Bradford's
charter was to identify and develop ideas for
new businesses which would be profitable, and
the operation of which would leverage off of
GTE's existing capabilities. As the search
process proceeded in late 1981, several factors
converged to bring about the birth of the idea
for a new communications service. In 1979,
GTE had acquired TeleMail, a system of trans-
mitting text via desk top data terminals. The
problem with such a system is that the sender
must have access to a data terminal and must,
ideally, possess some typing ability. Also,
Bradford was aware of the "personal touch"
created by telephone answering machines owing
to the fact that messages were transmitted in
the sender's own voice. Finally, he was aware
of an emerging technology through which sound
waves could be converted to a digital form to
be stored in and processed by a computer. The
technology, which was dubbed "voice store-and-
forward" (VSF), would make possible a

communications system which would not require
users to have a special data terminal or typing
ability (see Fig. 1).

FIGURE 1

Schematic of Voice Store-and-
Forward (VSF) System

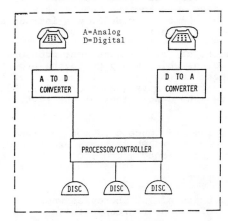

As he researched the new idea more carefully,
with the help of a consultant, Bradford began
compiling a list of key user benefits of a VSF
system. In short, VSF...

.....reduces time in call-backs; 70% of
all business calls are not completed
on the first try. This problem is
particularly acute for communications
between offices in different time
zones.

.....saves time in reducing "small talk":
the average person-to-person business
call is 7-10 minutes, most of which
is occupied by small talk. The
average VSF message is roughly a
minute.

.....reduces missed messages.

.....provides the personal touch of voice
communications.

.....enables a single message to be transmitted to hundreds of mailboxes/
telephones simultaneously.

.....allows the user to readily reply to,
save, delete or re-route a message.

Bill Bradford saw in the VSF the opportunity
for GTE to launch a new communications service,
a "voice mailbox" system. While such a system
could be used by individual consumers as an
alternative to an answering machine or telephone answering service, Bill thought the main
potential to lie in internal communications
within business organizations. Further, he
viewed the voice mailbox as having a good fit
with GTE's corporate image as a leader in the
communications industry. Down the road, he
foresaw possible integration of a voice mailbox system with other GTE services such as
telephone operations, TeleMail, and SPRINT.

In addition, because a VSF system could run on currently available computers -- customized software was required -- entrance into the new business required a rather modest capital outlay.

IN-HOUSE PRODUCT TEST

In April 1982, the voice mailbox idea was presented to the New Business Task Force and an agreement was reached to test a VSF system within selected GTE divisions. A hardware manufacturer, who also had developed a basic VSF software package, was located and the system, tentatively named VoiceMail, was introduced into a Telops Division for a trial run.

The results of the in-house test produced several findings which would guide the product development and marketing of the new service. In a memo to his boss (December 1981), Bradford summarized the conclusions of the test as follows:

1) The VSF concept is most useful to customers where there exists a close user group, members of which do not come into frequent face-to-face contact.

2) Usage of VSF increases where one member of the user group acts as a "champion" of the service.

3) System capacity does not appear to be a constraint.

4) Two additional features appear to be particularly desirable to customers: (a) message waiting indication; and (b) permitting outsiders (non-subscribers) to have open access to the system. ·

In addition, the in-house test produced implications for system development with respect to features such as length of message storage, message sequencing, mailbox labeling, formatting of key-pulsed commands and the like.

PROPOSAL TO TEST MARKET VOICEMAIL

In Bradford's view, the in-house test had been a success both in terms of fine-tuning the service concept and in terms of the VSF system's overall favorable reception by business users. At the same time, the six-month test did not provide data on which customer segments -- i.e., company size, location, industry group -- would represent the most productive target market for the VSF service. And the test provided little guidance as how the new service should be priced or promoted. Nevertheless, Bill Bradford was anxious to test the service under real market conditions, and in October 1982 he went to the New Business Task Force with a proposal to run a test market of VoiceMail for a year beginning in January 1983. In order to save money and to simplify the operational aspects of the test, a single city, Dallas, Texas, was selected as the test market. In his proposal, Johnson outlined five objectives of the test as follows: 1) to identify target customer segments; 2) to pre-test and fine-tune product offerings; 3) to test alternative pricing levels; 4) to develop

technical and operating expertise; and 5) to forecast demand. Figure 2 contains details of the Marketing Plan contained in the proposal.

FIGURE 2

Summary of Marketing Plan
for Dallas Test Market

Target Customers

- Business users

    - Small (2-9 employees)
    - Medium (10-99 employees)
    - Large (100 +)

Product

- Single product--messagebox for subscribers only

Price

- $30 per month
- $.50 per minute

Promotion

- Direct mail

    - "Improve Productivity"
    - "Save time, save money"

- Personal selling
- Advertising
- Sales promotion: "30 day free trial"

Bradford's proposal recommended that a business unit be established reporting to a General Manager (himself). Initially, the VoiceMail group would consist of two departments: Marketing & Sales, which would also handle in-field customer support; and Operations, consisting of installation, maintenance, customer support and training. Later, two more functional areas would be added: Finance and Product Development which would develop the system software.

The test market proposal met with a mixed reaction from the NBTF. Some NBTF members were favorably impressed with the progress made to date on what would be one of the company's first internally originated new products developed for an unregulated market. In addition, the potential synergy between VoiceMail and other GTE services was also seen as a positive point. On the other hand, certain NBTF members questioned whether the move to test market was premature, given the lack of research on defining target segments and their specific needs. In this group's view, further marketing of VoiceMail should be put on "hold" until Bradford and his group had in hand a thorough market study which described market segments and recommended specific marketing programs to meet their needs. While some members of the NBTF were encouraged by the absence of major competition in the VSF market, others took the apparent lack of interest by AT&T and IBM as a sign that GTE may be overestimating the potential size of the market. Finally, some NBTF members saw the revenue potential for VSF to be relatively small by GTE standards, and they reacted unfavorably to the fact that the break-even period for the new business might be as long as 24 months.

Of the situation Bill Bradford comments: "The objection that we needed more up-front marketing research really made me pause -- I began to wonder whether we were, in our enthusiasm, moving too quickly. At the same time, everything we knew about VSF told us that the concept itself would be very difficult to describe to respondents in a survey/market study format. In an early concept test that we did, most people came away thinking the product was just an elaborate answering machine. Therefore, I had serious doubts as to whether paper-and-pencil research could accurately forecast customer reactions to the actual service. I came to the conclusion that the only accurate way of gauging customer response was to observe real behavior under market conditions." After much debate, Bradford was given the go-ahead to test VSF in Dallas during calendar 1983. Initially he was elated at having secured the right to further develop a new market in which he saw GTE as establishing a leadership position. However, he was sobered by the fact that he had before him only 3 months to find a location, to recruit and hire personnel, and to plan and execute promotional programs.

SEARCH FOR A TRADEMARK

In preparation for the market test, GTE's advertising agency, Doyle Dane Bernbach (DDB), was asked to suggest a new brand name for the voice messaging service. Responding very quickly the agency submitted a long list of possible names including PhoneMail, PhoneMemo, Phone-A-Gram, TeleMemo, Voice Mailbox, and MaxiMail. DDB recommended that PhoneMail be chosen and Bill Bradford agreed. However, in late December 1982, a press release announced the launching of a new VSF service, named PhoneMail, by the Rolm Corporation. A few days later GTE's next choice, VoiceMail, was trademarked by another competitor. In frustration, Bradford asked the advice of the department secretary, Jan Bouchet, who immediately suggested the name Telemessage. Shortly thereafter, an "r" was added, the "m" was capitalized and TeleMessager (TM) was born.

THE DALLAS TEST

By December Bill Bradford had obtained office space in Dallas and had assembled a team of seven, all recruited from within GTE. Bradford comments: "Since I didn't have the financial resources to offer pay raises, the initial TM group was clearly motivated by the challenge of starting a new venture. Later, when we expanded to new locations, I found that the extraordinary level of commitment exhibited by this founding group was very difficult to duplicate."

A particularly fortuitous personnel move was the recruiting of Bob Wilson as Director of Product Development. Wilson, 25, had worked a six-month stint with the then Voice Messaging division as part of GTE's Associate Development Program for college graduates. Bradford recalls: "During this first assignment, I gave him a six-month

project which he completed in four months! As the head of Product Development, he managed to keep up with Marketing's demands to add new features on virtually a continuous basis."

With the TM organization in place in Dallas, marketing of the new service began in earnest in March of 1983. To kick off the marketing effort, a press release was issued and was picked up by key newspapers in Texas and New Orleans. Next, a direct mail piece describing the service and offering a 30-day free trial was sent to roughly 60,000 businesses, equalling the entire census of companies in the Dallas area. The brochure invited potential customers to learn more about TM by calling telemarketing reps located at the Dallas office. These reps were to further explain the Tele-Messager concept and to qualify the customer as a prime prospect. Qualified sales leads would then be followed-up by a TM salesperson.

The direct mail program, put together by a consultant, assumed that a mailing of 60,000 would yield 1125 qualified leads, 340 trial customers and 200 who would adopt the service. Each customer would average 10 messageboxes at a revenue of $42 per box. "The first three months was a disaster," Bradford recalls. "The phones were quiet. As of June 1, we got 60 qualified leads and sold six boxes. That was a very frustrating period. There was considerable pressure from GTE headquarters to discontinue the test market."

Arguing that the opportunity was too good to give up on, Bradford got approval to continue the test in Dallas, with the proviso that he would show improved performance within two months. At this low point, Bradford and his team shifted into high gear to implement changes based on their experience over the first three months of marketing TM. The direct mail piece, which looked too commercial and impersonal, was rewritten and personalized with the recipient's name. The original TM product which consisted of a single service -- Universal Messagebox -- was reconfigured into a five-product line, thus offering the customer more options. Pricing was revised to include quantity discounts at the 50, 100, and 200 unit levels. Finally, Bradford and his sales team realized that the TM product had considerable benefits for companies which operate multiple locations around the country. In this light the product needed to be marketed nationally as well as locally. They identified as a prime target, medium-sized companies which have sales reps, customers, or executives scattered across different time zones. Two of the TM sales reps spent many long hours in the Dallas Public Library identifying such prospects.

At this time, John Potts, TM's Marketing Director, proposed and received approval to offer a special sales incentive to TM's four sales representatives. The program, dubbed "Reach for the Beach," offered a vacation trip to Hawaii as the top prize if the quota for signing up new customers was achieved. Also at this time, one of the sales reps, Nancy Peterson, made the kind of sale that signals a business turnaround. The Dallas office of a large, multinational oil company, was spending $120,000 a year on Mailgrams to announce frequent price changes to salespeople and customers. Peterson presented the company with the TM feature known as "group calling" which enables a single message to be transmitted to many people. John Potts recalls: "They reached for their calculators, concluded we'd cut their communications cost 40 percent and suddenly we sold 200 messageboxes!"

With a sharper definition of the target customer and with new programs in place in the areas of product, pricing, and promotion, TeleMessager sales volume improved dramatically during the July-December period of 1983. Final results for the ten-month test are in Table 1.

All things considered, Bradford was satisfied with TM's performance. Despite the slow start, total sales of messageboxes had come in at (1910 ÷ 2000 =) 96% of target. While only 50% of the target number of customers was achieved, each customer on average purchased twice the target level of messageboxes. Revenue per messagebox came in at 75% of goal largely, Bradford thought, because of the quantity discount program implemented at midyear. On the positive side, total expenses came in somewhat below the original target.

TABLE 1

Dallas Test Market Results, 1983

	Target	Actual
Number of customers	100	98
Messageboxes/customer	10	19.5
Total messageboxes	2,000	1910
Revenue/Messagebox	$42.00	$31.20
Total revenue	$465,450	$312,500
Total expense	$965,375	$937,500

Source: Company records. Data has been disguised.

A PROPOSAL TO ROLL-OUT THE NEW SERVICE

Overall, the results of the Dallas test convinced Bradford that TeleMessager represented a major business opportunity for GTE. In late 1983, he put together a 100-page business plan containing marketing and operating plans, and pro-forma income statements for the 1984-93 period. In his cover memo to the NBTF, Bradford listed these five major conclusions based on the Dallas test market: (1) there is widespread demand for TeleMessager; (2) current product is acceptable, but ongoing enhancement is necessary; (3) pricing is acceptable, but further experimentation is recommended; (4) a cost-effective advertising program to increase customer awareness should be developed; and (5) the break-even period is short. The memo concluded that "a phased roll-out program should be undertaken to establish GTE leadership in the voice store-and-forward market."

The business plan recommended that the number of message centers be expanded to seven in 1984, to nine in 1985 and twelve in 1986 and beyond. GTE's long-run market share of VSF was projected to be 50%. At this level TeleMessager would breakeven in 1985. (An alternative income statement showed that even at a 35% market share TM would operate profitably in 1985).

Like the original proposal to open the Dallas test market, the proposal to roll-out TM met with a mixed reaction from the NBTF. Task Force members were, for the most part, dubious about the market share and financial projections. This skepticism was reinforced when Steve Washington, a marketing consultant to GTE, stated at a meeting between Bradford and the NBTF that there was a "zero chance" the TM group would deliver the numbers contained in the roll-out plan. Nevertheless, some NBTF members shared Bradford's optimism for TeleMessager, agreeing with him that the new venture bore a good fit with GTE's existing businesses and that it offered acceptable returns. Further they saw that the risk-level was kept low by the fact that the new business did not require the establishment of manufacturing facilities.

Other NBTF members remained skeptical of the TM roll-out proposal. In their view, a key weakness of the plan was the fact that the TM group still did not have a clear picture of the target customer. Marketing, therefore, would continue to follow a "shotgun" as opposed to "rifle" approach. Some NBTF members holding this view recommended that more marketing research be undertaken immediately. Others on the NBTF, Bradford thought, would be content to see the TeleMessager project scrapped without further delay.

Against these objections, Bradford countered that despite problems, the TM business had shown steady progress throughout the Dallas test. And while the test had not been a clear success from a numbers standpoint, a great deal had been learned about how to run the business. In net, he maintained, this was a business opportunity which GTE could not afford to walk away from because of its financial promise, its potential for synergy with other GTE offerings and its symbolic role as one of GTE's first internally developed new products under the aegis of the New Business Development organization.

Given all of the above, what would you recommend that GTE do?

POSTSCRIPT

After much debate, the NBTF approved the roll-out of TeleMessager. Overall, the decision was to proceed cautiously in order that Bradford and his group could continue to gain marketing and operating expertise.

In 1984, message centers were established in Los Angeles, New York, Chicago, San Francisco, Washington, D.C. and Boston. In 1985, three more cities were added; in 1986, five more U.S. cities came on-stream and operations were set up in seven foreign countries. The total number of messageboxes grew from 2000 in 1983 to over 55,000 in 1986. While the VSF market has attracted numerous competitors including Wang

Laboratories, GTE TeleMessager remains the industry leader.

The services provided by TeleMessager now cover several messaging media -- voice, text, facsimile, and video -- with selective integration of these media depending upon customer needs. A national and international messaging network is being introduced for cost effective transmission of messages. Special industry applications are being developed on a monthly basis in TeleMessager's own laboratories located near Dallas.

ADDENDUM: LESSONS LEARNED

1) Corporate Strategy

   - A well-defined corporate strategy can assist new product developers:

     - Define the boundaries of markets to be pursued.

     - Set forth criteria in terms of ROI, risk, payback, etc.

     - Outline the type and quantity of marketing research support required.

2) Product Champion

   - An able and committed "product champion" like Bill Bradford is key to the success of a new service.

3) Product Champion in Customer Company

   - Can be a major asset in spurring the adoption (on-going purchase) of a new industrial service.

4) Test Marketing

   - Can be employed in "learning" mode or in "sales forecast" mode but not both.

   - Single location test markets suffer from lack of representativeness, restrictions on experimentation and possibly too much TLC ("tender loving care" which can't be duplicated during commercialization).

5) New Product Marketing Research

   - Is particularly difficult when product is complicated and benefit-space is not clearly defined:

     - Attribute/image studies are harder to do.

     - Concept tests difficult.

6) Product Testing

   - Highly recommended prior to test market:

     - Aids product design.

     - Discover customer misconceptions.

7) Electronic Distribution Channels

   - Are easy to access but do not provide a barrier to competitive entry.

8) Advertising is Expensive but has Benefits

   - Boosts brand awareness; makes personal selling and direct mail more effective.

   - Enhances service "tangibility."

   - Provides reassurance of quality.

9) Sales Promotion

   - Generates trial by reducing customer risk.

   - Directs sales force efforts.

10) All Things Equal, the Service Concept is the Key Success Variable:

   - E.G., HMO's, drive-up windows and telemessaging are strong concepts. In Bill Bradford's words: "The TeleMessager concept was so appealing to customers that it survived the mistakes we made in learning how to market it."

Note: All persons' names and certain data have been disguised.

HOW ENVIRONMENTAL PRESSURES IMPACT MARKETING STRATEGY:
THE SUBURBAN CABLEVISION CASE

Kenneth L. Bernhardt, Georgia State University
James Novo, Continential CableVision

INTRODUCTION

Kim Harrison had joined Communications Industries, Inc. six months earlier, following her graduation from a well-known midwestern business school. Now, in late 1986, she had been promoted to Marketing Manager for Suburban Cable-Vision, a New England subsidiary of Communications Industries (CI), with the responsibility for marketing cable services in four suburban communities. Suburban Cable-Vision had just been acquired, and a new management team had been put in place.

Ms. Harrison had been assigned the task of developing a marketing plan for 1987. Given that the new year was only a few weeks away, she realized that she did not have much time. The problem was complicated by the regulatory changes that were due to take place on January 1. The new regulations allowed considerably greater flexibility in packaging and pricing of cable TV services. As she began to review the marketing files left by her predecessor, she realized that this holiday season was going to be very busy for her, very different from the previous few years when she was on Christmas Break from her university studies.

BACKGROUND ON THE CABLE TV INDUSTRY

The cable television industry was born in 1948. At that time, Ed Parsons of Astoria, Oregon lived at the foot of a mountain. The mountain was between his home, which contained a TV set with nothing but snow on the screen, and the transmitters for the television stations he wanted to watch. Parsons climbed the mountain with antenna in hand, secured it at the top, and strung a wire all of the way back down to his TV set. As the only person in town with good picture quality, he soon had friends and neighbors at his house all of the time. When neighbors asked him if he would hook up their sets to his wire, he quickly agreed, allowing him and his wife to have time alone together for the first time since he had climbed the mountain.

After this birth of cable television, the industry grew very slowly. In areas where there was poor TV reception, people put up towers and ran cable to those households willing to pay for better reception. By 1975, only about 10% of U.S. television households were cable subscribers. RCA launched the first communications satellite, SATCOM I, in 1975. Programs from the East Coast could now be received by the West Coast instantaneously. Home Box Office became the first company to provide programming specifically aimed at cable subscribers. Others followed and today there are over 150 programming sources. The rapid increase in programming led to a rapid growth in the number of cable subscribers.

Consumers were expected to spend more than $10 billion on cable television in 1986, more than they spend on going to the movies or renting home video programs. More than 77,000 people were employed by cable systems. The number of subscribers had doubled in the previous five years, and now 3/4 of all TV households now had cable available to them, but only about 60% of those households able to receive cable actually chose to buy it.

The number of subscribers had been growing at a compound annual growth rate of 14.2% between 1980 and 1985. This rate was expected to slow to under 5% between 1986 and 1990. An Arthur D. Little study indicated that spending on new cable systems would decline from a peak of $1.4 billion in 1982 to $160 million by 1990. Ms. Harrison recognized that the future of the industry lay in increasing the number of subscribers and revenue from existing systems rather than from laying new cable in areas that previously did not have cable TV available.

Planning for 1987 was complicated by the Cable Communications Policy Act of 1984 (CCPA). The Act took away the power of state and local authorities to regulate the rates that cable companies charge subscribers for basic cable service. At the same time the Federal Communications Commission was phasing out regulations such as the requirement that local cable systems carry all available local channels. Thus for the first time, starting January 1, 1987, local systems were free to raise rates and to put whatever programming they wanted on the channels.

The amount of money the average U.S. subscriber paid for cable TV services had nearly doubled between 1980 and 1986, to $21.00 per month. One leading cable-TV analyst has recently estimated that the average fee would grow to $28.00 in 1990 and $39.00 by 1995. Others in the industry were afraid that higher prices could drive away potential new subscribers and cause some existing subscripers to drop cable. Already, a number of premium channels such as Home Box Office (HBO), Showtime, and the Movie Channel had experienced a slowing in their growth patterns as consumers appeared to be rejecting expensive cable bills which included multiple premium services.

BACKGROUND ON COMMUNICATIONS INDUSTRIES AND SUBURBAN CABLEVISION

Communications Industries (CI) owned and operated four cable television systems servicing forty-three cities in the states of Delaware, Connecticut, Rhode Island, and Massachusetts. The four systems had cable passing 315,000 homes, 196,000 of which subscribed to basic cable programming services. More than 113,000 (62%) also subscribed to premium programming services such as movie channels or pay sports channels. CI was the 35th largest cable company, but was very small compared to the larger firms in the industry. Total revenues for CI were in excess of $100 million, coming from four television stations, six radio stations, and outdoor advertising services in addition to the cable TV revenues.

Suburban CableVision marketed cable services in four communities. The communities had very different profiles. Downing was a blue-collar, industrial town. Suburban had penetrated 75% of the homes in Downing with access to cable. This was the highest penetration of any of the cities in the area. However, the number of premium services subscribed to was lower than in the other areas. Some of the Suburban managers attributed this to the lower incomes of Downing's households—many could not afford basic plus several pay channels. They felt that the basic penetration was high because TV was a major form of entertainment for these people, and they were willing to pay for basic cable service.

The town of Anderson had a high percentage of the population employed in white-collar and managerial jobs. There was also a large elderly population. Suburban managers felt that these people would drive some distance to attend plays and the opera, so TV was less important to them. Those who did subscribe to basic cable, however, were likely to buy more pay services because of their relatively high incomes.

The towns of North Lexington and Middletown were rural, farm areas which were just beginning to be developed. Although these suburbs were relatively far from the downtown metropolitan area, a number of subdivisions were being created and many young families were moving into the area. The basic penetration and purchase of premium services were similar to the rates experienced in Anderson.

Although the population in Suburban's market area was growing relatively slowly, the company had experienced rapid growth. During 1985-86 there was only a 1.4% increase in the number of households with access to cable. For the system as a whole there were 22,675 households, and 14,600 of these were basic cable subscribers, (64%). Although the number of basic subscribers had grown by 7.8% in the previous year, the number of pay channel subscriptions, 17,200, was up only 2% over the previous year.

Channels 2-42 contained a wide variety of basic cable programming. Included were several news channels, network and independent broadcast stations, and specialized channels devoted to local programming, movies, children's programs, and music and culture. On channels 44-52, a number of premium channels were available for an extra charge above the basic cable service.

PRICING

Suburban's pricing structure was very complex. Basic service was broken down into five tiers. The lowest level of service generally available, "basic service," consisted of tiers one and two (channels 2-29). Subscribers signing up for this basic service were charged $7.25 per month. There were three other tiers available with options to add "super stations" (tier three, $2.05 per month), "family" stations (tier four, $3.10), and "sports" stations (tier five, $2.35). In addition, eight premium channels were available at prices ranging from $7.95 per month to $11.00 per month.

Table 1 shows a breakdown by level of service. Only 1,000 subscribers, 6.9%, subscribed to tiers one and two only. Ms. Harrison believed that the current system was much too complicated and caused problems in the development of advertising copy. In addition, it was difficult for Suburban's telephone sales representatives to explain the system to potential new subscribers. Thus, she felt that it was important to create a new system now that the company had the ability to change rates for the first time without having to get approval from each city council. She wondered whether she should include tier three as part of a basic subscriber package and felt that there was a marketing opportunity to simplify the system into "basic" and "super basic" (consisting of all five tiers). Other systems typically charged between $5.00 and $15.00 for basic service and anywhere from $7.00 to $12.00 for premium channels.

TABLE 1

Breakdown By Level of Basic Service

	# of Subscribers	% of Subscribers
Tiers 1 & 2 only	1000	6.9
Tiers 1, 2, & 3 only	4550	31.1
Tiers 1, 2, & 4 only	100	.7
Tiers 1, 2, 3, & 4 only	2950	20.2
Tiers 1, 2, 4, & 5 only	300	2.1
Tiers 1, 2, 3, & 5 only	150	1.0
Tiers 1, 2, 3, 4, 5	5550	38.0
	14,600	100.0

Ms. Harrison believed that Suburban made more money on basic service than on premium channels. The cost to Suburban for most of the premium movie channels was about $4.00 per subscriber per month, with some being slightly more and some slightly less. The premium sports channels cost about $3.00. Many of the basic channels did not cost Suburban anything, and most of the others only cost about $0.25 per subscriber per month. Counting all costs for billing, maintaining subscriber records, and programming costs, the average variable cost per month for basic subscribers (tiers one through five) was about $5.00.

Some cable executives believed that "basic subscriptions pay for the fixed costs of the system and you make your profit from premium channel sales." Others felt that subscribers perceived more value in the basic channels and that premium channels were already priced about as high as they could be. In fact, many felt that if basic channel rates were raised, that premium channel rates should be decreased to prevent pricing people out of the cable market. These managers believed that instead of downgrading their service (for example, having one of the premium channels disconnected), many people would just simply have the total cable service disconnected. Ms. Harrison had heard that some systems had substantially increased sales of the Disney Channel by lowering the price to $7.95. Ms. Harrison knew that she would have to give considerable thought to the issue of how she packaged the channels together and how she priced them.

ADVERTISING

Suburban had been experimenting recently with the use of direct mail in cooperation with premium channel programming suppliers. For example, they had recently completed a test of a promotion with the Disney Channel. The promotion, run in September, was centered around a free preview week-end. Direct mail and print ads informed consumers that they could preview the Disney Channel for free, and if they decided to sign up, a 50% discount ($5.00) was given toward the $10.00 installation charge. While she had not had time to fully evaluate the promotion, she felt that it had been a success. The advertising and mailing costs had been $2160.00, but the Disney co-op rebate had covered $783.00 of this. The Suburban customer service representatives were given $0.50 per new Disney subscriber as their commission. The gross margin (revenue less cost of programming) was $6.00 per subscriber per month. In addition, Suburban received the $5.00 installation fee per new subscriber to the Disney channel and incurred only about $0.25 in actual costs for the installation. Over the course of the promotion 188 subscribers took advantage of the offer and added the Disney channel to their service. This represented a 14% increase in the number of people subscribing to the

Disney channel.

A similar offer from HBO and Cinemax was far less success-ful. This promotion was communicated to subscribers via print advertising only. Only 12 subscribers added HBO as a result of the offer and nobody added Cinemax.

During the fall, Suburban also tested a heavy newspaper advertising campaign for adding the Movie Channel. New subscribers were given an AM/FM radio premium. Only 18 sales were attributable to the campaign, and Ms. Harrison thus had questions about the effectiveness of newspaper advertising and premiums.

A second direct mail campaign was tested, promotion the Sports Channel and the New England Sports Network. Sales of these two premium channels increased 25% and 17% re-spectively, at a cost per new subscriber of $2.58. No discounts or premiums were used.

As a result of the success with the premium channel direct mail promotions, Ms. Harrison decided to test targeted direct mail for basic subscriber acquisition. Eleven hundred mailers were sent to apartment addresses which had never had cable service. The mailers cost $0.25 each and 3 percent signed up. In addition, the mailer was sent to 321 homes where cable had been disconnected because the residents were moving. These homes represented 30% of the moves; the other 70% had been reconnected up when the new residents moved in. One-sixth of those receiving the mailing signed up for cable. Ms. Harrison thought that there might be potential with direct mail targeted to subsegments of the non-subscriber base, including the elderly, educators, managers, and those who disliked net-work TV.

In the early days of cable, there were a number of "truck chasers." These were consumers who would actually chase after the cable television truck when it was in their neighborhood laying cable. They would beg to get hooked up immediately, and direct sales people were used exten-sively to make door-to-door sales calls in neighborhoods where cable was being laid. With changing demographics, two-income families, and increased customer sophistica-tion, Ms. Harrison doubted whether door-to-door sales people would be effective today, but she wondered whether it would be worth testing. A good sales person would probably cost $25,000.00, including benefits.

She also wondered whether it might make sense to use public relations to help sell cable subscriptions. She was aware of Toys for Tots campaigns in various cities. In return for bringing a toy for an orphan, the in-stallation fee for new subscribers would be waived.

Ms. Harrison's predecessor had recommended a public relations program shortly before he left, but a decision had not been made on the program. He had recommended that Suburban sponsor a telethon in North Lexington in support of raising money for the renovation of the local library. There were 1,200 households in North Lexington that had never subscribed to cable, and anyone from these households who donated $25.00 or more to the telethon would be given free cable installation. Ms. Harrison made a note to review this plan to see whether if changed or in its present form it would be a good promotional vehicle for the coming year.

OTHER POTENTIAL SEGMENTS

Ms. Harrison was unsure about exactly which segments should be targeted. Much emphasis in the industry had been devoted to increasing the amount of revenue per cable household. Adopting this as a goal would mean that efforts should be directed at current subscribers with efforts made to increase the number of services to each household, increasing the total revenue.

One industry leader believed instead that it's easier to acquire a non-subscriber than to get someone who is already paying $20.00 a month to pay $30.00. This person recommended that cable systems target the "Young and Busies," conveying the message that cable provides a sense of control over one's viewing habits. He also recommended going after TV lovers already predisposed to the product category and promoting cable's variety and choices.

Still another target market recommended by others in the industry was videocassette recorder (VCR) owners. A recent study had shown that there was a relationship between VCR ownership and cable subscriptions. Only 18.5% of non-subscribers owned a VCR vs. 27% for basic-only sub-scribers. The precent owning a VCR increased to 33% for thoses who subscribed to one premium service, and to 34% for those who subscribed to two services.

Another recent study indicated that VCR ownership was related to cable subscriber behavior, depending on the degree to which the VCR owner rented tapes. Light renters of VCR tabes were more likely than average to upgrade (add premium services), and much less likely than average to downgrade (cancel premium channels) or disconnect the cable service. Ms. Harrison had read in a trade journal about one leading cable company which had been testing a strategy of positioning itself as an expert consultant on video electronics. This cable company promoted a $15.00 VCR hook-up kit, and even offered to come out and hook-up a subscriber's VCR for a fee. The company offered tech-nical assistance over the telephone to its subscribers, and had begun selling GE VCR's in several markets. The trade journal article reported that the company sold 389 VCR's in 1-1/2 months in a four market test. Special discounts were offered, tied to a pay channel upgrade campaign. Given that industry projections indicated that 50% of the population would soon have VCR's, she wondered whether Suburban should target VCR owners in its advertis-ing and promotional efforts.

Another potential market that she thought should be given some consideration was former subscribers. She thought a direct mail campaign targeted toward these households might have a high payoff. Many in the industry were concerned about "churn." Churn was a result of households downgrading their service or having it totally disconnect-ed and was computed by taking the number downgrading or disconnecting each month and dividing by the total number of subscribers at the beginning of the month. Depending on the season (it was higher in the summer and lower in the winter), the churn percentage for Suburban had been running between two and three percent for basic service, and between four and six percent for premium channels. If she chose to concentrate on increasing retention of subscribers (thus reducing churn), there were a number of promotional techniques which could be used. Some cable systems had experienced success in mailing letters to new subscribers explaining all aspects of cable. Thus, better educated, these people were able to get more out of their subscriptions. She felt that it would be import-ant to beef up customer service, since some people disconnected in frustration after having trouble getting billing and reception problems taken care of promptly and competently. Finally, she had heard that some cable systems had had some success in reducing churn by using advertising to inform people about programs on cable channels. Apparently bringing these programs to the attention of subscribers through advertising made them appreciate the services more, and thus they were less likely to downgrade or disconnect. Suburban's churn rate was about average for the industry and she wondered whether it made any sense to use her promotional budget to reduce churn.

Suburban's system used the latest technology, and was an
"Addressable" system. This meant that the subscriber's
service could be changed by merely pushing a button at the
central office. It also allowed the use of "pay-per-view"
(PPV) television. Basically, PPV is just what the name
implies--cable TV customers call their cable company and
order a particular movie (or other progam such as a sports
event) at one of the times it is offered. The cable
company transmits the movie and bills the customer accordingly. This means that cable companies can offer subscribers the ability to watch a movie at home without having to
pay a full month's price for services such as Home Box
Office or Showtime. It is also more convenient than renting a videotape. You don't have to have a VCR and you
don't have to leave your house.

One leading industry consultant estimated that by the end
of 1986 2.6 million households will have PPV available and
industry revenues are projected to reach $70 million. The
same consultant predicted that by the end of the decade,
pay-per-view will reach nearly 10 million cable subscribers
and generate revenue of more than $350 million. The
typical price of a PPV movie is $4.50 (rangins from $3.95
to $4.95 depending on the particular movie). The revenue
is usually split equally between the program supplier and
the cable company.

Currently movies are shown first in the movic theaters and
then are released on video tape to the tape rental stores.
Finally, they become available on premium movie channels
such as HBO. With PPV it is sometimes shown on cable TV
before it is released on video tape for rental. Suburban's
technology would allow the introduction of PPV movies, and
Ms. Harrison wondered whether that was the direction in
which to go.

Thinking about all of the available alternatives. Ms.
Harrison recognized the challenging opportunity in front
of her. She realized that putting together the marketing
plan for the new management team would be quite a job, and
thought that she had better get started.